RURAL LIFE IN VICTORIAN ABERDEENSHIRE

D1638047

RURAL LIFE IN VICTORIAN ABERDEENSHIRE

William Alexander

Edited and Introduced by

IAN CARTER

THE MERCAT PRESS
EDINBURGH
1992

This collection first published in 1992 by Mercat Press
James Thin, 53 South Bridge, Edinburgh EH1 1YS

Introduction © Ian Carter 1992

The Publisher acknowledges subsidy from the Scottish
Arts Council towards the publication of this volume.

British Library Cataloguing in Publication Data

Alexander, William
  Rural Life in Victorian Aberdeenshire
  I. Title II. Carter, Ian
  941.232081

  ISBN 1-873644-06-X

Typeset by Hewer Text Composition Services, Edinburgh
Printed and bound in Great Britain by
Athenaeum Press Limited, Newcastle upon Tyne

In memory of Gordon and Monika Horobin

Contents

Contents

Preface

Never go back, they say. I spent thirteen years teaching in Aberdeen University. I have spent the last nine years teaching in Auckland University. The initials are the same, but the places are separated by a world of water. Now I cross those twelve thousand wet miles to complete unfinished business.

In the mid seventies a postgraduate student, Robert Munro, told me about some essays which he had turned up in the *Aberdeen Free Press*. They concerned crofting in Aberdeenshire. Robert was working on folk song, and had no more than a passing interest in the essays. My enthusiasm was much keener. Ever since arriving in Aberdeen I had been fascinated by the social history of north east agriculture. I had a particular interest in the published work of William Alexander, the surest contemporary guide to the nineteenth century north eastern countryside. A glance at the essays confirmed that these were Alexander's work and, to the best of my knowledge, utterly unknown to scholars or to the general public.

Believing that they deserved better than to lie mouldering in bound volumes of the *Free Press* in King's College library stacks, I transcribed the ten essays. By themselves they were not enough to make a book, but they could form the kernel for one. Around them I arranged other material by Alexander that deserved an airing: two essays from long-forgotten journals; three chapters from his masterpiece, *Johnny Gibb of Gushetneuk*; sections from a lesser-known novella, 'Couper Sandy.' None of this was in print in 1975. *Johnny Gibb* had run through many editions between 1871 and 1947, but by 1975 it had been unobtainable for a decade except in second-hand book shops. 'Couper Sandy' had been published with similarly sardonic other stories in 1875, in a volume with the mock-couthy title *Life Among My Ain Folk*. A second edition appeared in 1882. There have been no more.

The collection was assembled, and submitted to a London publisher. It was accepted for that publisher's Library of Peasant Studies, and duly listed in the catalogue as a forthcoming attraction. It never appeared. The contract stipulated that the book would be published 'without unreasonable delay,' but that proved to be an elastic condition.

I give you these details not to feed – or illustrate – authors' paranoid suspicion of publishers, but to celebrate delay. For two reasons it was a very good thing that *Aberdeenshire Peasant Life* never hit the book stands. The first comes from the fact that in 1975 I was deep in research for a thesis that eventually became a book, *Farm Life in Northeast Scotland, 1840–1914*.[1] I was a lecturer, building an academic reputation. I was a sociologist, in a university many of whose senior inhabitants seemed to believe that sociology was one of the auld chiel's nastier inventions. I was defensive. To avoid historians' disdain *Farm Life* was massively documented. To throw dust in humanists' eyes it employed a deadeningly heavy theoretical machinery. The losers in all this were the people to whom I really had wanted to give the book: the men and women who had worked, or whose parents and grandparents had worked, the north-east land. My introduction to *Aberdeenshire Peasant Life* was written in treacle even thicker than parts of *Farm Life*. I rejoice in the chance to rewrite it in more accessible language. If north-east folk find it possible to reclaim some of their history through this process then my joy will know no bounds.

The second reason why delay was welcome concerns William Alexander. While his work was inaccessible in 1975, that is not quite true today. Approached by two local publishers for ideas about Aberdeenshire books worth re-publishing, I urged Alexander's merits on them. As a result, a new edition of *Johnny Gibb of Gushetneuk* appeared in 1979,[2] of *Northern Rural Life* in 1981.[3] Since then, William Donaldson has been delving in the *Aberdeen Free Press* files to excellent effect. He has put into print a hitherto unknown novel by Alexander, *The Laird of Drammochdyle and his Contemporaries*,[4] and two pieces that amble, in Alexander's customary fashion, across the boundary between fiction and documentary: 'Back to Macduff' and 'A Criminal Officer of the Old School'.[5] In his important critical study of newpaper fiction in Victorian Scotland Donaldson has provided, for the first time, a firm foundation for a proper literary appreciation of Alexander's work.[6]

This is very valuable, but an emphasis on Alexander's literary output, while entirely appropriate for William Donaldson's purpose, conceals almost as much as it reveals. Alexander's work is like the map of central Africa in his youth: a single undivided space. By the time that he died Africa was fully divided into different territories – often, as Lord Salisbury said, by people who had no idea what the boundaries signified. Today we may judge that sometimes Alexander wrote fiction, sometimes history, sometimes sociology. He would not recognise these distinctions. In defence of the people from whom he sprang, he just wrote what he felt he had to write.

In the introduction, and in notes to other chapters, I have not piled up footnotes in defence of every argument presented. Supporting evidence can be found in *Farm Life in Northeast Scotland*, which should be read as an appendix to this book. The source of the material included in this book is indicated in each chapter's notes. When Alexander quoted directly from other authors I have sought – not always successfully – to identify the exact source. Where possible I have left his text untouched; but some passages needed light editing. Alexander was famous among Aberdeen journalists for his ability to write clear and readable copy on the run. Experience gave him this skill. The earliest material in this book, the 'Sketches of rural life in Aberdeenshire' of 1852-3, shows his syntax tied, occasionally, in knots. A sprinkling of full stops and semi-colons helps to make the sense clear. Here, and in some other places, I have divided vast paragraphs into more managable chunks.

I am grateful to Auckland University's Research Committee for a grant that enabled me to search *Aberdeen Free Press* files in January and February 1991. I thank Norman and Tina Stockman for their hospitality, and for their habitual wonderful food. For advice on new work in Scottish agrarian history between 1982 and 1990 I thank Paul Dukes and Bob Tyson of Aberdeen University, and David McCrone of Edinburgh University.

Mount Eden April 1991

NOTES

1. Edinburgh, John Donald, 1979.
2. Turriff, Heritage Press.
3. Finzean, Robin Callander.
4. Aberdeen, Aberdeen University Press, 1986.
5. In W Donaldson (ed), *The Language of the People: Scots Prose from the Victorian Revival* (Aberdeen, Aberdeen University Press, 1989) pp 93–107.
6. W Donaldson, *Popular Literature in Victorian Scotland* (Aberdeen, Aberdeen University Press, 1986) pp 101–44.

Introduction

When, after death, I find myself wandering in the Elysian fields I shall not immediately join the long queues of folk waiting to talk to Socrates or Shakespeare, to discuss the ecumenical movement with Calvin or military tactics with Attilla the Hun. I shall seek out a tall stooping man with a bushy beard, a wooden leg and a strong Aberdeenshire accent. He will be found far from the fashionable salons of the dead, probably leaning on a gate and casting a critical eye over the Elysian turnip crop. No queues will bar my approach to him, though William Alexander once had a considerable reputation – an obituary described him as 'unquestionably the most distinguished of Aberdeen citizens'.[1]

Those days are long gone. Until recent years he had been forgotten. There are many reasons why this neglect is not justified. In the last five years William Donaldson has laid out one of the most important. Alexander was the jewel in the nineteenth century movement for a Scots vernacular literature. This was a literature published in cheap newspapers rather than costly books, a democratic literature that sought to reflect the lives that real people enjoyed and endured in Victorian Scotland, and to help those people think through their current difficulties.[2]

Donaldson builds a strong case, but as a literary specialist his prime target is the common view that Victorian fiction was weak, backward-looking and sentimental, examining rural Scotland through the rose-coloured glass of the manse window. In properly debunking this 'kailyard myth' Donaldson emphasises that Alexander in the *Aberdeen Free Press*, and fellow writers in other cheap Liberal papers like the *People's Journal*, did write about contemporary life in Scottish towns and cities. So they did, and we should honour them for it. But one can overstate the point.[3] Alexander turns again and again to rural matters, and to the past. This was no weakness. He looked backwards to get his bearings so that he might go forwards. He wrote about those who had lived – and still lived – in the Aberdeenshire countryside not to avert his gaze from the horrors of contemporary urban life, but to contribute to vital debates about the proper social shape of that countryside.

We live in a time when such debates are stilled. Since the British state began to intervene consistently in agricultural markets from the middle of this century, discussion about the shape of rural society has been dominated by agricultural economists. The notion of 'rural' has shrunk to make the word equivalent to 'agricultural'. And agriculture has come to mean simply the production of food and fibre products at minimum unit cost. When social matters intrude, it is through the notion of 'rural adjustment': making the pattern of social life correspond to an unquestioned economic pattern by bribing or forcing small farmers off the land, and consolidating farms in ever larger units. Despite its origin in the political defence of French and German peasant farms, the common agricultural policy of the European Economic Community reinforced this tendency. For almost fifty years the amount of capital needed to work each acre of cultivated land has risen inexorably. Crop yields have risen, but more slowly than levels of debt and fossil fuel use. In Aberdeenshire, as elsewhere in Britain, an agriculture which once produced more energy in 'horn and corn' than it consumed in artifical manures has moved into chronic energy deficit. This profligate production employs ever fewer people, and generates a landscape of surplus produce: mountains and lakes of beef, grain, butter, wine and olive oil – not much of the last two from Aberdeenshire! – that threaten to destroy coherent agricultural production arrangements in other parts of the world. British agriculture is tied into forms of production that everybody recognises cannot be sustained in the long term; yet nobody can think through alternatives.

William Alexander had an alternative. It is beyond the scope of this introduction to consider how adequate it would prove today,[3] but there can be no dispute that his vision was different. His essays, journalism and fiction run directly counter to the policies that we have taken for granted for two generations. While recognising that agriculture was the leading industry of the nineteenth century Aberdeenshire countryside, he showed that many people who lived and worked in the country were not farmers. Alexander was born in a time when a whole range of rural craftwork, once combined with agriculture on farm and croft, was collapsing: spinning and handloom weaving, stocking knitting, illicit distilling.[4] He was a Liberal passionately devoted to free trade, and hence despised protectionism. But he was a radical liberal. His shade would ask awkward questions today about who has benefitted from protection, and it would challenge things that we take for granted. Chief among these are the automatic virtues of increasing scale in agriculture, and the prerogatives of landed property. Born into a social world of crofters and small farmers, Alexander spent his life passionately denying that such folk had to be destroyed so that an efficient 'large farm system' could take their place.[5] This challenge led him to develop, more or less clearly in different places at different times, an image of what relations between landlords, large and small tenant farmers, and farm-servants ought to look like. It was in the space between what ought to be and what was that he wrote his essays, journalism and fiction. Thus all Alexander's work on rural Aberdeenshire is deeply political, though the climate of local and national politics determined whether the politics appeared on the surface or were deeply buried under his ironic facade.

William Alexander had one aim in all his writings: to present and defend the world view of the class from which he sprang, the crofters and small farmers of Aberdeenshire. That aim is reflected even in his style. His English sometimes strikes us as stilted and mannered, while when writing in his native Doric[6] his style is fluent, even racy. A perceptive early commentator noted that although the Doric was largely impenetrable to people born outside north-east Scotland, 'yet Mr Alexander uses it as if it were international, and English a subordinate dialect'.[7] Alexander's commitment to his peasant origins, symbolised in his lifelong tendency to think in the Doric and translate his thoughts into English, is his great strength as a commentator on rural life. The selections in this book show him worrying away at the opportunities and dilemmas, the advantages and drawbacks, the combination and division of Aberdeenshire crofting and small farming. Taken as a whole, his rural writing is a matchless account of the aspirations – ultimately to be proved hopeless – of a peasantry resisting full incorporation into capitalist agriculture.

William Alexander was born on 12 June 1826, the third child and eldest son of James Alexander and Anne Wilson, his wife. They had seven more children after William. James Alexander was a blacksmith and crofter at Rescivit, Chapel of Garioch – a central Aberdeenshire parish that straddles the hill of Bennachie, that potent symbol for so many emigrants from the county. James Alexander gave up smithing while his eldest son was still a child and took the lease of Damhead, a small farm in the same parish. William received the usual elementary education of the Scottish rural loon of his day – rudimentary enough by our standards but as good as could be found in any other country – and he began to work on the family farm when he left Daviot parish school. It is not unlikely that his career would have resembled that of so many peasant sons in nineteenth-century Aberdeenshire: to work at home until the family farm was in labour surplus, and then to go to farm service until the age of thirty or thirty-five. After this age he probably would have returned to take over the lease of his father's farm, have taken the lease of a croft elsewhere, have left farming for the town or, like his brother James, have emigrated to start farming in North America. But William lost a leg in an accident while still young. His farming career was over, but he never forgot what it was like to work on the family farm. His injuries necessitated a long convalescence, which he devoted to extending and deepening the basic education that he had received at the parish school.[8] He became active in his local Mutual Instruction Class – the Garioch swarmed with earnest autodidacts in the 1840s, all writing politico-philosophical essays and reading them to each other[9] – and he came to the notice of the patron of the mutual improvement movement, William McCombie of Cairnballoch, Alford.[10]

McCombie was a model Aberdeenshire self-educated man. A 'walking liberal education',[11] he was a small farmer, a fervent Baptist, a rabid Liberal, and part-proprietor of the *North of Scotland Gazette*. William Alexander joined the *Gazette* as a reporter late in 1852. His wooden leg meant many bone-jolting journeys in an unsprung cart to report meetings, but it did have its uses. In 1855 a proposal to drive the line of a new railway across Aberdeen Links led to a fiery public meeting in the city. At one point protesters rushed the platform, and Alexander claimed to have saved his fellow journalists from injury by thrusting his wooden leg between the platform and the table at which they were sitting.[12] In 1853 the *North of Scotland Gazette* was merged in the new *Aberdeen Free Press*. The new paper had a rather tentative beginning, but soon prospered and became one of the most important Liberal newspapers north of the Forth. It paid much closer attention to agriculture than any previous Aberdeen paper and was rewarded by a near monopoly of circulation among Aberdeenshire farmers and crofters. Characteristically, the almost pathologically modest William Alexander ascribed the *Free Press*'s pre-eminence in the Aberdeenshire countryside to its first editor, William McCombie;[13] but his biographer and former colleague makes it clear that the credit was due to McCombie's sub-editor and reporter, Alexander himself, who concentrated on local and agricultural questions while McCombie took national and international political matters.[14] By common consent Alexander's coverage and treatment of agriculture was in a class of its own when compared with his competitors. William McCombie died in 1870, and Alexander became editor of the *Free Press*. Under his control it flowered and prospered; in 1872 it changed from weekly or twice-weekly publication to become Aberdeen's first daily paper. But Alexander's health, never robust, gave him more and more trouble, and in 1882 he gave over the *Free Press* editorial chair to his younger brother Henry. He took on the lighter duties of editing the new *Aberdeen Evening Gazette* until he died, quite suddenly, of pneumonia in February 1894. He was sixty seven years old.

At his death Alexander might have seemed the model provincial burgess. He had a house in the granite villa'd fastness of Aberdeen's West End. He was an elder of East Free Church. In public life he was an elected director of Aberdeen Royal Infirmary and a member of the city's Public Library Committee. His intellectual and antiquarian interests were reflected by his membership of the governing bodies of the Aberdeen Philosophical Society and the New Spalding Club. The local university had given him an honorary degree in 1886. The full panoply of respectable Aberdeen was arrayed at his funeral, led by the Principal of the University, the Lord Provost and the town council. Crowds lined the streets as he made his last journey to Nellfield

Cemetery, where his fine granite memorial still stands. It could have been the funeral of any Aberdeen manufacturer or wholesale butcher of cultivated taste – until one begins to hear the discords that sound through fulsome tributes to his memory. Thus in the funeral service the minister of St Clement's noted that Alexander's views 'were pronounced and his advocacy of them unflinching and persistent'.[15] His eldership in the Free Church did not lead William Alexander to the more bigoted paths of that often grim Kirk. He was the leading local supporter of William Robertson Smith when, in 1881, that brilliant early sociologist of religion was removed on a charge of heresy from his position as Professor of Old Testament Exegesis in Aberdeen Free Church College.[16] Passages in 'The Peasantry of North-East Scotland' refract familiar contemporary Free Church arguments about lairds' and large farmers' responsibility for 'immorality' – read sex – among farm-servants; but Alexander's close knowledge of farm life makes him more generous than monstrous Edinburgh divines like Rev James Begg. His treatment of Jinse Deans's premarital pregnancy (see below, pp 132–6) and his more extended reworking of the same theme in 'Bawbie Huie's Bastard Geet',[17] is extraordinarily unpunitive for a man of Alexander's sect and time.

He was widely appreciated in respectable circles in Aberdeen and the surrounding counties, yet he remained his own man. He had made no comfortable political compromise with local ruling groups. To the end of his days he remained a fiercely radical Gladstonian Liberal. The fissure in the Liberal Party over Irish Home Rule divided him in bitter acrimony from more conservative journalists on the *Free Press* and the *Evening Gazette*, led by his brother Henry. It is likely that his radicalism had as much to do with his leaving the *Free Press* editorial chair in 1882 as had his health. Despite the strength and principled persistence of his beliefs, however, William Alexander lacked the brash self-confidence that one might expect in a man with his history. He was continually surprised at the success of his books, and agonised over his sense of unworthiness before agreeing to take the honorary degree offered by Aberdeen University. This peculiar combination of personal beliefs and attributes was no accident; it came from his class commitment, his identification with the people from whom he sprang. This was no mere sentimental attachment. It was rooted in a thorough analysis of changing productive methods in Aberdeenshire agriculture, and the social pattern that was erected on that base. We may distinguish these two strands in his work but, as we shall see, Alexander was interested in agricultural production so that he could get a handle on social and political problems in the Aberdeenshire countryside.

'The Making of Aberdeenshire' was published in 1892, in the *Transactions of the Aberdeen Philosophical Society*. It is Alexander's most concise account of the process by which agriculture in the county was transformed to the pattern which, in essence, we recognise today. Heather moors and boggy

mires were reclaimed. Arable land was enclosed within stone walls or wire
fences, allowing regular rotation of crops among corn (lots of oats, less
barley and little wheat), turnips and temporary grass. With transport
improvements came a specialised cattle breeding and feeding industry that
carried local agriculture – in more or less comfort – through the nineteenth
century: in 1871 a southern visitor noted that in Aberdeenshire 'all the
operations of husbandry are subordinate to the requirements of the byre'.[18]
Six years before that, the first Scottish agricultural census had shown how
important Aberdeenshire was in the national picture. It held sixty per cent
more land under crops than any other Scottish county; this figure included
twice as much land under corn and almost three times as much under turnips.
It held more than eighty per cent more cattle than any other county. Only in
sheep numbers did the county trail others. In 1867 Aberdeenshire had an
eighth of Scotland's entire tilled acreage, and a slightly higher proportion of
the nation's cattle. Crucial to those beasts' survival through the winter was
the fifth of the entire national turnip acreage that lay within this single
county. In 'The making of Aberdeenshire' Alexander quoted figures for 1887
that show not much had changed in twenty years.[19]

    Alexander celebrates the development of Aberdeenshire agriculture. In a
short compass in this essay, at much greater length in *Northern Rural Life*,[20]
he rejoices at the physical transformation of the county. But he is a man of his
time. Relying on narratives by lairds like Archibald Grant of Monymusk,
contemporary surveys by Andrew Wight, James Anderson and George
Skene Keith, and odd studies like Cosmo Innes' *Lectures on Scotch Legal
Antiquities* (1872), he tells us that the 'improvement' of agriculture took a
relatively short time, and that landlords were the key agents of change.
Subsequent scholarship suggests that change was slower, and extended over
a longer period, than this account would suggest.[21] Fired with enthusiasm
for new methods, eighteenth- and nineteenth-century writers buried
previous arrangements under heaps of insults. Taking the pamphlets at
face value, Alexander followed their lead. Earlier practices have little more
than curiosity value, like the intriguing discussion of the herd's club in
'Couper Sandy' (pp 141–2). None of this matters very much. As a Liberal
with a Whiggish faith in progress, the great fact for Alexander was the
wonderful transformation of Aberdeenshire agriculture. The timing of
change mattered little.

    Landlords' part in that transformation is a different kettle of fish. In
Alexander's time almost all Aberdeenshire farmland was held on lease.
Nineteen years was the usual term for a 'tack', based on a half-forgotten
belief in a nineteen-year cycle of good and bad growing seasons. Some small
farmers and many crofters held on shorter leases than these, and a few
continued to be sub-tenants of larger farmers; but very few farmers, whether
large or small, owned their own land. Thus the matter of the proper relation

between a landlord and his (rarely her) tenant farmers was a key contemporary social question. As a radical Liberal Alexander's natural tendency was to suspect the motives of landlords, and to suspect their agents — factors — much more deeply and much more quickly. Yet improvement writers insisted that landlords had kick-started the wonderful transformation of Aberdeenshire agriculture. Committed to following these authors' accounts of the transformation, Alexander had to handle their celebration of lairdly enterprise. He solved the conundrum in 'The Making of Aberdeenshire' by dividing the improvement period in two. In the eighteenth century, he argues, landlords like Grant of Monymusk, Lord Pitsligo, Fraser of Strichen, Garden of Troup and Gordon of Fyvie were thoroughly progressive, forcing change on their estates against the ingrained conservatism of their tenants. But after the turn of the nineteenth century, and particularly after the inflationary years of the French wars with their high prices for farm produce, the progressive baton passed to the tenantry. The 'idle sport-loving laird' became more common, and it was his tenants who introduced the use of artificial manures, took advantage of improved transport to ship fat cattle to London markets on the hoof or as dead meat, and through-drained the laird's land with government money for which they paid the laird a steep premium. The relation between landlord and tenant was transformed. Hitherto the progressive social force, landlords as a class now were parasites, living off the back of their newly-progressive tenantry. This is one of Alexander's fundamental tenets, underlying everything that he wrote about contemporary rural life. It is expressed most neatly in *Johnny Gibb of Gushetneuk*, where the high-living laird, Sir Simon Frissall of Glensnicker, is forced to borrow money from the thrifty small farmer, Johnny Gibb. The loan provides the plot lever with which Johnny prevents Gushetneuk being collapsed into a neighbouring large farm; but it also symbolises landlords' parasitical dependence on tenants' enterprise.

There is a curious echo of that unflattering opinion of tenant farmers before the modern age which Alexander laid out in 'The Making of Aberdeenshire'. In the first section of 'Sketches of Rural Life in Aberdeenshire' he tells us that the small farmer Peter Stark, though admirable in many ways, is not in the forefront of change. He has been known to yoke a horse and an ox to the plough. The structure and furnishing of his house are old-fashioned. Ten years later, the portrait of Peter is reworked and developed as Johnny Gibb. Johnny, too, is cautious of change until it has proved its worth. Given Alexander's commitment to progress, are we to decry Peter and Johnny? The answer must be 'no'. These men are rather elderly: Johnny retires from farming near the end of his book. But both train up excellent, progressive young men to follow them. One of Johnny's former farm-servants, 'the gudge,' follows him as the tenant of Gushetneuk.

We may expect that Peter Stark's former servant, the 'saving ploughman' Jamie Dawson, will follow much the same road. Despite their slight tincture of conservatism, Peter Stark and Johnny Gibb stand at the moral centre of Alexander's work on rural Aberdeenshire. Emblematic of the virtues of small farmers and crofters, they provide the benchmark against which all other groups are measured. Although farming small acreages, both need to hire farm-servants because they have no sons to work on the family holding. Peter Stark is a bachelor living with his sister. Johnny Gibb's marriage has proved childless, but a niece lives with Johnny and his wife. The lack of male children allows Alexander to contrast the way in which Peter and Johnny treat their farm-servants with the manner in which that is done on neighbouring large farms. Beyond that, it reveals Alexander's total commitment to the class from which he sprang, the class for which these men are standard-bearers. Johnny Gibb's household has exactly the same shape as Alexander's own: a barren wife, with a niece living in. This cannot be accident. Johnny Gibb is the small farmer that Alexander would have striven to be had he not lost his leg.

'Sketches of Rural Life in Aberdeenshire' was William Alexanders' first excursion into social description and analysis. Published intermittently between December 1852 and December 1853, soon after he had joined the *North of Scotland Gazette,* these essays bridged the time – May 1853 – when the *Aberdeen Free Press* emerged from the *Gazette's* chrysalis. As the title hints, they are a bit of a ragbag. One week readers were shown a feeing market; later Alexander took them to the parish school, a ploughing match, a country ball, a wedding, and a farmhouse party. Several pieces attacked the demon drink; a topic that the teetotal Alexander treated at greater length in *The Laird of Drammochdyle.* The first essay, included in this book, introduces us to a small farmer, Peter Stark: but it ends with an anecdote in which Peter gains a local reputation as a 'politician'. This has little to do with what has gone before, but sets the scene for several essays in which Peter discusses issues of the day with his friend, the school teacher Tammas Gray. These are good examples of Alexander learning to use the Doric for literary and polemical purposes. They read well in context, but turn to *Johnny Gibb* and one sees how much the author developed in a decade. The dialect is still a little stilted in the 'Sketches'; in *Johnny Gibb* it ripples and swirls to wonderful effect.

Six sketches are printed in this book. In the newspaper files, scattered among dialect debates and genre pieces, they make a muted effect. Pull them together, however, and they become the first published statement of themes to which Alexander would return throughout his writing life. Thirty years later, he wrote his essay on 'The Peasantry of North-East Scotland', included here. Written for a church magazine, it assumed that readers would recalled a recent furious controversy in which ministers denounced the immoral effects of inadequate housing for farm-servants. Despite this particular setting, the underlying analysis in the essay is little different from that in the earlier 'sketches'. At the heart of both is the question of how farmers should treat their hired servants, and the need for landlords to provide adequate housing on leased farms. Before considering the arguments we need to spend a little time on their context.

The uncompromising nature of its geology and soils meant that much Aberdeenshire arable land came under the plough very late.[22] Reclamation had been carried on in earlier centuries, but in 'The Making of Aberdeenshire', published in 1892, Alexander calculated that a quarter of the current arable, some 170,000 acres, had been cut from the waste since 1800. Landlords could not afford to hire labour to do this work. They did not have to pay. With the strong 'yird hunger' on them, men took patches of moor or bog on improving leases. These leases required the tenant to pay no rent or a nominal sum for the first few years, and a low rent for the next few. Only in the last third of the lease, say seven out of twenty-one, was he charged an economic rent. In return for the magnanimous laird foregoing the tiny rent that these acres would bring for rough grazing or shooting, the colonising crofter made him a new 'placie'. The colonising crofter dug granite and schist boulders from the earth and built them into walls around his small parks. He built his own house and steading. He laid drains under the new fields. Again and again Alexander insists on the herculean labour that this involved for the crofter and his family; labour often poured into the croft after the tenant had finished a full day's work for wages elsewhere.[23] At the end of the lease – or when he was evicted if, like Donald Jack, he had no lease[24] – the crofter gave to his laird valuable arable land where waste had been before. The laird could now let the croft again, perhaps at an enhanced rent. Alternatively, he could engross the land, either by adding a single croft to a neighbouring larger farm or by combining several crofts to form a new single farm. 'The Aberdeenshire Crofter' shows how widespread engrossment was; but these essays also show that estates varied in their policies towards crofters, from the benign Haddo to the rapacious Aden.

The reservoir of improvable Aberdeenshire land had very important social consequences. It meant that peasant agriculture – crofting and small farming, using family labour rather than hired labour – was constantly rebuilt on the margins of cultivation as more and more arable land was consolidated in big farms worked by hired labour. In Alexander's day most land was leased by big farmers, but these men made up only about one tenant in seven. Small farmers (those who had just about enough labour in the farm household to work the holding) and crofters (who had too much family labour for the holding, and had to sell some of it on a permanent, part-time or seasonal basis), were invaluable to neighbouring large farmers. When the big men moved rapidly into specialised cattle feeding as steamship and then railway communication with the south opened up a profitable dead meat trade, so they needed an assured supply of high quality beasts to fatten. They got the beasts from their small neighbours, who lacked the capital to benefit from the new opportunities.[25]

They got something even more significant. Big farmers had to hire all or most of the labour to work their holdings. Neighbouring crofters could help in the fields at turnip-hoeing and corn hairst. Permanent servants – a grieve to manage the farm if the tenant lived elsewhere, horsemen to plough and cart, 'coo baillies' to look after cattle beasts, 'orra men' to do odd jobs, 'deems' (maids) to work in the farmhouse – could be hired in the twice-yearly feeing markets held in every district. These servants were the children of crofters and small farmers, children whose labour was no longer needed on the paternal holding. And children many of them were. Explicitly in 'The Peasantry of North-East Scotland,' implicity elsewhere, Alexander insists on the youth of farm workers. Feeing first in their early teens, like Peter Stark's mathematical foreman, most servants would have left the farms within twenty years. Some would have gone to the towns, some to the colonies. A surprisingly large number would have turned to farming in a small way themselves. The complex social mixture of large farms, small farms and crofts ensured that Aberdeenshire 'muckle farmers' enjoyed a continuing supply of highly skilled and experienced farm-servants. At the same time, it bound together the social categories of farm servant, crofter and small farmer. With relentless thrift and industry it was possible for a 'saving ploughman' to scrape together just enough capital to allow him to lease an existing croft or hazard an improving lease.[26] As Malcolm Gray was the first modern writer to point out, in nineteenth century Aberdeenshire farm service was not a career in itself, but a stage in a career that began for almost all in family farming, and would end there for a proportion of servants.[27] Even in the middle decades of the century enough folk rode what Leslie Mitchell later would call the 'strange, antique whirlimagig of the Scottish peasantry' to ensure that the machine kept spinning. William Alexander called his essay on farm service 'The Peasantry of North-East Scotland' because in his time English hired farm workers were conventionally – though incorrectly – described as peasants.[28] But the error conceals a deeper truth. Aberdeenshire farm-servants, crofters, and small farmers were three fragments of a single peasant class.

That class differed in some ways from its pre-'improvement' ancestor, but there were strong cultural continuities. Widespread witchcraft beliefs were put to good use to construct a primitive trade union in the Society of the Horseman's Word. A farmer who fell out with his farm-servants' spokesman, the foreman, faced other communal sanctions. Like the tenant of Hillhead in the first of the 'Sketches of Rural Life in Aberdeenshire', like Peter Birse at almost every term day in *Johnny Gibb of Gushetneuk*, he would face a 'clean toon'. Every servant would leave at the term, and the farmer would have to recruit an entirely new squad in a market where the reasons why the clean toon had been enforced were widely known. The enormously strong and vital north-east ballad tradition was employed to powerful effect through bothy ballads, to blacken the reputation of villainous farmers in the feeing market. More generally, throughout the nineteenth century the huge numerical superiority of small farmers, crofters and farm-servants over large farmers constrained 'muckle farmers' in dealings with their servants. In principle Thomas Carlyle's 'cash nexus' alone connected them: the farmer contracted to buy the servants' labour power for an agreed period at an agreed rate of money wages and perquisites. In practice, the cash nexus collided with a widespread sense of 'kindly relations'; an assertion that a farmer, no matter what scale his operations, should act towards his servants in the light of a rather rosy version of the relations between a crofter or small farmer and his sons and daughters.

We now see why Peter Stark and Johnny Gibb are such central figures in William Alexander's world view. Forced through family circumstances to hire labour even for a small farm, they treat their servants as if they were sons. Johnny Gibb sends out into the wider world a stream of well trained young men. We first meet Peter Stark on an evening when he and his sister are visited by two cousins who once, at different times, worked for Peter. It reads like a visit from relatives, not former hired workers. These two young men, Geordie Brown and Jamie Dawson, will have different careers. Geordie is outgoing and gregarious. Quickly winning a name as a skilled ploughman, he seems to have a bright future. Jamie is much quieter, buying a lamp so that he can read books in the Wardend chaumer after the skinflint farmer refuses to provide candles for his servants. Yet when we leave them in the last sketch included here it is Jamie, the 'saving ploughman', who has a bright future. Geordie has got a girl pregnant, and has to borrow money from Jamie to pay for the wedding. He has saved nothing from his wages, and faces a bleak prospect. He discovers just how bleak it is likely to be when he falls in with a former workmate, Rob. Once the admired foreman on a large farm, injudicious courtship has reduced this labour aristocrat to day labouring, and to living acrimoniously with a wife whom he had despised before he got her pregnant. Visiting the hovel that this unhappy family occupies — with another of Rob's love-children making up the number — leads Geordie to think again. But he is trapped, and the marriage will take place.

Alexander is doing two things in these essays. The first is to describe for people who had not seen it first-hand the life led by Aberdeenshire farm-servants. There was nothing terribly novel about this. Many farm-servants wrote essays on the condition of their class in the 1850s and 1860s, usually trying to win prize competitions. These competitions were established by philanthropic groups concerned with the 'moral depravity' of servants: a concern fuelled by the sky-high Aberdeenshire illegitimacy rates revealed to a scandalised respectable public in the 1850s. Genteel explorers soon began to write their own essays about the moral situation of farm-servants. Unfortunately most farm-servants wrote a stilted prose, and ministers, doctors and lawyers were unable to distinguish 'roch' conditions from the usual manner in which servants were housed and fed on Aberdeenshire farms. A practising journalist who had been on the farms, Alexander steered between these hazards. In his 'Sketches of Rural Life in Aberdeenshire' he merely outlines life in the Wardend chaumer, the end of the stable where the servants slept: but his fuller description of life in an unnamed farm's bothy is masterful. When chaumered, servants were fed in the farm kitchen as part of their fee. In the bothy they were provided with agreed supplies of food, and had to cook it themselves. The fourth essay included here shows them doing this in the usual haphazard way, but it shows other things that respectable explorers missed: the rigid etiquette of bothy life, codified in written rules and enforced with physical vigour; and the strict hierarchy within any farm squad, with the foreman as cock of the walk. When Tam Meerison (Rob's literary descendant) fees as foreman of Clinkstyle in *Johnny Gibb of Gushetneuk* he is required by virtue of that position to act as the servants' spokesman in dealings with the farmer, Peter Birse, and his lady wife — known to the servants as 'the auld soo'. When she beats him down in their presence, the other servants despise their foreman.[29] Tam Meerison's career and the 'Sketches of Rural Life in Aberdeenshire' give us an insider's view of what it meant to work as a nineteenth century Aberdeenshire farm servant.

Genteel clerical explorers focused on housing conditions as the cause of Aberdeenshire farm-servants' 'gross immorality'. For unmarried servants, the great bulk of the county's hired farm labour force, William Alexander denied this simple equation. In 'The Peasantry of North-East Scotland' he noted that sleeping conditions in the chaumer (and the uncommon bothy) were spartan enough on many farms, but 'if the general relationship between master and servant were adjusted on sound principles, such details might be regarded as subordinate'. The problems were rooted in social relations, not architecture. But he joined many other free church commentators in deploring the shortage of farm cottages for married men. Tam Meerison has to start his married life fee'ed as a single man, tramping at weekends to visit the pregnant Jinse Deans in her mother's hovel at the foot of Bennachie, for local lairds ensured that he would find no cottage to rent. Here and in other places Alexander asserts that in the 1840s landlords destroyed cottages wholesale on farms and crofts to pre-empt the possibility that they might be required by the new Poor Law of that decade to maintain a pauper population. In Alexander's view morality should precede expediency. An adequate land policy for Aberdeenshire would see landlords providing cottages on farms for married servants, and maintaining a proper balance between crofts, small farms and large farms on their estates. Big farmers might have to give up swallowing croft land, but in return they would enjoy a reliable supply of seasonal crofter labour, and crofts and small farms would continue to breed up skilled servants for the muckle farmer to hire.

The second thing that Alexander does in these essays is contemplate what Robert Anderson has called the 'myth' of the lad of parts.[30] Anderson does not mean that such folk did not exist, though they were less common than enthusiasts suggested. Rather, the myth distilled the different experience of many men, forming a guiding principle, a moral code, for others to copy. Teetotaller, Free Churchman, radical Liberal: every element in William Alexander's beliefs led him to celebrate lads of parts like Jamie Dawson and Johnny Gibb's 'gudge'. He wanted farm-servants to save their wages, not spend them on whisky. He wanted them to read improving books in their scant spare time, not stride around the countryside all night visiting friends on other farms and trying to cuddle the kitchie deems. It sounds worthy and dull; but Alexander told his moral tales in an attempt to persuade young men that it would be worth it in the end.

But in one place he inverts the argument. In the extracts from 'Couper Sandy' included here, Sandy Mutch rises from humble origins to lease one of the best farms in his district. We might expect Alexander to approve this success. He does not. The lad of parts deserves his social mobility. He has admirable personal qualities: that thrift, independence and sobriety that Alexander valued so highly. Sandy Mutch is unworthy of his rise to the ranks of the large farmers. He has a natural talent for cattle dealing, but otherwise he is unredeemably stupid. He tries to break a bargain with a crofter from a secluded part of the county. The fact that Alexander's description of the crofter makes him seem Johnny Gibb's brother tells us who we are to support in this struggle. Ruined, Sandy rebuilds his fortune by passing off meat from diseased cattle as fit for human consumption. We leave him (in the extract included here) at the peak of his fortune, as he is about to take the tenancy of Mill of Meadapple. Once there he will be manipulated by Tammas Rorison the banker and Muirton, the tenant of a neighbouring large farm. Rorison is interested simply in increasing the profits of his bank. Muirton's interest in Sandy is more subtle. He has managed over the years to garner almost all the local big farms into the extended family of which he, Muirton, is the head. Only one plum has eluded his grasp — Mill of Meadapple. He completes his monopoly by matching his daughter to the weakly protesting Sandy Mutch.

In this sour novella Alexander stands the myth of the lad of parts on its head. Outwardly, Sandy Mutch is a paragon; but we know that he is a cretin, a crook and a fool. He is wealthy, and tenant of a very good farm; but no muckle farmer is to be admired unless his personal qualities make him admirable. Neither Sandy nor Muirton meets that stern test. Peter Birse had failed it hands down in *Johnny Gibb of Gushetneuk*. His harridan wife feeds the servants very badly. What really annoys them is the knowledge that food for the family 'ben the hoose' is very different from what they are given in the kitchen. Once again, it is the lack of 'kindly relations' that rankles. Peter takes no interest in his servants, so they take no interest in his farm. He can keep servants no more than one six-month term, except when Tam Meerison returns and then stays (to the disgust of his fellow servants) in order to be near Jinse Deans. Alexander knows where muckle farmers keep their better nature: in their pockets. Take an interest in your servants, he tells them, and they will increase your profits.

If Peter Birse is feckless, his wife is venal. She exploits the Clinkstyle servants to scrimp more money to spend on the genteel education of her children, and to purchase the equipment for her own pursuit of gentility: notably the 'viackle', a lumbering coach in which, together with her husband, she will encounter the laird on the kirk road, and be acknowledged as gentry. Note how, in the 'Sketches of Rural Life in Aberdeenshire', the gudewife of Wardend anticipates Mrs Birse. She too seeks gentility, but more modestly; through having her daughter copy the 'wine rubbers' that a neighbouring farmer's wife has conjured. Her husband's parsimony with candles for his servants prefigures Peter Birse. Again we see how these sketches prefigure themes developed much more fully a decade later in *Johnny Gibb*.

Alexander despises social pretension. The idle, sport-loving laird and the muckle farmer's wife trying to catch hold of the gentry's tail are equally to be deplored. Pretension is contagious, and it can be deadly. Mrs Sheepshank has only the slightest attack at Wardend. Mrs Birse catches pretension much more seriously at Clinkstyle, and it destroys her family and their hold on the farm. Alexander fears that the contagion will spread to farm-servants, crofters and small farmers. He praises the simple dwellings, food and dress of Johnny Gibb, Peter Stark and their fellows in 'The Aberdeenshire Crofter' because this shows that they yet remain untainted. Plain living and high thinking is the only way that Aberdeenshire peasant groups can survive in the nineteenth century. And all Alexander's rural work seeks to justify that survival.

His tactics varied over time. When he wrote the 'Sketches of Rural Life in Aberdeenshire' and *Johnny Gibb of Gushetneuk* agriculture was generally prosperous. Alexander could not use economic arguments to support his defence of peasant interests. He had to rest the defence on the politically weaker ground of social morality. Less than two decades later, the situation was very different. When he wrote 'The Aberdeenshire Crofter' in 1886 political circumstances were unusually fluid. A rare historical moment had arrived when political action could have a dramatic effect on rural class relations. This opportunity emerged from 'the lower range of prices such as seems likely to be now permanently established' (see below, p 45); the fall in cash crop prices after 1875 in 'the great depression'. The prosperity of the three preceding decades, a prosperity that had encouraged large farmers to expand their holdings at the expense of small farmers and crofters, disappeared with the arrival of large consignments of prairie grain from the middle 1870s and of frozen and chilled beef from Australia, New Zealand and South America from the middle 1880s. Aberdeenshire farmers were cushioned against the worst effects of 'the great depression'; but low prices still hit agriculture hard, and had important social effects. Engrossment almost stopped. Large farmers petitioned lairds for a permanent or temporary remission of high rents contracted in the good years and often got it; for landlords soon learnt that large farms would be difficult to let on the open market. Rents for large Aberdeenshire farms fell by anything from twenty five to fifty per cent between 1878 and 1895, depending on local conditions. By contrast, small farms and crofts held their rent. Since wholesale prices fell by a third over this period small farmers and crofters paid a much higher real rent than had been the case in the fat years before 1875.

William Alexander now had a firm base for his campaign. Landlords' rent rolls depended much more on peasant rents than had been the case for several decades. But the growing indispensability of the small farmer and crofter for his laird did not mean that their problems were over. The nightmare of engrossment had been removed, but the problem of how to pay the rent loomed ever larger. A strong continuing demand for small farms and crofts meant that occupants of these places frequently did not share the rent remissions that big farmers wrestled from their lairds. Finding the rent was more difficult. The ancient artisan buttresses of the peasant economy – weaving, distilling, and so on – had been effectively extinct for decades. Large farmers feeding cattle for the London market could maintain profit margins and pass price fluctuations to the smaller men who raised the cattle. In good years this meant prosperity for crofters and small farmers; in depression it meant penury. Large farmers cutting labour costs through mechanisation (of the harvest, for instance) meant that less casual wage-work was available. The Aberdeenshire small farmer and crofter stood at the classic crossroads of a peasantry in lean times. To make ends meet they had either to reduce household consumption or increase commodity production. The first solution meant saving their family economy at the cost of a yet more ruthless exploitation of family labour. The second solution meant giving up peasant production, and seeking to transform their holdings into minute capitalist enterprises. In the long run this could be no solution, for economies of scale on large farms would blast out of the water small places that tried to compete on equal terms. The only hope was legal protection for crofting and small farming.

Alexander saw his chance in the early 1880s, and seized it. Under his influence the *Aberdeen Free Press* had been urging radical Liberal land policies for almost three decades. Irish peasant political action had wrung the 1881 Irish Land Act from the British legislature. This external example, plus a series of very bad harvests without corresponding scarcity prices for grain – the result of American imports – at last stung Aberdeenshire farmers into action. Land agitation ignited spontaneously in Skene and Insch in August 1881, and quickly spread to every parish in the county and to neighbouring counties. From his editorial chair on the *Aberdeen Free Press* Alexander publicised and chivvied the infant movement, driving it in ever more radical directions. The agitation culminated in a 'great Meeting' in Aberdeen city, attended by more than 6,000 farmers, in early December. From this meeting came the Scottish Farmers' Alliance. Throughout its brief history the SFA was based firmly in Aberdeenshire, Banffshire and Kincardine.

The SFA's political posture proved to be fatally ambiguous. For the more conservative section of the movement the main objective was tenant right – compensation for improvements carried out by the tenant during his lease – and that fairly superficial reform of land laws (the abolition of entail and primogeniture, for example) that for decades had been the small change of discussion within the Liberal Party. These policies favoured large farmers, since they gave the farmer greater protection for his invested capital and removed obstacles to investment by his laird. Alexander supported these demands but he went much further. A radical section of the SFA – for which Alexander provided the intellectual ammunition – argued that tenant right was not enough to ensure a 'sound rural economy'. It had to be supplemented by a Land Act closely modelled on the 1881 Irish measure. This would give the tenant farmer security and heritability of tenure at a rent fixed by a Land Court. At a stroke engrossment and rack-renting – the twin nightmares of Aberdeenshire small farmers and crofters – would be a thing of the past. The peasantry would be safe, at least for a time.

In 1886 it seemed that the millennium was at hand when even the most radical demands of Alexander and his friends would be achieved. The reason for this optimism was the passage through parliament of the Liberal government's Bill to give Highland crofters security of tenure under conditions very like those of the 1881 Irish Land Act. As principal theorist for the SFA, William Alexander was casting bullets for a significant political movement. The Alliance had won a modest victory in 1883, when a new act ensured that landlords had to pay some compensation for tenants' improvements. Having achieved their principal objective many larger farmers abandoned the organisation. The weakened SFA changed its name to the Scottish Land Reform Alliance in January 1886, in an attempt to attract new and different members. Now firmly under radical control as satisfied conservatives left, the SLRA's parliamentary spokesmen pressed for the Crofters' Holdings Bill to be extended to Aberdeenshire and the other north-eastern counties.

This parliamentary agitation gave birth to Alexander's essays on 'The Aberdeenshire Crofter'. His other works were written to create a climate of opinion favourable to peasant farmers; only in these ten essays does he turn his attention to a pressing political issue. In the early essays he comments several times on how much more scandalous was the treatment meted out to some Aberdeenshire crofters than to some of their brethren in the area soon to become 'the crofting counties'. This reflects the nineteenth-century Lowlander's characteristic, and essentially racist, denigration of Gaeldom: but it also was an attempt to tie the interest of Aberdeenshire small farmers and crofter to the clearly successful argument being waged in Westminister by the crofter members. His emphasis on the small average size of Aberdeenshire holdings (smaller than that in Argyll, soon to be a 'crofting county'), on the survival of the Gaelic language on upper Deeside, and on historical evidence of common grazings in the county are all responses to increasingly desperate efforts by the Liberal government to find a rational basis on which to limit crofting legislation to the counties of Argyll, Inverness, Ross and Cromarty, Sutherland, Caithness, Orkney, and Shetland. Every time that the Lord Advocate dug up a new distinguishing factor, SLRA spokesmen shot him down with ammunition provided by Alexander in these essays. Not surprisingly, the Lord Advocate eventually wearied of the game. Only those counties visited by the Napier Commission[31] would, he declared, be covered by the Bill. SLRA spokesmen opposed this blatant evasion of the issue, but in vain. By 126 votes to 87 they lost an amendment in committee to extend the area under the Bill. That vote was the death warrant for the Aberdeenshire peasantry.

When this fateful vote was lost Alexander had written six of the ten essays in 'The Aberdeenshire Crofter'. The series was then quickly wound up. The tenth essay noted the need to 'intermit' the series for a time; in fact the thread was never taken up again. With more than a century's hindsight, this was a tragedy. 'The Aberdeenshire Crofter' greatly increases our knowledge of crofting life in late nineteenth-century Aberdeenshire, but the essays leave some areas untouched. For instance, Alexander concentrates almost exclusively on colonising crofters. In an early essay he notes the rapid decline of 'crofts scattered about among large farms in various districts of Deeside' (p 85) and promises to take up the matter in detail in a later essay. He never does so, apart from some very general comments in the tenth essay on the desirability of mixing large and small farms. Thus we are given no detail about the integration of crofters, small farmers and large farmers in different districts – the most shadowy topic in nineteenth century Aberdeenshire rural class relations.

The second problem with these ten essays is their geographical range. Alexander starts his tour on Deeside and then moves up the Formartine and Buchan coasts, often relying on correspondents to give him local material.

He never gets round to looking at the area that he knew best – the Garioch, his birthplace. He never looks at Strathbogie. Crucially, he never looks at Donside, where much of the most radical agitation was centred. In Leochel Cushnie, for example, the common greeting in the market had changed from 'Stormy Weather and bad trade' to 'Skye begun in Cushnie': a reference to the contemporary Highland land war, complete with government gunboat. In Kemnay the leader of the SLRA's political wing held two 'monster protest meetings' to oppose the planned engrossment of a croft, at one of which the local laird was burnt in effigy. We should be grateful for the invaluable material that Alexander gives us in these ten essays, but he could have given us so much more.

Why were the essays never resumed? The immediate reason for their 'intermission' was Gladstone's conversion to Home Rule for Ireland, which precipitated a general election. The *Aberdeen Free Press* had to clear its decks for the campaign. When he wrote these essays Alexander had been exiled from the *Free Press* for four years. His expertise on rural matters – acknowledged in one of the letters included here in an appendix to the essays – meant that the proprietors had to bring him in from the outer darkness of the *Aberdeen Evening Gazette* to act as their 'Crofter Commissioner'. But his politics were dangerously predictable. The 1886 general election split the Liberal Party into a Gladstonian and a Unionist faction. Alexander supported Irish home rule, and stayed in the Gladstonian camp. The more conservative *Free Press* proprietors opposed Home Rule, and decamped to liberal unionism. It is unlikely that the radical demands implicit in 'The Aberdeenshire Crofter' would have found a platform in that paper again. There is evidence that he came under pressure to tone down his criticism even as he wrote: the last three essays, written after the crucial vote had been lost at Westminster, are markedly more conciliatory in their attitude to landlords. The battle had been lost. North-east Scotland clave to Gladstone in the 1886 election, but elsewhere the flight of the Old Whigs spelt the end of 'the people's Wullie's' ministry and took land reform off the agenda of British politics. 'The Aberdeenshire Crofter' had been written for a specific political purpose, and that purpose had disappeared.

If the interests of Aberdeenshire crofters and small farmers could not be represented adequately within the Liberal Party then why did Alexander stay within Liberalism's debilitating embrace? Part of the reason may have been simple habit – he was sixty years old in 1886. But he had always been an 'advanced' Liberal, and in many parts of his analysis – his distinction between productive farmers and unproductive landlords, his analysis of the historical role of landowners – he looks towards a socialist rather than a Liberal philosophical tradition. Yet he never crossed the bridge. We come at last to the paradox buried at the heart of Alexander's analysis. Contradictions within the Liberal Party forced him to act circumspectly, but in all his writings he proposed radical – and often ultra-radical – solutions to the problems of Aberdeenshire crofters and small farmers. These solutions were always arcadian, proposing a return to the 'kindly relations' of a recollected, simpler world. He could not countenance socialist remedies to problems because those solutions – as understood in his day, and often in ours – would have destroyed the peasantry as completely as the final penetration of capitalist relations was later, in fact, to do. But the peasantry must survive. It carried everything that Alexander loved about Aberdeenshire social life: the marvellously supple and resourceful dialect that he used to such great effect, the political and religious independence that he found so attractive, the deep commitment to education and to individual social mobility through intrinsic worth and effort (the myth of the lad of parts). The final dissolution of the peasantry would mean not simply a major change in social structure but the dissolution of that vital culture into which Alexander had been born and which gave his life meaning. Aberdeenshire crofters and small farmers were caught between a rock and a hard place. Just as firmly caught was their most distinguished spokesman, William Alexander.

Alexander was one of history's losers. With his friends, he lost the 1886 battle to list Aberdeenshire in the crofting counties. Within a generation it was clear that the Aberdeenshire peasantry was dwindling fast. The death of this class meant the collapse of the culture which it had carried. No bothy ballads were written after 1914. The supple local dialect withered, until today it has to be taught as a foreign language in evening classes – with *Johnny Gibb of Gushetneuk* as the textbook. But if Alexander's defence of peasant interests was unavailing at the last, then we should celebrate the fact that his lifelong fidelity to the class into which he was born has given us a matchless account of the dilemmas and opportunities of crofting and small farming in Aberdeenshire. To the best of his very considerable abilities, he represented his fellows. He would ask for no other epitaph.

NOTES

1. *Aberdeen Free Press*, 23 March 1894.
2. W. Donaldson, *Popular Literature in Victorian Scotland* (Aberdeen, Aberdeen University Press, 1986).
3. The debate between Alexander's vision, usually described as 'neopopulism,' and proponents of large scale production will be found in development studies. The best introduction to the debate is G Kitching, *Development and Underdevelopment in Historical Perspective* (London, Methuen, 1982).
4. R E Tyson, 'The rise and fall of manufacturing in rural Aberdeenshire,' in J S Smith and D Stevenson (ed), *Fermfolk and Fisherfolk* (Aberdeen, Aberdeen University Press, 1989), pp 63–82.
5. Evidence from non-European societies shows that this is not rural Luddism. Large

farms produce more efficiently in the sense that profit per acre is maximised. Small family farms produce more efficiently in the sense that production per acre is maximised. These definitions of efficiency cut across each other, but neither is self-evidently true. We choose which view to take, and from that choice flow large social consequences.

6. This was, of course, a regional form of vernacular Scots, and thus ultimately a dialect of English; but I prefer to follow local custom and call it the Doric.

7. *St James' Gazette*, reprinted in the *Aberdeen Free Press*, 17 December 1881.

8. Donaldson, op cit, p 104 suggests that the detailed knowledge of parochial school teaching scattered widely through Alexander's work may mean that he taught such a school at this time.

9. I Carter, 'The Mutual Improvement Movement in North-East Scotland in the Nineteenth Century', *Aberdeen University Review*, 46, 1976, pp 383–92.

10. A MacKilligan, '*Johnny Gibb of Gushetneuk* and its Author', *Transactions of the Buchan Field Club*, 13, 1926, 96–122. Together with Donaldson, op cit, pp 101–6 this is the best biographical sketch.

11. Donaldson, op cit, p 105.

12. W Carnie, *Reporting Reminiscences* (Aberdeen, Aberdeen University Press, 1902), pp 150–1.

13. W. Alexander, *Twenty-Five Years: a Personal Retrospect* (Aberdeen, no publisher stated, 1878), pp 6–8.

14. MacKilligan, loc cit, p 100.

15. *Aberdeen Free Press*, 26 February 1894.

16. B Turner, 'Neutrality, Secularisation and the Robertson Smith Case', *Bulletin of the Scottish Institute of Missionary Studies*, 9, 1971, pp 10–17.

17. W Alexander, *Life Among My Ain Folks* (Edinburgh, Douglas, 2nd ed, 1882), pp 204–30.

18. H M Jenkins, 'Report on Some Features of Scottish Agriculture', *Journal of the Royal Agricultural Society of England*, 2nd series, vol 7, 1871, p 192.

19. See below, pp 30–1.

20. W Alexander, *Notes and Sketches Illustrative of Northern Rural Life in the Eighteenth Century* (Edinburgh, Douglas, 1877).

21. See, for example, A Fenton, *Country Life in Scotland: Our Rural Past* (Edinburgh, John Donald, 1987); I Whyte, *Agriculture and Society in Seventeenth Century Scotland* (Edinburgh, John Donald, 1979).

22. For summary accounts of the great differences in agriculture among Lowland Scottish counties see M Gray, 'The Regions and Their Issues: Scotland', in *The Victorian Countryside*, ed G E Mingay (London, Routledge and Kegan Paul, 1981), vol 1, pp 81–93;

23. See below, pp 81–2.

24. See p 81.

25. But see p 89 for an example of a Deeside crofter selling one fat beast each year in the Aberdeen Christmas market.

26. See pp 52, 87, 94, 103, 113.

27. M Gray, 'North-East Agriculture and the Labour Force, 1790– 1875', in *Social Class in Scotland: Past and Present*, ed A A Maclaren (Edinburgh, John Donald, 1976), pp 86–104. For differences in the structure and organisation of hired farm labour in different Scottish districts see T M Devine (ed), *Farm Servants and Labour in Lowland Scotland, 1770–1914* (Edinburgh, John Donald, 1984).

28. See, for instance, R Heath, *The English Peasant* (London, Fisher Unwin, 1893). (Reprinted in an abridged form as *The Victorian Peasant*, ed K Dockray (Gloucester, Sutton, 1989).) See also R M Garnier, *Annals of the British Peasantry* (London, Swan Sonnenschein, 1895).
29. See pp 127–8.
30. R Anderson, 'In Search of the "Lad of Parts": the Mythical History of Scottish Education', *History Workshop Journal*, 19, 1985, pp 82–104.
31. Royal Commission on the Condition of the Crofters and Cottars of the Highlands and Islands of Scotland, *Report and Minutes*, Parliamentary Papers, 1884, XXXII–XXXVI, C3980.

PART 1   ESSAYS

PART I ESSAYS

1 The Making of Aberdeenshire[1]

The subject upon which it is my purpose to offer a few discursive remarks seems to me one of very considerable general interest at any time; and at present, when questions affecting the welfare of that part of the population who make their living directly off the land claim a large share of public attention, that interest must naturally be deepened. By the making of Aberdeenshire is meant the development of its agriculture, and the related social progress of its inhabitants; the conversion of the county from a bleak, comparatively treeless, wholly roadless region, abundantly dotted with undrained swamps and dominating stretches of heather and stony waste, to one of the most skilfully cultivated counties of Scotland, and certainly the best for cattle-rearing.

The period of time to which I shall have occasion to refer extends over about a century and a half. The history of agriculture, and of social progress generally, in Scotland, is an extremely interesting one, had we time to dwell upon it with anything like adequate fullness. Going back to the thirteenth century, we should find a long period of peaceful progress, during which the tillers of the soil seem to have lived happily and contentedly, while the tide of civilisation continued to flow steadily northward. With the death of Alexander III, 'the peaceable king', in 1286, this state of matters came to an end, and 'the prosperity of Scotland suffered a long eclipse'. The dire struggle which closed its first scene on the field of Bannockburn had commenced; and the termination of that struggle was followed by the departure of the great Anglo-Norman lords, who, holding vast possessions in both countries, had long maintained benorth the Border an example of English wealth and refinement that, in the eyes of the common people, contrasted strongly with anything they had been accustomed to see. It has been said, and not untruly, that 'Scotland, at the death of King Alexander III, was more civilised and more prosperous than at any period of her existence down to the time when she ceased to be a separate kingdom in 1707'. And it is certainly rather remarkable to find it on record that the estimated number of sheep in Scotland in the reigns of Robert I and Robert II was equal to half the estimated number so late as 1814 even. Thus far of the events leading up to the War of Independence and of the consequences, in a material sense, of that great struggle. Whether, had no such struggle become necessary, the tide of a higher civilisation, bringing with it increased industrial enterprise and greater material prosperity, would have been earlier felt thus far north we need not speculate; we only know that at the commencement of the eighteenth century the state of agriculture in Aberdeenshire was about as wretched as it well could be; that the tenants were poor and inefficient cultivators, destitute of means, and equally destitute of a desire to adopt improved modes of husbandry.

In describing the general state of rural occupation in Scotland at an early date, Mr Cosmo Innes brings a heavy charge against 'the lawyers' of systematically lending their services to aid the barons of old in depriving poor tenants of their grazing grounds, and, without justification, bringing those grounds within terms of the charters of those who claimed to be feudal superiors. He then says: 'The land held in common was of vast extent. In truth, the arable, the cultivated land of Scotland, the land early appropriated, and held by charter, is a narrow strip of the river bank, or beside the sea. The inland, the upland, the moor, the mountain, were really not occupied at all for agricultural purposes, or served only to keep the poor and their cattle from starving'.[2] And so late as 1702, an Englishman, Rev Mr Thomas Morer, minister of St Ann's within Aldersgate, then chaplain to a Scotch regiment, speaks of the surface of the country in Scotland as 'generally unenclosed'.[3] And in describing the best cultivated parts, he states that 'the arable land ran in narrow slips, with stony wastes between, like the moraines of a glacier. The soil of the country', says Mr Morer, 'seems to the eye very indifferent; and though they have many fine valleys, which might be improved into a competitorship with our English meadows, yet for want of sufficient industry and care, they become almost useless, on the account of frequent bogs and waters in such places'. Artificial drainage was practically unknown in those days; and it thus came to pass that cultivation was carried out exclusively upon lands that were naturally dry; and this, in turn, accounts for the fact that traces of old cultivation are in some instances to be found at altitudes so great as to puzzle the modern farmer. 'The Highlanders', continues Mr. Morer, 'are not without considerable quantities of corn, yet have not enough to satisfy their numbers, and therefore yearly come down with their cattle, of which they have greater plenty, and so traffic with the Lowlanders for such proportions of oats and barley as their families or necessities call for'; and he repeats that, for the supply of cattle, the Lowlanders depended much on 'the yearly descent of the Highlanders'. Let us endeavour now to obtain an idea of the state of the county of Aberdeen, in its agricultural aspect, as it was at the beginning and up to fully the middle of the eighteenth century, noting, in the first place, its extent, generally, and in cultivated acreage.

In point of extent Aberdeenshire is the sixth largest county in Scotland. Its total area of land and water is 1,258,510 acres. Inverness-shire, including its island adjuncts, has an area considerably more than double that of Aberdeenshire. Argyllshire and the combined county of Ross and Cromarty each exceed two millions of acres in extent; Perthshire is larger than Aberdeenshire by more than a quarter of a million of acres, and Sutherlandshire by more than a hundred thousand acres. Thus far of total areas. When we come to the total acreage under crops, bare fallow, and grass, however, Aberdeenshire takes the first place by a long way amongst the counties named, and in all Scotland. The area so classified in the Agricultural Returns for 1887[4] was: in Aberdeenshire, 612,724 acres; in Perthshire, which comes second, 347,723 acres; Dumfries, Lanark, and Forfarshires are each somewhere about a third less than Perthshire; while Inverness-shire has 150,417 acres; Ross and Cromarty, 134,870 acres – not much over a fourth of the arable area of Aberdeenshire; Argyllshire, 128,258 acres; and Sutherlandshire, only 32,302 acres under crops, bare fallow, and grass. The acreage under cultivation in Aberdeenshire at the present time has been more largely increased in proportion to total area than is the case in, perhaps, any other county in Scotland. According to the most reliable estimates known to me, the total cultivated area of the county now exceeds the total cultivated area at the close of the first decade of the present century by not less than 170,000 acres, or more than one fourth of the whole. And prior to even that date the area reclaimed from the waste – bog, marsh, and heather – and brought under the plough, amounted to a good many thousands of acres, as we shall see later on.

A brief reference to the division of the land in the matter of occupation may here be made. In his *General View of the Agriculture and Rural Economy of the County of Aberdeen*, drawn up for the consideration of the Board of Agriculture and Internal Improvement by Dr James Anderson, the author, in speaking of the size of farms, says:

> 'There is not perhaps an extensive corn country in the globe in which the farms are in general so small as in Aberdeenshire, these rising in general from £2 of rent to £100: but as farms of this size are rare, they cannot on an average exceed £15 or £20 . . . About the middle of last century farms in Aberdeenshire were of much greater extent than they are at present; and, from many incidental circumstances that occurred to me during my residence in that county, it seems evident to me that farmers were then in general a more wealthy and respectable body of men than they are at present'.[5]

Dr Anderson does not specify the precise grounds upon which he arrived at the conclusion that the farms were of greater extent, and the farmers a more wealthy and respectable class about the middle of the seventeenth century than was the case a hundred years later, but, so far as my inquiries have led me, the chief difference would seem to have been that at the earlier date the form of occupation was more in the direction of one principal tenant, with a cluster of others under him — 'sub-tenants', 'cottars', 'grassmen', or 'yeomen', as we occasionally find the designation to be in the Poll Book[6] — than was the case later on. But, however that may be, it is of practical interest to note the fact that, as it concerns occupation at the present time, as for many years byegone, the average size of the holdings in Aberdeenshire is smaller, and the grading from the smaller to the larger sizes more pervasive than in almost any other county in Scotland.

This point will be best illustrated by quoting actual figures bearing thereon. In 1868 a careful classification of the holdings in Aberdeenshire according to amount of rental as entered in the Valuation Roll was made up by Mr Alexander Fraser, at that time assessor for the County of Aberdeen, under the Lands Valuation Acts, and now Inspector of Stamps and Taxes, Edinburgh. A summary of that classification appended to the Valuation Roll for the year named brings out in a striking way the very small proportion of really large farms in the county, as large farms are reckoned elsewhere, relatively to the great number of medium-sized, small, and very small farms, and crofts. Mr Fraser's figures, given somewhat less in detail than he presented them, show that the total number of holdings was 11,462, ranging thus:

Rental (Pounds)	Number of Holdings
600 and under 700	5
400 and under 600	31
250 and under 400	201
100 and under 250	1,366
50 and under 100	1,837
15 and under 50	3,329
4 and under 15	4,693
TOTAL	11,462

It is thus seen that the number of farms in Aberdeenshire in 1868 with a rental of £400 and upwards was only thirty-six, while the number of small farms and crofts under £50 of rental was close upon 8,000, the classes of farms ranging from £50 to £400 rental numbering somewhat over 3,000, and the proportions have not changed appreciably since.

We shall now glance briefly at the state of matters at, and prior to, the time when agricultural improvement first commenced. In a well-known passage applicable to the date 1716 Sir Archibald Grant, second baronet of Monymusk, one of the earliest and most spirited of early agricultural improvers in Aberdeenshire, speaks of 'all the farms' on his own estate as being 'ill-disposed and mixed, different persons having alternated ridges;

not one wheeled carriage on the estate, nor, indeed, any one road that would allow it'. And he adds – 'In 1720 I could not, in chariote, get my wife from Aberdeen to Monymusk'.[7] In the year last mentioned, indeed, the county gentlemen met and resolved 'that the whole highways and bridges within the said county should be repaired, amended and built with all convenient diligence'. But matters did not go rapidly in those days, and a generation had yet to elapse before much progress in road-making was achieved. For Dr James Anderson expressly states that 'about forty or fifty years ago' (that is, about the middle of the century) 'there was no road in this county on which wheels of any kind could be dragged'.[8] And even later on the roads were few and bad, their construction amounting to nothing more than a little levelling out, and depositing a few big stones in the soft and swampy places, care being taken to make the line of road followed wind about well up the brae sides, to get advantage, as far as might be, of a dry, hard bottom. It was not till the year 1800 that the first turnpike road was opened in the county.[9]

And as with road-making, so with agricultural improvements generally. Though the Society of Improvers in the Knowledge of Agriculture in Scotland was instituted so early as 1723, no general progress was made for a full half-century after that date. The body of tenants and sub-tenants continued to live on in their old meagre way; a good deal of the land was in run-rig, with a common fold for the cattle; there was no rotation of crops, cereals – oats, and bere or barley – being grown continuously, till the land, exhausted and full of weeds, would yield no more, when it was allowed to run out and lie fallow for some years. In winter, when the cattle could not be herded out, they were fed almost wholly on oat straw; and when the winter happened to be long and severe, the poor starveling animals were reduced to skin and bone, while occasionally the weaker ones actually died before they could be turned out to crop the early spring grass. The ordinary dietary of the people, moreover, was what the poorest labourer in town or country would not submit to now. The regulation 'pottage' for breakfast, 'sowens' for dinner, and 'brose' for supper had little variation indeed in the best of times, and when seasons were adverse, or anything went out of joint, it was not always they could be had in sufficient allowance. The bitter mugwort was pulled in the fields and cooked; the harsh red kail was carefully stacked for winter use; and even the revolting expedient of drawing blood from the necks of the live cattle to be cooked and eaten, was not unknown among the rural population of Aberdeenshire.

I may not stay to speak further of the domesticities of the people, the degree of comfort they enjoyed, or the epidemic diseases from which they suffered: deadly fevers, small-pox, and the like; but cannot quit this part of my subject without quoting a paragraph from the analysis of Sir John Sinclair's Statistical Account[10] on the prevalence of ague among the rural

population, showing as it vividly does, the condition in which the soil of the
country generally was, through lack of drainage of marshes, and the like:

> This disease, so enfeebling to the constitution, formerly prevailed over a
> large proportion of Scotland. It was so common in spring and autumn, and
> sometimes even in summer, that the farmers found it difficult to carry on
> the various operations of husbandry at the proper seasons, their servants
> being so much afflicted with ague. It was not unusual, when any piece of
> work was to be executed, to order six labourers instead of four, from the
> probability that some of them, before the work could be finished, would be
> rendered unfit for labour by an attack of this disorder. Indeed, in several
> parishes, the inhabitants, with very few exceptions, had an annual attack.
> That the ague, [adds Sir John] has become less common, and, indeed, has
> been entirely banished from a number of districts, is so highly honourable
> to agriculture, that it is impossible for the author to mention it without a
> high degree of pride and pleasure.

The date at which these remarks were written was about 1795. In the
immediately preceding year Dr Anderson, in describing the general
appearance of the 'surface' of Aberdeenshire, had written that 'in its
present state the appearance of the country is rather bleak and uninviting on
account of the general want of wood around the hamlets, the imperfect
culture of the fields, and the too frequent marshy appearance of the low
grounds'.[11]

The seven closing years of the seventeenth century were marked by great
inclemence, leading to not only miserably deficient crops, but to a great
many deaths from famine in various parts of the county of Aberdeen.
Numbers of tenants were ruined, and their farms thrown into the hands of
the landowners, who had great difficulty, even when they broke them up
into smaller holdings, and offered the bribe of a team of oxen or a few milk
cows as a present, in inducing tenants to accept the farms. I have heard the
story of a Garioch laird of a much later time, who had spent good part of a
day riding about in search of tenants for his vacant farms, and, as it should
seem, without much success; and late in the afternoon he pulled up his horse,
in passing, for a talk with Saunders —. The laird felicitated himself on the
fact of that worthy having stuck to him. 'Ou, weel, sir, ye needna care, I'm nae
able ta pay ye nae rent,' was the reply. 'Yes, yes, Saunders,' said the laird, 'but
ye aye keep in the rigs.' The laird deemed himself fortunate in being able to
retain a man who would honestly till his acres, even when he could pay no
rent. It is upon record that 'of so little value was land in this county' at the
period referred to that there were instances of 'considerable tracts of corn
lands being so totally abandoned as to be allowed to pass from one
proprietor to another, merely by a prescriptive title of occupancy, for

upwards of forty years without a challenge'.[12] And all this, no doubt, tended to make the progress of early agricultural improvement slow and difficult. In speaking of the proportion of cultivated to waste land, in the county of Aberdeen, at the date of his *General View* (1794), Dr Anderson says he supposes

> 'that in the district of Mar, not much above one-fourth part of the whole surface has ever been brought under the plough – in Formartine, perhaps two-thirds – in Buchan, three-fourths – and in the Garioch, about one-half has been at one time or other under culture. Of the lands that may now be reckoned waste, perhaps one half of these are susceptible of being brought under the plough . . . The enclosed ground does not, I should suppose, exceed one-twentieth part of the present arable, and not perhaps above one-hundredth part of the arable ground occupied by farmers is enclosed'.[13]

The earliest valuation of land available in Aberdeenshire was made in 1644. There had been earlier valuations of lands, of which nothing very definite is known; but in Cromwell's time revaluations of all the counties in Scotland took place, in accordance with which taxes were imposed, till the restoration of Charles II. The 1644 valuation stated the 'suma of the valued rent of the whole shyre of Aberdene' at £263,308. 9s. 1d., Scots money. Five years thereafter, in 1649, the sum total of the valuation was practically the same, the total land valuation of Scotland at that date being £441,148 sterling. And in 1674, when the valuation of the lands in the county, technically known as the 'valued rent', was made under a commission from the Privy Council, the amount was stated at £236,240. 13s. 9d. Scots money. This valuation, 'as appears from the attestation subjoined to the record of it, was the real rent of the lands at the time when it was made, and it has ever since been the rule for proportioning the cess and other taxes on land in Aberdeenshire'.[14] The valuations given being expressed in Scots money, we find that the total rent valuation of Aberdeenshire in 1674 was only something like £19,616. 14s. 5d. And it is noteworthy that, at that date, it was less by £2,256 than it had been thirty years previously. And a full century later, in 1786, the valuation of the county, per Land Tax Roll for the service of the year, was slightly less, being £235,665. 8s. 11d. Scots, or about £19,418 sterling. So far as appears, the valuation of the land of the county had not in the slightest degree increased during the space of time indicated. Agricultural improvement had indeed begun, but its influence in increasing rentals was as yet practically unfelt. The next quarter of a century told another tale, however, for in 1812 the rental or yearly value of real property in the county of Aberdeen stood at £301,098 sterling, and in three years thereafter, in 1815, under the stimulus of high prices for cattle and grain

caused by the Peninsular War then going on, the valuation had risen to
£325,218 sterling; and thenceforth it continued to mount upward. In 1842-3,
when income tax was first imposed, the value of land assessed under
schedule B (exclusive of mansion houses, policies, &c.) was £420,608; in
1852-3, it was £445,316; in 1862-3, £540,955; in 1872-3, £625,080; in
1883-4, £672,153; and in 1885-6, when probably the maximum was
reached, it was £668,237, being an increase of no less than £247,629 in
forty-three years. Last year (1886-7), there was a slight decrease of some
£1,400,[15] and, as matters stand, the likelihood seems to be that the next, and
some coming years will show a more serious declension, although, let us
hope, matters will not go so far in that direction as to portend anything
approaching to the unmaking of Aberdeenshire.

The era of effective agricultural improvement commenced about the
middle of the eighteenth century, or a very little before it. And in giving
some brief details bearing on the progress of that improvement I would
desire to notice three points in particular: (1) that in its inception and
intelligent prosecution for a full half century, the credit of the making of
Aberdeenshire, agriculturally and otherwise, was almost wholly due to the
landed proprietors; (2) that during the greater part of the time indicated, and
especially at its commencement, the tenants were all but universally poor in
means, and inefficient as cultivators; that they were, as a rule, averse to
change in their old and outworn modes of husbandry, and, in many cases,
not only slow to adopt improvements, but stoutly opposed to those forced
upon them; and (3) that, for the past three quarters of a century, the situation
has been so far reversed that the tenants have either directly carried out, or
borne the charge of carrying out, the great part of the improvements
effected.

1. In his report of 1794, already quoted, Dr James Anderson remarks that
everyone who reads his faithful delineation of 'the general practice of
agriculture in Aberdeenshire will execrate it'.[16] But while that applied to the
'country parts generally, let it not', he says, 'be conceived that better modes
of culture are not known in it. This is far from being the case. Every
gentleman of landed property in Aberdeenshire cultivates a farm by means
of his own servants, and in general these farms are managed in a neat,
husband-like manner – most of them enclosed, and many of them very
highly improved'.[17] In the list of subscribers who took each ten copies of an
Essay setting forth a 'true method of treating light, hazelly ground', issued
by 'A Small Society of Farmers in Buchan' so early as 1735,[18] we find the
names of a number of proprietors, as Lord Pitsligo; the Hon Alex Fraser of
Strichen, one of the Senators of the College of Justice; Sir James Elphinstone
of Logie; James Ferguson of Pitfour; Alexander Garden of Troup; James
Gordon of Ellon, Ernest Leslie of Balquhain; George Skene of Skene; and
William Urquhart of Meldrum. And, as already indicated, one of the chief

agricultural improvers of the time was Sir Archibald Grant of Monymusk, who, in addition to promoting improved modes of cultivation, took the lead in pushing on the construction of roads. His greatest achievement was, however, in the planting of forest trees. When the estate came into his hands, there was not, he says, one acre upon it enclosed, 'nor any timber upon it, but a few elm, sycamore, and ash, about a small kitchen garden, adjoining to the house, and some straggling trees at some of the farmyards, with a small copsewood – not enclosed, and dwarfish – and browsed by sheep and cattle'.[19] But before he had finished his life he had planted some fifty millions of young trees; and it was the belief of Dr Anderson that 'no other man ever existed on the globe who had planted so many trees'.[20] So much of the secondary maker of one of the most magnificently wooded estates in Aberdeenshire. Another famous planter of timber trees in the county was James Farquharson of Invercauld, who, during the latter half of last century, is said to have planted sixteen million firs and two million larches on his property at Braemar, through which he constructed more than twenty miles of roads. General Gordon of Fyvie is credited with having planted three million trees; and justly proud the General was of his handiwork. It was of him the story was wont to be told that, in taking a survey of his thriving saplings along with his forester, he pulled up with the remark: 'Well, I should not be surprised to see some of these fit to be the mainmast of a three-decker sixty years hence!' 'Aye, sir,' said the matter-of-fact forester, 'but I doot neither you nor me has much chance o' seein' that.' 'Ah!' exclaimed the General, 'there's the – plague – of it!'

Dr Anderson's general statement on this subject, towards the close of the century, was that 'There is scarcely a private gentleman in Aberdeenshire who owns an estate of £500 or £600 a year, who has not planted many hundred thousand trees';[21] a noteworthy statement certainly. In his interesting *Memoirs of the Life and Works* of his father, Archdeacon Sinclair gives a glimpse or two of Sir John Sinclair's intercourse with Dr Johnson, whose 'sarcasms upon Scotland had', Sir John admitted, 'been as useful as they were severe: and more particularly that his sneers at the dearth of timber had been the means of clothing the nakedness of the land'. And in closing the Archdeacon says, 'I may be allowed to add one further anecdote, in which my father took great pleasure. Dr Johnson, descanting upon the bleak and treeless aspect of Aberdeenshire, remarked to a native proprietor that if he searched his whole county he would not find a tree older than the Union. "At all events," replied the sturdy laird, "we have no such era in Scotland as the Conquest!"'[22]

Dr Anderson himself came from Hermiston, in Midlothian, to occupy the large farm of Monkshill, on the property of Mr Udny of Udny, under a long lease, granted him for the express purpose of showing an outstanding example of improved agriculture. And Mr Udny must have considered his

purpose very well served, for while Dr Anderson, who married Miss Seton
of Mounie, by whom he had a family of thirteen children, farmed
considerably over a 1,000 acres with energy and skill on advanced lines,
he kept his pen going with equal vigour in the discussion of agricultural
questions, and the denunciation of absurd and obsolete practices. Mr Udny,
who had been a Commissioner of Excise, was himself a very enlightened and
enterprising agricultural improver; or, as put by Mr Andrew Wight,
Surveyor for the Commissioners of the Annexed Estates, he was 'long a
zealous promoter of husbandry by showing frequent examples to his
neighbours both of skill and success'.[23]

Mr Wight's report indeed, gives us very vivid glimpses of the course of
agricultural improvement at about its most interesting stage. His visit to
Aberdeenshire was made in 1779. Of the county generally at that date, he
says:

> 'This county is populous and is turning more so daily . . . Wages for men-
> servants are moderate; for women they are much higher than in the
> Lothians, owing to the extensive manufacture of stockings at Aberdeen,
> which has taught all of them to knit; and so industrious they are that in
> travelling the high road they knit as busily as at home . . . The horned
> cattle, in general, are of a good kind, but ill-managed . . . The poverty of
> the pasture here is the bane of improvement, as likewise the number of
> cattle that are kept . . . The native breed of sheep is diminutive, and no
> wonder, for the custom is to tether them; and yet I could observe no grass
> till I alighted and put on my spectacles!'[24]

Other improving proprietors mentioned by Mr Wight are Mr Buchan of
Auchmacoy, and Miss Fraser of Inverallochy, to whom he says, 'every one
agrees to assign the first place for knowledge in farming', and from whom he
solicited a communication descriptive of her methods, which he inserts in his
report. Mr Garden of Troup, Mr Fraser of Strichen, Lord Saltoun, and others
in Buchan are also commended for their improvements. Of Sir Archibald
Grant's farm Mr Wight, who, be it remembered, was a skilled East Lothian
farmer himself, says, 'The culture of this farm is equal to any I ever saw'. And
of Mr Baron Gordon of Cluny, he remarks that while formerly more devoted
to the study of law than husbandry, he 'has now become a champion for the
latter'; and Mr Burnett of Kemnay's 'Herculean labour of purging his land of
stones' excites his admiration.

Before passing from this point it may be remarked that in introducing
their improvements, and as a means of furnishing example and stimulus to
the native tenantry, not a few of the proprietors obtained the services of
overseers from the Lothians, or some other region in which improved
agriculture prevailed. And a common case was to find these men, after

serving the laird for a term of years on the home farm, put into farms of their own as a fitting reward. An example is found at Monymusk, whither, says Mr Wight,

> 'John Bookless was some years ago brought from East Lothian by the late Sir Archibald to be overseer of his farm. Sir Archibald rewarded his services by putting him in possession of two farms – one of a hundred and forty acres, whereof forty were planted with firs six years ago, the rent £50 sterling. Bookless has undertaken the care of this plantation, for which he is to have half the value of the trees at the close of his lease, which is given for twenty years certain, and during his own and his wife's life if they survive the twenty years. The other farm, containing 350 acres, is rented at £100. Bookless has been well rewarded [adds the Surveyor] and ought to be grateful. He sets out well, and ought to be disgraced if he exert not every power of body and mind upon this farm. I am hopeful that my countryman will give an example of well-conducted husbandry to the tenants around him, particularly of good tillage which is much wanted in this district'.[25]

Not the least interesting part of our Surveyor's report, is that in which he speaks of what had been accomplished in the immediate neighbourhood of Aberdeen itself.[26] 'There is, perhaps no place in the world', says he, 'where a spirit of husbandry has made such a figure as about Aberdeen'. With the exception of a corner between the sea and the rivers Dee and Don, which had been for many years skilfully cultivated,

> 'the town of Aberdeen was, on all hands surrounded with a dry, barren, stony muir, close to the houses . . . It might appear vain to think of improving that soil for profit, but the citizens, prone to bestow that way any money they could spare, fell to work, and persevered without regarding the expense. From £20 to £25 per acre was not sufficient to deter them. And now the fields about Aberdeen, to the distance of three or four miles, carry as rich crops as are to be seen anywhere in Britain'.

He mentions the operations of Adam Duff, Esq, late Provost, as an example to all around him. Mr Duff had feued 150 acres 'as stony and barren as any in the neighbourhood' at thirteen shillings per acre of feu-duty; and though at the time not worth a penny per acre, Mr Duff, by his skilled operations, had brought it to yield thirty-three to thirty-eight shillings per acre for pasture. Others mentioned as agricultural improvers, 'for men of all ranks here are struck with the enthusiasm of farming', are Mr Angus, late bookseller, who had reclaimed about forty acres of the same stony muir; Mr Paton of Grandholm; Mr Mossman, advocate; Mr Hugh Lesly, son to Professor Lesly in the Old College of Aberdeen; and Mr John Auldjo, 'a most respectable citizen, and eminent in the mercantile line', who had purchased an estate on the side of the river Dee, and showed great skill in the preparation and application of extraneous manures, including the carcases of defunct sea-dogs. Speaking of these improvements generally, Mr Francis Douglas remarks that, when the soil and other circumstances were considered, the improvements carried out 'are really astonishing.' He wished to obtain particulars of the costs of improvement and the returns obtained, with a view to showing how far the improvements paid, but did not find that liberal spirit of communication that he had expected, and he evidently felt disappointed. 'There is certainly a pleasure', says Francis, 'in improving ground, of which none but the illuminati are conscious; for after a man has fairly got into the spirit of it, his hopes get entirely the better of his fears'. But, he admits, 'these improvers have unquestionably great merit, and though some individuals may have suffered, the gain to the public is too evident to be disputed'.[27]

2. I have dwelt so long upon my first point that I must be comparatively brief upon the others. What has been already said must have gone far to show that the tenant farmers of last century were as a rule poor as regards means, lacking in enterprise, and averse to change. That, in these respects, they were worse than the average of human nature under similar circumstances, I should be loth to assert, but as simple matter of fact they were both lazy and perverse. Except during seed time and harvest they knew little or nothing of hard work, but lived or loafed on contentedly in their idle, haphazard way; great fellows of any age from nineteen to twenty-five herding the cattle, while the rent, such as it was, was not seldom earned through the spinning and knitting done by the women. It took a full half-century of persistent effort to stir them out of their old slovenly methods, and beget a more enlightened and progressive spirit; a fact which, I cannot but think, ought to read something of a lesson to those who are disposed to come so heavily down on the unlucky Highland crofters, who have never had the slightest example set to them, on the ground of their laziness and want of efficiency as cultivators. The mass of the tenants of Aberdeenshire 120 years ago were just as inefficient and indolent cultivators as the Highland crofters are today; and but for the stimulus continuously and resolutely applied in the way of both precept and example by early improving proprietors, it were difficult to say what their stage of advancement might have been even now; certainly some thing a long way short of what it is.

In a New Year address to his tenants, of date 1756, Sir Archibald Grant of Monymusk, already repeatedly referred to, supplies incidental evidence on this point. While administering much excellent advice to the tenants, the worthy baronet complains strongly of their laziness and perversity, if not even of something worse. The many evident proofs he had given of his real desire for their happiness had by many of them been misconstrued, and received with sentiments which were both 'unjust and ungrateful'. But though all his past endeavours for their welfare had had very little effect amongst them, which 'justly discouraged him to continue them', he 'could not resist an inclination to try once more to rouse' them to a serious consideration of their own interest, as the best New Year gift he could bestow. And he proceeds with his very plain-spoken homily in this wise:

'Others are more virtuous: they don't lie and pilfer, nor allow it by encouraging or concealing those about them who do;...you know how blameable many of you are in these respects; and deceive yourselves by very false notions, that taking or destroying grass, corn, fuel, or trees are not evils or injuries, and, therefore, you practise these and don't inform against others; you imagine also that it is base to inform against or discover transgressors, by which you encourage them, and make them wicked, and are in part guilty by this evident mistake. I know you will say that few or any labour or slave more than you do, or live more frugally. Such of you as are diligent misapply it, and won't take advice from those who know better, nor will you follow good example when you see it has good effects; but will keep strictly to the old way; but also a great many of you are idle, and trifle away a great deal of your time: many hours of it are often spent in idleness, or sauntering about, or upon trifles, and when you are at work you don't work with life and spirit, but as if half-dead, or asleep, and many half-hours which you don't value might do much good. As to your poor living I am sorry for it, but it is your own fault, for by industry and advice you might live and be clothed much better, and have all the comforts and credits of life. For God's sake then, be roused by the example of others, and by your own reason, to pursue your true interest'.[28]

Their true interest they took to be a stout adherence to what their forefathers had taught them, and a dogged resistance of every innovation attempted upon their old methods, such as by establishment of a rotation of crops, or the introduction of turnip cultivation.

Without enlarging further upon the point, though abundant evidence to the same effect might be found, I content myself by quoting a single sentence from Francis Douglas illustrative of the spirit in which the common people viewed the efforts of improving lairds. He is speaking of the case of a proprietor on the lower Don, who was an early improver. 'Such enemies were the common people then', he says, 'to every kind of improvement, that in the night time they threw down his enclosures and pulled up thousands of his young trees by the roots'.[29] That, I take it, was not much more commendable than certain proceedings that have recently been heard of in the Outer Hebrides in the way of making raids into deer forests, and breaking down farm enclosures.

3. It is not easy to form a reliable estimate of the actual extent of land

reclaimed in Aberdeenshire during the latter half of last century. Mr Wight does not give any statement on the point. As it concerns the extent of barren land feued out for reclamation by the town of Aberdeen, we find in Francis Douglas's pages a detailed statement, which shows that between the years 1747 and 1782, when his book was published, the extent of barren ground so feued was 1,313 acres.[30] As indicated, an enormous area was reclaimed and well utilised by being planted with timber trees. Keeping in view the number of millions of trees known to have been planted, and not forgetting that a single million of young trees will plant several hundred acres, not less than 50,000 acres must have been in this sense 'afforested' by the race of early proprietor-improvers, of whom mention has been made. If, in addition to that, we credit them with having brought another 30,000 acres under the plough – and that is probably an under-estimate – we arrive at this result – that the total extent of land reclamation for arable purposes in Aberdeenshire, first and last, has been not less than 200,000 acres, or 50,000 acres more than the whole cultivated area of Inverness-shire.

When the early improvers began their operations the average rent of land in Aberdeenshire was probably not half-a-crown an acre. The estimated average rent about the middle of the last decade of last century was five shillings an acre. Through the improvement effected by the gradual adoption of better methods, and specially the general introduction of turnip husbandry and a regular rotation of crops, the five shillings average had got to be quite doubled by the end of the first decade of the present century; and from that date until the close of the Peninsular War agricultural prices and rents continued to advance. When the laird could command a fairly good rent for the acres which had been worth but little to his careful and industrious forebears, it was not unnatural, perhaps, that the mere ownership of land should be felt to put a man, from his birth upward, in a distinctive social position; that the idle, sport-loving laird, who was above understanding his own business, and above attempting to manage it, otherwise than by deputy, should become more and more common. For a period of years after the close of the Peninsular War, agricultural progress was but slow. The next great impulse it got in Aberdeenshire, indeed, was by the introduction, somewhat over fifty years ago, of extraneous manures; bone dust first, then guano, and soon thereafter by the establishment of direct shipment of fat cattle to the London market. The 'enthusiasm of farming' then exhibited itself afresh by further extensive land reclamations, and more thorough drainage of land than had been hitherto attempted.[31]

But there had now come the system of government loans, of which the early improvers knew little or nothing, and under which money was advanced for drainage; and, by and by, for farm buildings, fencing, construction of accommodation roads, improvement of waste land by trenching, planting for shelter, deepening and straightening of existing water courses, and so on. Tenants now were not like the tenants of old. They were eager to be improvers, and ready to offer high rents. It was not difficult, therefore, for the proprietor who chose so to do, to make the tenant do either of two things – carry out improvements directly at his own charge, which not a few did; or bear the charge indirectly by himself obtaining a loan of public money, at, say, three or three and a half per cent, and then getting the tenant to pay a rate as much in excess of that as practically repaid the loan before the end of his lease. And in the case of the earlier drainage loans in particular this course was adopted to a very large extent, six or seven per cent being quite a common charge against the tenant upon loans got at not exceeding three and a half per cent. I have not been able to obtain anything like a complete estimate of the amount of public money applied to land improvements in Aberdeenshire during the period under notice; but am able to say that, on estates representing an annual rental of £143,000 the amount of such expenditure, within less than the whole period under consideration, has been £630,000 and as the gross rental of Aberdeenshire is £668,000, it is not difficult to believe that the gross total borrowed for improvements at low interest, which the tenant has been asked to do something more than cover, has amounted to a very large sum. One better able to estimate it than myself has put it at not less than a couple of millions.

But apart altogether from government grants, or other aid, the tenants of Aberdeenshire have to be credited with a substantial contribution to the making of the county. Under improving leases many hundreds of acres were reclaimed and made arable by tenants, larger and smaller, whose only inducement was the security of possession given by an ordinary nineteen years' lease entered upon at the full value of the holding at the date of entry, while in not a few cases the capital they could command, apart from their own habits of indomitable industry and rigid thrift, was marvellously small. I may best illustrate this point, perhaps, by briefly narrating a case, the main facts of which are known to me personally. In 1832 a tenant entered upon a holding not inappropriately known as the Reisk. The extent in arable land of very poor quality was about twenty acres, and there was double that extent in heather, whins, and wet clayey waste. The rent was £15. His capital consisted of a halfworn mare and cart, a couple of cows, and less than £10 in cash. He had a wife and child, and the farm-steading of thatched clay-walled buildings, which were far from new, had certainly not cost over £30 in their original construction. The tenant, who spent several years towards the close of his life in Aberdeen, and died not many months ago, an octogenarian and something more, sat in his holding for something over 'two nineteens'. Before the end of his first lease, by almost incredible personal industry – literally keeping his own hand incessantly at plough, pick, or spade – with what help his growing young family could give him, he had extended his arable area from twenty to nearly sixty acres. The annual value had been raised from £15 to £60, in other words, from five shillings to twenty shillings an acre, without a penny of expenditure to the landlord. And so long as matters went on upon the old lines, the laird not pushing too closely for his rent when seasons were backward, the tenant, by his own admission, continued not only to make ends meet, but gradually to 'fog' a little. The times were good, and if his reclaimed land was but thin, it was still 'sharp', and for the time 'answered' well to a little extra manuring. It was only when he and the laird, by common agreement, burdened the Reisk with the annual interest charge applicable to the capital outlay necessary in providing a slated dwelling-house and new steading that matters began to get too tight, and that then rather than see his capital gradually diminishing, as his own physical strength had now begun to do, he gave up the lease and realised what was his by a displenish sale.

The case which I have narrated in brief outline, with as near as may be literal adherence to the facts, was, perhaps, above average notable as regards the amount of hard labour performed by the tenant with his own hands, for no man who had not more than average power of physical endurance could ever have gone through it. But in its main features it was in all respects typical of hundreds of similar cases. In the same parish, indeed, they could be traced out by the dozen, and if in many of the cases the tenants failed to come quite up to the same standard as makers of their holdings, they as a rule realised correspondingly smaller returns. The tenant I have specified retired an old man, with a capital of some £300; not a few of his contemporaries reached the close of the working period of an industrious and thrifty life, largely spent in improving farming, without being able to do more than barely hold their own; and an appreciable proportion did not find it possible to do even as much as that. I know what can be said, generally, on behalf of the lairds on this head; but may not enter upon that at length. I therefore content myself by saying that while freely admitting the claim of not a few landed proprietors of the present and recently past times to have discharged their duty towards the land and towards their tenants in a spirited, equitable, and even generous manner, I must still stand by my contention that for the past three quarters of a century the tenants have either directly carried out, or borne the charge of carrying out, the greater part of the improvements effected.

A glance at the figures will show that the increase in the valuation of land in the county in the thirty years 1842–72 was very great, amounting to fully £200,000 or not much short of a half added to the previous rental. The apparent prosperity was not well guided for either landlord or tenant. As it concerns the latter he went blindly on under the exhilaration of rising prices, making himself bound for too much in rent and otherwise, in view of his limited tenure, and the one sided state of the statute law affecting landlord and tenant. And the natural result was that he often did not obtain the just return to which his enterprise and active exertions entitled him; with the general consequence that at the present hour our tenant farmers, as a class, are much poorer than they ought to have been. In the case of the landlords the temptation to take the highest rents offered was undoubtedly great – not to say irresistible, where the money was pressingly wanted. So also was the temptation to spend too freely personally, and in the maintenance of establishments, and to do certain other things not too wise in their way, as persisting in the obnoxious, unjust, and destructive policy of close game preserving on arable land and in a not inconsiderable number of instances, making a disproportionate expenditure on the erection of modernised farm steadings.

When the principle of the Agricultural Holdings Act was first spoken of, it was roundly denounced from the landlord side as an intolerable interference with what was called 'freedom of contract'. When the principle found embodiment in an Act of Parliament it was denounced from the tenants' side as 'a pure sham'. My own opinion is that had the Act in question become law, precisely as it stands, a quarter of a century earlier than it did, it would have served the true interests of both proprietor and tenant very materially, by sensibly moderating the unwise competition for farms, and correspondingiy checking undue inflation of rents; thus leaving the tenants in better heart in a pecuniary sense, and abler to meet the pressure of the times than they are, and in like manner improving the laird's chances of getting his rent regularly paid without serious reduction in the amount. Recent experience has not been of the pleasantest to either proprietor or tenant farmer. But if the lessons of the past generally are properly laid to heart, there ought to be no cause for taking an unduly pessimistic view of the situation. For their respective parts in the making of Aberdeenshire, proprietor and tenant may each in turn claim a goodly measure of credit; and now that it has been made in a sense peculiar to itself as regards the large area reclaimed, and the division into holdings of limited size, occupied by skilful and industrious working farmers, chiefly engaged in the rearing of cattle, it seems to me that, with a moderate reduction on existing rents, say twenty to twenty-five per cent on an average, and due security for tenants' improvements, no county in Scotland is in a better position than Aberdeenshire to hold on its way successfully under a lower range of prices such as seems likely to be now permanently established.

NOTES

NB Notes marked [WA] were written by William Alexander.
1. Reprinted from the *Transactions of the Aberdeen Philosophical Society*, 2, 1892, pp 102–22.
2. C Innes, *Lectures on Scotch Legal Antiquities* (Edinburgh, Edmonston and Douglas, 1872), pp 154–5.

3. T Morer, *A Short Account of Scotland* (London, Morphew, 1715), p 4.

4. Board of Agriculture, *Agricultural Returns for Great Britain*, Parliamentary Papers, 1887, LXXXVIII, C5187.

5. J Anderson, *General View of the Agriculture of the County of Aberdeen* (Edinburgh, no publisher stated), 1794, p 142.

6. J Stuart (ed), *List of Pollable Persons Within the Shire of Aberdeen, 1696* (Aberdeen, Bennett, 2 vols, 1844).

7. A Grant, 'Description of the Present State of Monymusk (1716)', *Miscellany of the Spalding Club* ed J Stuart (Aberdeen, Spalding Club), 1842, vol 2, p 96.

8. Anderson, op cit, p 20.

9. For Alexander's extended discussion of turnpike building in Aberdeenshire see W Alexander, *Northern Rural Life in the Eighteenth Century* (Edinburgh, Douglas, 1877), pp 83–91, 216–9.

10. J Sinclair, *Analysis of the Statistical Account of Scotland* (Edinburgh, Arch Constable), 1831, p 135.

11. Anderson, op cit, p 10.

12. Alexander, *Northern Rural Life*, p 47.

13. Anderson, op cit, p 127.

14. Stuart, op cit, p xii.

15. The temporary abatements voluntarily made are, of course, far in excess of this amount. [WA]

16. Anderson, op cit, p 5.

17. Ibid, p 65.

18. J Arbuthnott, *A True Method of Treating Light Hazelly Ground: or an Exact Relation of the Practice of Farmers in Buchan* (Edinburgh, Cheyne, 1735).

19. Grant, loc cit, p 96.

20. Anderson, op cit, p 33.

21. Ibid.

22. J Sinclair, *Memoir of the Life and Works of the Late Right Honourable Sir John Sinclair, Bart* (Edinburgh, Blackwood, 1837), vol 1, pp 50–2.

23. A Wight, *Present State of Husbandry in Scotland* (Edinburgh, Creech, 1778–83), vol 4, pp 606–7.

24 Ibid.

25. Ibid, pp 598–9.

26 Ibid, pp 585–602.

27 F Douglas, *General Description of the East Coast of Scotland* (Aberdeen, Chalmers, 2nd edn, 1826), p 147.

28 H Hamilton (ed),*Selections fromthe Monymusk Papers, 1713–1755* (Edinburgh, Scottish History Society, 1945), pp 1xx–lxxi.

29 Douglas, op cit, p 183.

30 Ibid, pp 145–6.

31 In his *Journals*, writing under date 6 May 1838, Lord Cockburn says:

I know of no part of Scotland so much and so visibly improved within thirty years as Aberdeen shire. At the beginning of that time the country between Keith and Stonehaven was little else than a hopeless region of stones; there was nothing but large white stones, of from half a ton to ten tons weight, to be seen. A stranger to the chracter of the people would have supposed that despair would have held back their hands from even attempting to remove them. However, they began, and year after year have been going on, making dykes and drains, and filling up holes with these materials till at last they have created a country which, when the rain happens to cease and the sun shines, is really very endurable.

This passge is repeated in the recently published *Circuit Journeys* of Lord Cockburn, and is emphasised by at least two additional references to the subject of Aberdeenshire enterprise in reclaiming the soil and changing the face of the country. [WA] For the source of the main quotation, see A Cockburn, *Journal* (Edinburgh, Edmonston and Douglas, 1874), vol 1, p 172.

2   The Peasantry of North-East Scotland[1]

The typical peasant or farm labourer of north-eastern Scotland, viewed simply as a sample of humanity, is wanting neither in physical nor mental stamina. I very well recollect an estimable and philanthropic member of the legal profession, who for many years took a strong personal interest in the class, giving me an account of his first impressions of the scene at the half-yearly feeing market. A member of the Edinburgh bar, and not unaccustomed to the rural life of the Lothians, his purpose for the time was to gain some knowledge of the persons who occasionally figured in the sheriff-courts of Aberdeenshire as culprits accused of breaking the public peace, and of the surroundings amid which the brawls in which they were implicated originated. And while the robust physique, and boisterous animal spirits, characteristic of the younger men and lads, explained to him how heavy rounds of fisticuffs, with much attendant noise, might become possible, it only required the too convenient stimulus of bad whisky to precipitate somewhat pronounced breaches of law and order, where normally there was little or no disposition toward lawlessness. The other points remarked upon, as contrasting with what the observer had seen elsewhere, were the outspoken freedom, and even sauciness, with which servants seeking engagements addressed, or retorted upon, masters inquiring after their services, but who did not find favour in their eyes,[2] and the rude familiarity that marked the behaviour of the young men towards their companions of the opposite sex, even in the presence of their more sober-minded seniors. The general conclusion, and a very sound one in my opinion, was that, with much to lament in their moral habits and social condition, the peasantry of the north-eastern districts, as a class, exhibited more than average force of character and shrewdness, rendering them capable, under favouring circumstances, of working their way successfully in almost an exceptional degree.

Over twenty years have passed since the opinions thus generally outlined were expressed. But in the interval circumstances have not greatly changed. One broad result of the policy of engrossing crofts and demolishing farm cottages in order to avoid a heavy Poor Law assessment was to compel married farm labourers to seek their homes mainly in the larger villages and burghs situated in different parts of the county, and often at several miles' distance from the farm upon which the head of the family worked. The manifold evils involved in such an arrangement scarcely require to be dwelt upon. Very obviously, a ploughman whose wife and family lived four or five miles away from the scene of his daily labour, and who was able to visit them and spend a night under what was understood to be his own roof not oftener than once a fortnight, could not by possibility either discharge fully and properly the duties devolving upon him as head of a household, or enjoy as he ought the society of those dear to him.[3] And as a consequence, many of the best and most thoughtful of the class, who found themselves in this position abandoned the plough, and regular service on the farm, to become day-labourers, or accept such other unskilled occupation as they could get, simply that they might be enabled to live with their families. It was not that they preferred the change – the very opposite in many cases – but that they had in them the natural affections that bind men to their own flesh and blood, and the laudable feeling that makes a man prize his own home above every other place. And nothing of all this had entered into the calculations of the laird or tenant in settling the economy of the farm.

In Aberdeenshire the prevailing arrangement for the accommodation of the servants upon the farm is not that known as the bothy, where the men live apart and cook their own food, but the farm kitchen, where the men and women servants have their food in common, and the men sleep in an outside 'chaumer', in some part of the farm-steading, generally over, or adjacent to, the stable. But that custom of long standing has obscured its defects in the eyes of those directly responsible, the farm kitchen system would be seen to be about the most objectionable arrangement possible in a moral point of view. Under it the farmer, who of course takes his meals apart with his family, exercises no direct supervision over the labouring portion of the household who have their food in the kitchen; and it depends entirely upon the character of the man who happens to be 'grieve', or 'foreman', upon the farm, what the behaviour and style of talk indulged in at meals, and during the leisure time after hours, amongst the company of lads and young women who assemble in the kitchen shall be. His influence may be for good; but it may be also for evil, and the master is practically helpless to find it out or check it. Even where the master seeks to satisfy his sense of duty by 'going about' family worship, and the like, with the household, including servants (and such cases form a very small minority of the whole), the arrangement, founded as it is upon a subversion of the principle of the family, is wholly unsatisfactory. In saying so, I speak from sufficiently intimate personal knowledge to feel perfectly sure of my ground in so far as the average farm kitchen is concerned. The average farm 'chaumer' or sleeping-place is perhaps not much to boast of; and such primitive arrangements as that of placing the beds for the men directly in rear of the horses on a stone-causewayed floor, without any dividing wall whatever between quadrupeds and bipeds, are not unknown; only it may be argued that for sleeping purposes the essential requisites are adequate shelter and a fair measure of breathing space. And if the general relationship between master and servant were adjusted on sound principles, such details might be regarded as subordinate.

Glancing for a moment at the composition of a staff of eight or ten servants upon a farm of what would be deemed rather over medium size in Aberdeenshire, we shall find the facts and circumstances to be of this sort. The entire staff are there under half-yearly engagement, at fixed money wages, with bed and board; or if one or two of the leading men are provided with cottages upon the farm upon a yearly tenure and engagement, such cases form the exception and not the rule. The prevailing method of forming engagements is through feeing markets. These occur in each district at the terms of Whitsunday and Martinmas. And at least two such markets are held in Aberdeen, – one before the 'term day', the other, known by the suggestive name of 'rascal fair' – and at which men and lads who have entered service with a new master, and promptly deserted it, may offer themselves afresh for engagement with some farmer who is still unsupplied – after it. A not unusual position with the farmer, on the morning of the feeing market day, is to find that, with the exception, it may be, of his 'grieve', or 'foreman', or perhaps his female servants, he has got to select and engage his whole staff from the miscellaneous crowd gathered from long and widely separated distances on the market site. Anything like careful inquiry into the character and antecedents of the servants spoken to is a simple impossibility; and oftener than otherwise the engagement turns almost wholly upon the account the man gives of himself, and the promise of working capacity to be gathered from the development of bone and muscle he presents to the scrutiny of would-be employers. And so the working staff of the farm, composed to three-fourths of its extent, or it may be wholly, of young people of either sex ranging in age from fifteen to thirty or thereby, is made up. Brought together, in a large proportion of cases, almost entire strangers to each other, they are destined to be closely associated together for the next six months, without anything like adequate household superintendence – not unfrequently without anything that bears even the semblance of superintendence. How could it be otherwise than that evil results, morally and socially, should but too frequently follow?

But the evil has been even further intensified through the direct results of the policy already described. As a consequence of the farm labourer's family having been driven off the soil into village and burghal communities years ago, the supply of labour, in place of being found, as it should be, upon or adjacent to the land to be cultivated, is largely drawn from the communities spoken of – consists, in short, of young people whose earliest years are associated, not with the occupations and pleasures of rural life, but with the gutter doings and furtive pleasures and mischiefs, of a sort of modified slum existence, and who enter upon their service, not with the almost intuitive knowledge of the ways of the farm and interest in its ongoings that belong to the true 'hind's bairn', but with a feeling of utter indifference about the work undertaken, coupled with a feeling of direct antagonism towards or distrust of the farmer, and concerned only to avoid being compelled to give more than the legal due of service for the wages promised. And, having no local ties attaching them to the scene of their labour for the time being, it is hardly matter of wonder that young fellows, brought face to face with the struggle of life in the fashion described, should in many cases come to feel, practically, that where all are alike aliens to them, they have no character in particular to maintain, and to act upon the principle that if they do get into some disgraceful or embarrassing scrape, the readiest means of extrication from whatever annoyances or burdens it may entail upon them is to take advantage of the next half- yearly 'flitting term' to place a good many miles distance between them and their present place of sojourn, and begin a new record where the old is unknown. In the light of what has been said, it is not difficult to understand how it should be the complaint not of one but of all the Churches, that the class of farm servants has, during the past quarter of a century or more, to a large extent gone, if not beyond their pale formally, at any rate beyond their influence for wholesome moral and Christian ends. Their nomadic and unsettled habits are as antagonistic to the restraints of religion as they are to the demands and amenities of a sound domestic life; and until the peasant has had restored to him his just right to a comfortable and settled home upon the land he cultivates, there is small hope of the farm labourers of the north-eastern districts taking the place they ought in relation to Church membership and Church life.

The picture I have endeavoured to give is undoubtedly a somewhat dismal one. But, however imperfectly limned, its general accuracy will hardly be called in question. It were, however, to convey an utterly erroneous impression of the peasantry of north-eastern Scotland were I to leave my readers to imagine that the many 'Buirdly chiels an' weel-faur't hizzies', bred in the manner described, were fit only to serve in the prime of their years as homeless, thriftless, and reckless farm hands, to break down by little after mid-life, and seek a last earthly refuge in the poorhouse. The case is far different from that. I have already at the commencement of this paper given the estimate formed by one independent outside witness of the capacities, mental and physical, of the Aberdeenshire peasant. I now give that of another, a teacher, who, after several years' experience in conducting a school attended chiefly by the children of hinds and others in similar grades of life in a southern county, conducted a school in Aberdeenshire the pupils of which were drawn from the socially corresponding classes. And the unhesitating testimony was that, in point of native shrewdness, aptness to learn, and the desire to get on, the

Aberdeenshire bairns were so far ahead of their southern compeers as to form a complete contrast to them.

It is this desire and determination to better their position that forms the distinguishing characteristic of the cooler-headed, sober-living portion of the younger men amongst the class of farm labourers in Aberdeenshire; and among the other section, who may not have been remarkable themselves for either cool-hneadedness or sobriety of conduct, the desire that their children should succeed in life is equally strong. And this in face of all the disadvantages of the position. It is surprising to find how many of the more thoughtful and energetic, whose leanings have gone strongly in the direction of agriculture, have contrived to become tenants of small farms — husband and wife alike, by their industry and thrift, making up for their necessarily very limited capital. Of this order was no inconsiderable proportion of the men who, when agriculture was more prosperous than it is at present, and the demand for farms keen, 'took' small holdings upon what were termed 'improving leases', and after indomitable industry and perseverance had enabled them to reclaim as much of the barren waste as completed their farms, found, at the expiry of their tenure, that it was considered not only legal, but perfectly just, to invite all and sundry outsiders to bid against them for continued occupancy!

But while the ranks of the smaller tenantry have obtained many valuable recruits from the farm labourer class, a vastly greater number have pushed their way into other occupations. While the more reckless and morally obtuse are content to go on indefinitely, leading the life of the farm kitchen or bothy nomad, the man of steadier and more reflective character, whose aspirations would be met in a general way by the opportunity of settling down in moderate comfort as a married ploughman, in view of the dismal prospect before him determines to try something else; even should it be, as already indicated, something that he likes less, the feeling that he can have a home of his own is sufficient incitement. Rough day-labour, much harder than the ploughman's task, is accepted by not a few, as are the toilsome duties of the town carter and shop porter. Very many find their way into the ranks of the police, town and county; and — according to the very competent testimony of Colonel Kinloch, who was for several years chief constable of Scotland — of the Aberdeenshire men who have become police constables, a quite exceptional proportion have risen to the rank of sergeants, inspectors, and superintendents. This may in part be due to the fact that the educational advantages of Aberdeenshire have all along been greater than those enjoyed in most other Scottish counties; but it is not unreasonable to believe that it is due in part also to that innate 'hard-headedness' and general capacity which have enabled many of the more enterprising of the Aberdeenshire peasant class to push their way successfully in nearly every walk of life, not excluding the learned professions.

In any case, the general result of a land policy at once selfish and economically unsound has been, in the first place, to weaken the peasant class in the north-eastern districts by producing an abnormal depletion of its best constituents, who under more just conditions would have remained on the soil in greater numbers; and, in the second place, to deteriorate the average character, morally and socially, of those who perform the manual service of the farm. And, as invariably happens, the policy which in its inception was selfish, has also proved to be short-sighted in its bearing upon the interests of both the landlord and the tenant farmer, inasmuch as through its operation the supply of farm labour has been both greatly deteriorated in quality and largely enhanced in cost.

NOTES

1. Reprinted from the *United Presbyterian Magazine*, 1, 1884, pp 377–9, 426–9.
2. In *Johnny Gibb* Peter Birse is sent to the feeing market by his wife, to find a farm servant who can drive her absurd carriage, the 'viackle', on Sundays. He is rebuffed. '"Na sang,"' one likely fellow tells him, '"gin we work sax days i' the ook we dee brawly; ye can ca' yersel' to the kirk, laird. Ye'll need-a try some ither ane to be a flunkey to ye; we're nae come to that yet freely."' W Alexander, *Johnny Gibb of Gushetneuk* (reprint of 8th edn, Turriff, Heritage Press, 1979), p 261.
3. The point is elaborated in a short story, 'Francie Herriegerie's Sharger Laddie', in W Alexander, *Life Among My Ain Folk* (Edinburgh, Douglas, 2nd edn, 1882), pp 183–203. Francie is forced to lodge his wife and family in a cottage in the burgh of Innerebrie – probably Inverurie – while he fees some miles away as a single man. In the unhealthy town Francie's son sickens and dies. The father's tragedy is double: first, that the lack of farm cottages for married servants forces him to lodge his family in the burgh, and second that the distance between Innerebrie and Mains of Puddleweal, the farm on which he is fee'd, prevents him from being with his son in his last illness.

PART 2   JOURNALISM

3 Sketches of Rural Life in Aberdeenshire

'To catch the manners living as they rise.' – Pope

1

It is a frosty moonlight night near the middle of November, the season at which our homely rustics begin to be alive to the pleasure of roasting round the kitchen ingle, with their toes turned up to the blazing peat-fire. If the reader pleases, we will enter the snug 'stob-thackit' dwelling of my friend, Peter Stark, and quietly shutting the 'inner door', take a survey of the 'ben-end', without disturbing its inmates.

Peter's domicile is one of those quaint old-looking structures that may occasionally be met with in out-of-the-way corners of the land; and it is furnished in strict accordance with its owner's notions of what a house ought to be. Along the front wall stands the ponderous time-honoured 'dais',[1] whereon Peter delights of an evening to stretch his wearied limbs; the opposite corner is occupied by an old easy chair, while the blue smoke curls up the huge aperture of the 'hingin' lum', unencumbered by a 'swing', or any other modern invention; the sturdy 'crook' hangs dangling from the 'rantle-tree', built into the wall at a great elevation, and the glowing peats on the hearth are confined on each side by an unhewn stone, somewhat resembling a milestone laid on its edge. Yet, lest the reader suppose that anything untidy is to be seen – let him look round on the rows of brightly scoured tin dishes, the rack with its gorgeous array of crockery, and the neat time-piece ticking on the opposite wall, and he must acknowledge that a sense of homely comfort meets his eye: albeit Peter is not a little indebted to the tidy house-wifery of his sister, Martha, for the neatness of his domestic arrangements, even from the trimly swept earthen floor to the whitewashed 'coom' ceiling, to which are suspended sundry small parcels of 'kail-seed', and other such odds and ends, along with a rusty fowling-piece.

On the particular night on which I would introduce the reader to this quiet abode, the family were engaged, much as was their wont at such times. In front of the 'dais', on a hard, old-fashioned chair, with a high back, sat a sturdy little man, some fifty years of age; the closely cropped black hair, with a few tufts straggling over his forehead – the broad face of iron hue, with ample nostrils, and closely compressed lips, as he turned over the leaves of a venerable volume that lay upon his knees, bespoke perseverance and successful industry. This was Peter; and, ayont the fire, in her linsey-wolsey dress, and with cap of snowy whiteness, sat his sister, Martha – a mild-looking woman, several years younger than her brother. Martha was busily engaged in knitting, her favourite cat reposing in comfort between her and the hearth; while, by her side, sat a curly- headed boy of about a dozen years of age, occupied with a slate and pencil, making a sketch of the lamp that hung between him and his master, and every now and then showing his superior skill by asking Martha for a solution to some dreadfully-puzzling question. This was the servant man, or, as he was often styled, the 'foreman'; for Peter is one of those old-fashioned small farmers, in whose 'hearts' the 'virtues of our fathers' appear to 'glow the same'. With something approaching to an infringement of the Mosaic law, he drove his plough with a bullock and a horse; and well does he love to tell how many 'threaves' he could thresh in a long winter morning, hinting, at the same time, that the young men now-a-days could not 'stan' the flail' like men he had known, – leaving his hearers sometimes with a vague notion that he means to include himself among those ancient worthies.

The boy had finished his drawing; and, after it had been duly inspected and praised by Martha, he commenced a manful struggle with a question of how long a man with a pair of horses would require to plough an imperial acre, the plough going at the rate of three and a quarter miles in two hours (including stoppages), and cutting a furrow six inches in breadth?

The question was perplexing, and Martha could give no assistance; but she remarked, 'I'se warran' some o' our first-prize ploughmen cudna count that question, Charlie.'

'I daresay they cudna,' said Charlie, 'but I will count it yet, an' I'll maybe puzzle some o' the chaps wi't some day. Jock Gordon blaws aboot fat he can dee wi' a high cuttin' plough; but he'll need a whilie to finish this acre, I'm thinkin'' – and Charlie laughed at his own wit.

'Lat's see the sclate, laddie,' quoth Peter, reaching round the corner of his chair, and putting past his book. 'Lat me try't.'

The 'sclate' accordingly was handed to the gudeman, and Charlie gazed with no little interest in his face, as he proceeded studying the question. Now he commences, 'skallie' in hand – figures, and again rubs out; he is on a wrong tack.

Musing a while, and scratching his head, he asks Charlie what the answer is; this he refuses to tell, until the question is 'wrocht' – at the same time looking slyly up to his mistress.

'I cud work it, but' – and Peter was proceeding to point out some grievous fallacies in the question, when he was interrupted by the noise of persons speaking outside, and presently the door was opened. 'Collie', as the fat short-winded cur of doubtful breed was called, came lumbering out from the rear of the old arm-chair, resolved to stand in the front rank, if danger was near.

No sooner did the lamp shed its light on the new comers, than his fears were allayed, and wagging his stumpy tail at a rate that might have shaken it off had its length been greater, he bounded forward to give them welcome.

'Come awa', lads,' cried the worthy farmer, as a couple of boys, some sixteen or seventeen years of age, emerged from the entrance; 'are ye baith brawly the nicht?'

They immediately assured him that they were, and with a little bustle on Martha's part, the young men were soon seated in front of the fire. Peter, settling himself on his chair, and laying one leg over the other, was evidently resolved on having a crack with them. The elder and stouter of the two was a fine open-faced fellow, with a neatly combed head of brown hair, inclining to curl; the gorgeous red plush vest and jauntily cut coat showed he had something of the beau in him. This was an elder brother of Charlie's; his companion, of a slighter make, and dressed with less pretension, was a quiet-looking, fair-haired boy, with the down of manhood on his lip; and as he sat patting the head of Collie, who had now confidently placed his snout across one of his knees, or exchanging small gossip with Martha and the boy, while the other was rattling on with Peter, among ploughs and horses, the training of colts, and the feeding of cattle, a stranger would have said, he was much less fitted for pushing his way in the world than his companion. The young men were cousins, and had been companions from infancy. Each in his time had been foreman to our host, and now they were both serving a neighbouring farmer.

'Ye'll be baith bidin' at Hillhead through the winter,' said Peter, addressing his young friends, during a momentary lull in the conversation.

'I'm nae thinkin' that,' was the ready response; 'Hillie's been gaun throw't wi' the foreman, noo an' than a' simmer; an', for a chance, there'll be a clean toon.'

'Weel, I'm sure I'm nae wantin' to flit,' said our fair-haired friend, somewhat thoughtfully.

'Nor I either, Jamie,' returned his companion; 'but, fan it comes to that, I'm as independent o' my maister as he is o' me.'

Seven o'clock had arrived, and it was time to supper the cattle. Charlie was stirring, and had got hold of a capacious wooden 'booet', whose windows had evidently been cut of a size to fit the glass, and not the glass to fit them. He drew two inches of a candle from the interior of it, lighted, and put it in again; and was then marching off, when Peter requested the young men to accompany him to 'see the beasts' – an honour which (like many more opulent farmers) he was in the habit of conferring upon all and sundry of his visitors.

By the time they had dandered round to the stable, the work was proceeding apace; the horse and ox stood side by side, each in his stall, and Charlie, pitchfork in hand, was busy arranging their litter; so there was little for the gudeman to do, and he accordingly shut the door, and, hooking his thumbs into the armholes of his waistcoat, stretched himself up to his full height, and proceeded to descant on the merits of his cattle – for it must be observed Peter considers himself a perfect judge of horse or cow, and no mean cattle-doctor to boot. Farriery, in fact, is a sort of hobby with him, and well does he know how to concoct a balsam for a sprained joint, and many a precious receipt is he in possession of, for mixing healing potions. The venerable book we found him reading, which has unfortunately lost both title-page and preface, is his standard authority in the veterinary line. It belonged to his grandfather, and along with the *Monthly Visitor*, a volume of the *Cheap Magazine*, and the *History of the House of Douglas*, by the worthy Hume of Godscroft, forms the main portion of his library. He was wont to declare that no such books were printing now-a-days; but his prejudices against the press of the present day were somewhat shaken by the following incident.

Peter's neighbours, taking into consideration the great benefit they had derived from his gratuitous service among their ailing cattle, wisely resolved on presenting him with a testimonial. A committee was accordingly formed, subscriptions raised, and, in a short time, a deputation of the subscribers waited on him at his own residence, with a handsome time-piece, acompanied by a neat tea-service of china for his sister, as a small acknowledgement of the value of his services, and their esteem for him as a neighbour. When all this was set forth with becoming gravity in the newspapers of next week, with the addition, that Mr Stark replied in a neat and feeling speech, it need not be wondered at, if Peter held his head a little higher for some time. To be sure, the testimonial was of no use, as he had an eight-day clock before, and Martha never dreamed of making further use of her tea service, than taking them out on cleaning days, wiping the dust carefully from each piece in succession, and again locking them into the wa'-press. Yet, Peter had the consolation of thinking that testimonials, in general, are presented with a very slight regard to the actual benefit the recipients are to derive from them. He was, moreover, a little taken aback at first, to find the few stammering words he had uttered lauded as 'a neat and feeling speech'; but, as this was a matter between the deputation and himself, he thought it best to keep his thumb on it. Sarcastic people, indeed, sometimes hinted, that a copy of the newspaper, containing the identical paragraph, was somewhat ostentatiously displayed for a time in our friend's dwelling; but, be that as it may, would it not have been something strange, if a man who had been thus prominently noticed in the public papers, could not have given ignorant people some useful hints as to how matters were managed in a printing-office? Certain it is, Peter became, from this time, more of a 'politician,' as his neighbours called it, although his political reading, like that of many of our country friends, was confined rather too much to hunting out paragraphs of import similar to the one we have mentioned – conning over the advertisments, or reading aloud any 'horrible occurrence' for the benefit of the household.[2]

2

The early evening of the day after the term was gloomily closing down upon the hills, as Geordie Brown, after tramping a distance of nine or ten miles, neared the farm of —. He passed the front of the stately farm-house, taking a sly peep at it through the garden hedge; and a hundred yards farther on stood the out-houses. Here he found the grieve just entering the stable, for the purpose of leading the horses out to watering, before it became dark. There was no other servant on the premises but a 'rowd-shoulder'd mannie,' with soil-stained habilments, who was busy among the cattle; and as the grieve had been obliged to groom and look after six or seven horses for the last day and a half, he was disposed to be in rather a friendly humour at our hero's making his appearance. As Geordie looked round on the sleek, well-fed horses, and the polished harness hanging to the smoothly-plastered walls by many a convenient hook and beam, he could not help contrasting these things in his own mind with the gear he had been accustomed to at Hillhead. His thoughts instantly reverted to his old companions, and he felt a little elevated at the idea of driving such a well-appointed pair.

'An' that's your beasts at the backside, lad – ye may tak' them oot to get a drink.' Geordie pulled off his coat, and ordered one of the beasts to 'stan' roun',' preparatory to loosing it. The animal gave a caper, and threw out its heels, he escaping the stroke but a few inches. The grieve was narrowly watching his new man, apparently with the view of ascertaining whether he would show pluck. On catching Geordie's eye, he said 'They're some idle enoo, ye see, but she's quite peaceable; only min' yer eye a little wi' the tither ane – I wudna promise muckle upo' him takin a nip o' ye. I never likes to lat a young loon gae in amo' them wantin warnin.'

And here, we cannot help making a passing remark on the grieve's very considerate conduct in giving this warning. Masters and grieves who are in the habit of changing their servants often, seldom think it necessary to do anything of the kind; and although the matter caused very little remark among those most deeply concerned, yet it does seem a piece of unnecessary barbarity to allow a man to go at random in amongst animals, that may inflict serious injury on him, in an unguarded moment, leaving him to discover the vicious tempered by experience.

The horses were duly watered, and Geordie having been consigned to the care of the baillie, they proceeded together to the bothy. Here a fire was kindled with some small trouble, and the boiler put on to get hot water for the brose. When the lamp was lighted, Geordie had an opportunity of viewing the servants' dwelling. It was an old house, which at one time had been the farm-house; one end of it was now used as a lumber-house, the other as the bothy. Immediately fronting the door stood a trap stair, which led to the sleeping apartment above; and, at the back wall, were two meal girnals, each divided in the interior into three compartments, for the purpose of keeping every man's meal by itself. When the lids were closed, they did duty commonly as tables, for breakfast, dinner, and supper. In one corner hung a girdle, and beside it, the 'bake-board,' formed from the floor of an old bee-hive. Above these was a shelf, crammed with old bottles, blacking-brushes, pieces of leather, &c. A rickety chair, two or three long stools, and several round blocks of wood, sawn off about eighteen inches in length, formed the seats. The middle of the floor was occupied by nearly a barrow load of sticks, partly chopped, with an axe lying on the top of them. The water bucket stood by the door, with the cat's dish by its side – the custom being, to have the latter dish commonly filled to overflowing, but never cleaned out. Moreover, there was a hole broken in the bottom of the door for pussy's especial convenience in getting ingress and egress. One more thing that particularly attracted Geordie's attention, was a long strip of soiled paper, stuck up above the fire-place, on which was inscribed the rules and regulations of 'this bothy.'

When supper was over, the baillie drew one of the chairs very close to the fire, and sat down to enjoy his smoke. If one might judge by appearances, he was afraid of catching a cold in his head; for, while he did not think it necessary to put on a coat at all, his bonnet was drawn down over his ears. The cattleman being rather a taciturn sort of gentleman, our friend felt the time hang heavily on his hands, and could not help wishing that to-morrow were come. In the course of the evening, one or two more of the servants dropped in. The grieve came up to give some orders about suppering the cattle, and asked whether Rob — was yet come. On being answered in the negative, he said rather angrily, 'He sud hae been or noo. Weel, weel, lads, gae awa t' yer beds in gude time, an' I'll be up i' the mornin to tell you fat to dee.' The lads accordingly retired in good time. The cattleman knew the advantages of a good sleep, and slipped off to bed as soon as the grieve left. The others, being strangers to each other, had little choice but follow his example.

Early in the morning, the servants were roused by someone shouting loudly at the door. Geordie, thinking he had overslept himself, was at the floor feeling for his clothes before his eyes were well opened. On listening again, however, he recognised the voice of Rob —, calling on the inmates of the bothy, whoever they might be, for a parcel of 'lazy scoundrels', to 'rise an' lat him in'. Informed by Geordie how matters stood, the rest of the lads kept their beds, and he hurried down to get a light and open the door. And, presently, Rob got admittance, with a new whip strapped round his shoulders, and a bundle below his arm. 'Hilloa, Geordie,' quoth he with his usual frankness, 'is that you there, half-naket? Fan cam ye? Is the second horseman come?' On being answered these queries, Rob continued – 'I b'lieve I sud hae been here the 'streen tee, but, sang! I was anither gate; but fat time i' the mornin is't?' and he pulled out his watch. It was but a little past three o'clock, and Rob swore 'he wud get an hour in's bed yet. Come awa up, Geordie, or we see aboot it.' On reaching the sleeping apartment, Rob seized the light to have a look at his new 'neebours'. He knew none of them, however, but that 'aul sinner,' the baillie, who grumbled rather audibly at being thus unseasonably disturbed. 'Weel, Geordie, ye maun tak in han' to waken me at five o'clock.' Geordie promised he would try, at least; and Rob, throwing off his coat and shoes, jumped into one of the beds, without farther ceremony, shouting out, 'Aha! lads – I've been here afore.'[3]

3

We introduced our readers to a bothy some weeks ago, and at closing, left the inmates all safe in bed. Wishing it to be supposed that said inmates had risen at the proper time, and gone about their labour day by day, for a period of nearly three months, we will again pay them a visit, as some of our readers may have but an imperfect knowledge of how matters are managed in these institutions. It was past mid winter, as we have said, and the sun was gradually encroaching on the long winter nights, giving promise of a returning seed time; ploughmen might now, by dint of economising time, manage to work their regular hours, that is, take their horses to yoke at six in the morning, and have daylight for being a-field till six at night.

Rob and his fellow ploughmen had just concluded a day's labour, the cattlemen had their charges settled up for a night; and they, one and all, began to drop into the bothy; one proceeds with kindling the fire, another sets off to fill the water bucket, and by the time the last straggler has reached the bothy, the kettle is almost invisible in the fierce blaze of crackling firewood. In a few minutes each man is ready with his caup and spoon, and as soon as the water has reached its boiling point, Rob shouts 'Whaar's the police?'

An orra man at the other side of the fire, picked up a piece of an old stuff hat in the corner behind him, and reached across to Rob with a 'Hae ther's.'

Rob having got the so-called 'police', seized hold of the handle of the kettle, which was nearly red hot by this time, and having got his supply of water, immediately handed it to the next in succession, and thus it went on till it came to a blunt-looking youth, who had been but a few days in the bothy, having been hired as an additional spring hand; this poor fellow was dumbfounded by someone at his back shouting out 'Thoomb him, thoomb him,' immediately on his commencing to pour water.

What could the uproar mean? Alas! he was soon to be taught to his cost; in holding his dish, he had placed his thumb on the edge of it, and had thus unconsciously broken through the rules; a smartish looking chap, who was jocosely delving in his brose dish, at one side of the fire, reached suddenly across with the intention of giving him a tremendous slap with his spoon on the offending digital; but he, starting aside to escape the blow, unfortunately lost his hold on the caup, which rolled on the floor, scattering his meal hither and thither, and scalding his fingers to boot; the cry now was 'Ram him;' the poor simpleton looked half inclined to cry. Some said it 'wasna fair to ram him, he bein' but new came in'; others were of a different opinion, but it was ultimately referred to Rob, who declared it 'cudna be pass't: na, na, sang he'll ken better the neist time.' The fellow who had missed the opportunity of thoomin', being the last punished, started up with alacrity and laid hold of the axe, being glad, no doubt, at the prospect of being liberated from the duties of axe-man. The culprit was then placed upon the lid of his meal girnal, and submitted, with a very bad grace, to three pretty severe blows on the heel, with the head of the axe, which had the effect of putting him completely out of humour for the rest of the evening, and he accordingly slunk off to his bed in a very short time.

'Are ye a' through wi' the fire?' cried the baillie coming forward with a small pot of potatoes, which he proceeded to boil; another had commenced making porridge, while a third came elbowing his way to the fire with a piece of suspicious-looking cake, which he declared was become so hard that 'a dog's teeth wadna chaw it.' In a short time all were through, saving the baillie, who, having got himself seated on a block of wood, continued to watch the boiling of his potatoes with great assiduity, his face lighted up with the fitful glare of the half- burnt sticks.

'Sit roun, Willie, an' lat in aboot the form,' – the baillie moved with a half audible grumble, withdrew his pot, and having poured out the bree, returned to give his potatoes a toast preparatory to commencing eating. 'Are na ye giens' a tattie, Willie?' exclaimed two or three voices, at the same time, that as many hands – some of them not particularly clean – were unceremoniously thrust into the pot.

Willie, seeing that he was likely to be left but a slight supper, and knowing how needless it was to remonstrate, put on a resolute countenance, and seizing his pot of imperfectly dried potatoes, marched off to the other end of the bothy, to enjoy his meal in peace and darkness. Part of the lads now grouped themselves about the fire, and commenced filling their pipes; one of the orra men stretched himself on the top of the meal girnals; and, in a short time, was fast asleep.

Rob was stirring about. 'I think we'll awa an' gie our bridles a tip up for the morn,' said he, addressing his fellow ploughmen; on the morn, it must be understood, a ploughing match was to take place, at which Rob and his companions were to compete, and the rest of the harness being cleaned, he meant by 'gien the bridles a tip up', they should give them the finishing polish. They accordingly proceeded to the stable, and began to examine the bridles with no little earnestness.

By and by Rob commenced giving them a biographic sketch of a chap who had gained an extraordinary number of prizes at ploughing matches, enlarging on his extreme youth at the time he gained the first of them. Here the second horseman, who was better informed than Rob was aware of, gave him a slight correction on one or two points. Rob could not contradict him, seeing he quoted authorities, but he merely remarked 'That's ae way o't.'

The other, not a little elated at his success, proceeded, 'Ye'll need to see an' cast a bit o' a dash the morn, Geordie, bein' ye're first outset.'

This was addressed to Geordie Brown, but Rob replied, 'Aye but he'll dee that; sang, Geordie an' me'll cast a dash mair ways nor ane the morn, maybe.'

'Hoo mair ways nor ane, d'ye mean that ye'll tak' prizes for ploughin an' groomin' baith?' said the other with an inquiring look.

'Oh, Davie, man, there's little i' ye,' replied Rob with a scornful laugh. 'I dinna care that for their prizes,' snapping his fingers, and clinching the expression with an oath.

'Oh, ye'll be gaun to the ball, are ye?'

'Na, we're nae gaen to the ball either, Davie. Ye'll need to stick up better fan we gae back yon'er again, Geordie,' with a sly wink to our friend, who began to look rather uncomfortable.

'O ho! I see ye noo, Rob, it's the lasses ye're after; didna Geordie shew richt pluck the last nicht tha' ye was o' the spree?'

'It's nane o' your bisness, Davie, ye ha'ena great spunk amo' the lasses fatever.'

Davie was not to be thus put down, however, but immediately commenced telling them of a remarkable feat he had performed on a love expedition 'fan he was but a gey loon'. The story was interrupted by uncontrollable bursts of laughter from the narrator; but, as it was not of general interest, we need not give the details.

Its only effect on Rob was to make him labour still more assiduously at his bridles, and by the time Davie had got his eyes dried, he had perversely struck off at a tangent, and was again enlarging on well-cleaned harness, and fleet cutting ploughs, from which subject he would never have wandered, had not Davie, in utter defiance of the rules of good conversation, thrust himself forward to the first place in the conversation, when ordinary discernment might have shown him that it became him to take the second. However it he did not echo his leader's sentiments, as in duty bound, for the rest of the evening, he at least had the prudence not to expend more of his choice anecdotes so profitlessly. As the remainder of the conversation turned chiefly on technical points, we shall not follow it farther, seeing it would involve a world of explanation to bring it down to the capacity of the general reader. For it is well known that all classes of men take a lining to their phraseology from their own peculiar avocation, even from the statesman down to the itinerant fish-vendor, or as much lower as you please. So, hoping to see our friends a-field on another day, we say good night.[4]

4

The farmer of Wardend was a stout burly sort of personage, who might be seen at times driving a load of corn to market, or seated on the fore breast of the cart, with his 'journey' clothes on, wending his way home from the town of —, with a boll or two of coals, and a number of miscellaneous articles in the cart; but, in general, he kept himself, or rather his wife insisted on keeping him, above drudgery work. He kept a man for driving his pair of horses, a mannie to wait on his cattle, and a halflin to manage his orra beast. This latter individual was our friend, Jamie Dawson.

Wardend's wife, too, was a remarkable woman in her way, her father and grandfather had been so well known; in fact, her 'ation' had taken root deeply and spread widely in the district. Who did not know the Benzies? Her father had two or three sons, and a whole half dozen daughters. For his sons, he had, by great foresight and prudence, managed to procure wives and farms as soon as they came of a proper age, and though his daughters had been rather a drug in the matrimonial market, yet they had never stooped so low as to become servants, though officious people sometimes wondered what 'aul Benzie did wi' sae mony muckle dochters aboot's han'. Moreover, Miss Benzie thought that, in bestowing her hand on the farmer of Wardend, she rather conferred an honour on the worthy man; for, though there might be wealth on his side, she could boast of a long and unsullied pedigree. All those matters would the gudewife gravely discuss with her servant girl when in a gossiping humour, albeit she had a just and proper sense of what was due to a servant, and never failed to tell the damsel so when a suitable opportunity offered.

Another person at the farm of Wardend demands a special share of our attention. Andrew Gibb, the foreman, was a rather small-sized, fair-haired man, and among his companions universally allowed to be a fine creature. He had flitted and flitted from master to master, round the whole neighbourhood, sometimes jumping a distance of twelve miles or so for six months, and then returning to his old locality till he found himself unwillingly verging upon forty years of age, without having saved a single sixpence of the many fees he had worked hard to earn. He knew he might have saved something, and was willing to acknowledge that he might have been better settled in life; but, 'he was aye ower free-heartit and independent for that – he cud gie a dram or tak ane,' and 'he would never haud in wi' maister or mistress for ony sake o' keepin' their favour.' Andrew had a very extensive acquaintance among the horses and horsemen of the district. It may seem somewhat incongruous to put the quadruped before the biped; but the fact is, Andrew had fully as great an affection for the one as for the other. And in speaking of even the hugest and most unwieldy animal, he invariably employed the diminutive 'horsie,' like a certain fond mother of our acquaintance, who always distinguishes her youngest son – a great overgrown fellow of sixteen – by the title of 'my tchil'. His ambition had led him, at one time, to think of learning the trade of a shoemaker, but he found it impossible to tear himself away from his beloved animals; and, though the farm of Wardend lay in a somewhat remote corner – there being only one country road passing it at the distance of nearly a mile – yet even at that distance, Andrew, if not able to determine exactly, could generally form a very probable conjecture of the identity of every farm horse that passed, and consequently of its master. More fleetly mounted equestrians were rare and puzzling to account for – like meteoric stone to the astronomer. Then he would tell his companions such a 'shortsome' place as Knowhead was, where he had been serving at three different times: the turnpike passing close by, 'there was never an hour o' the day, but something was to be seen.'

Andrew had great abilities too, in the hair-cutting line. Every other night, two or three fellows would be dropping in to have their locks shortened, and he would cheerfully trudge a distance of two or three miles through dub and mire to perform the like operation on any one who might choose to ask him; not that the barber part of his business was a very paying concern, for Andrew had only the rather vague promise of 'I'll be due ye a dram, Anro, an' ye wud clip my head,' generally, to rely on for remuneration, yet he pursued his philanthropic labours most unflaggingly, and would have been quite unhappy if any of his subjects had taken it into their heads, to apply to a professional hair-cutter. The truth is, Andrew felt the long winter evenings hang heavily on his hands, and though it might be irksome to tramp some miles on a dark night, yet when his labours were over, he would get an hour or two of glorious smoking, and talking about horses and ploughing matches, in somebody's cham'er or bothy.

It was on the night following one of Andrew's professional tours. He had just got his horses suppered, and had retired to the cham'er, or, to speak more plainly, to his own end of the stable. Wardend's steading or offices had been built anterior to the period at which men struck out the happy idea of building farm out-houses in squares. A long barn stretched one way, with sundry 'back and fore doors;' some cattle-sheds, with an enclosed space in front, stood over against it; small houses were strewn broadcast here and there; at the top of the close was the stable, with a byre or two at one end of it. The three horses stood with their heads to the gable wall at one end, and directly in their rear, at the back wall, were the servants' beds – there being no attempt at a partition to separate the men from the horses; for Andrew declared, with something like pride, that 'he had kent the mearie mair than ance brak loose o' the nicht, and come ben snuffin for him in's bed.' The servants' trunks stood in front of the beds, at a distance of a yard or so from them, beside a space railed off for holding a 'pickle strae' and some old harness.

Andrew had got himself seated on his 'ain kist lid', with his hands thrust into his pockets, and was attempting to whistle a tune, but every now and then yawning portentously. Jamie Dawson having his trunk-lid opened, was examining some books by the aid of a lamp.

'Boys,' said Wardie, softly opening the door of the stable, and thrusting himself half in, 'ye wunna need to bide there burnin awa licht.'

Jamie was evidently the culprit; but Andrew, rousing himself up, declared, 'It wasna three minutes sin' they had deen supperin.'

'Oh! maybe that,' rejoined the farmer mildly; 'but ye've been i' the practice o' bidin' oot for some nichts back, ye ken, and it'll hardly dee, Anro.'

Andrew replied, that 'he thocht there cudna be muckle said to them, fan they got licht i' the house nae langer than just to lat them see to tak their supper.'

'Deed, boys, but them that needs licht at ony ither time, maun just afford it to themsells, for I canna keep a licht bleezin' aye mornin and evenin' in this lang dark nichts; it wud herry me.'

So saying, the farmer went away, and Andrew proceeded with 'lowsing his points', rating farmers, in general, severely for their niggardliness, Wardend, of course, coming in for a liberal share of his censure. The light was put out, and he went to bed directly to get up his arrears of sleep, advising Jamie to 'drop that reading o' buiks, for he never saw naebody mak' muckle by that.'

This advice had but little effect, however, as Jamie had the hardihood to buy a small lamp for himself; and he might be found, night after night, when the weather was not too cold, in the noways desirable chamber, engaged with his books, and though his master looked with rather an unfavourable eye on the matter, he never again attempted putting a veto on his proceedings.[5]

5

On a certain night, near the end of April, the farmer of Wardend was sitting by the kitchen fire musing, with his chair tilted up on two legs, and his heels stuck into the aperture formed by the arm of the swing.[6] He was evidently indulging in a pleasant reverie, when the servant girl came with a pot of water to hang on the fire; by pushing back the swing she unfortunately deprived Wardend's feet of their resting place, and they came to the hearthstone with some violence, bringing him rather suddenly to a bolt upright position on his seat. Wardie rose to his feet a little nettled, the lassie looked foolish and endeavoured to stammer out something like an apology. The deed was evidently done through ignorance, not through malice, and the gudewife assured her husband, if he 'wud sit roun' a bittie he wudna be nane i' the road;' but the gudeman's equanimity was disturbed, and he would not resume his seat — 'he was gaun oot at ony rate to see fat the boys war deein.'

'Tell Jamie to come in an' speak to me than,' said the gudewife as he vanished from the doorway. A faint 'aye, aye,' was heard as the door was shutting.

Wardend found the boys standing sheltered from a hail shower at the front of the cart shed. The reason of his wishing to know so particularly what they 'war deein' on that particular evening was this. After a rather backward season, Wardend had succeeded in getting his sowing nearly finished, but, being an improving farmer, he had resolved, previous to laying down his grass seeds, to give a certain portion of his cleaned land a 'gude coat o' lime'. The fashion of liming previous to sowing was not then so much in vogue as now; and, as Wardie had been hitherto hindered in getting a supply of lime, he had resolved on sending his men and horses for a 'draught' on the morrow. Now, the small seaport town, at which the worthy farmer procured his artificial manures, lay at a distance of some sixteen miles from his place of abode, and that the journey to and from might be performed in a day, it was customary for them to set out at one o'clock in the morning. Jamie Dawson had never been on this jaunt, but his master, in consideration, no doubt, of his faithful service, had promised to allow him to accompany Andrew with the orra beast.

So finding the carts were greased, and provender for the horses prepared, and having given Jamie a hint that the gudewife 'wuntit to speak till him', he then strolled away round to examine a mole trap or two that he had industriously kept setting and re-setting for two or three weeks, though unfortunately no mole had stumbled into either of them to reward him for his pains. On his way he met his neighbour, Yonderton, who had been on some business jaunt, and the two worthies entered into a stiff controversy as to the expediency or inexpediency of capturing moles; Yonderton being inclined to afford them protection, in consideration of their subsoiling and draining powers, while Wardend had, as he declared, a 'mortal hatred' at them, because they uprooted his plants. The arguments, pro and con, were scarcely worth recording, however. Yonderton touched with a sort of general benevolence, spoke much of the cruelty of bowstringing the poor creatures, though he admitted he had sometimes been put a little out of humour by seeing a drill of newly sprung turnips, 'sheel't up boss fae en' to en'', as his neighbour expressed it. It was at such times as the turnip hoeing season that Wardend might be seen half frantic with rage at the destruction committed by the moles; then would he declare that, if he 'war spared till the beginning o' anither season, he sud pay a mole-catcher, and hae his lan' cleart o' them, though it sud cost him five poun'.' But by the time that 'gentle spring came roun' again', he was always cooled down, and set about amusing himself at the old process of trap-setting, only it is but fair to say that he did sometimes catch a more than usually blind mole; and then would he expatiate to the gudewife on the foolishness of paying 'a man to dee fat he cud dee brawly himsel', – at the same time exhibiting the dead mole in triumph, and perhaps relating an anecdote of the 'half-witted auld lairdie', who on one occasion refused to bargain with a mole-catcher to rid his farm of the obnoxious grubbers for a few shillings, at the same time gladly consenting to give him twopence for every head of the enemy. Imagining that the man could not gain above a shilling by the speculation, judge then of his surprise when, on going out to take a walk next morning, he met 'moley' coming groaning and sweating in at the gate, pushing a wheelbarrow before him heavily loaded with strangulated moles. Wardend declared he verily 'danced with rage', they said, but having only received the story at second hand it, of course, marred the effect a little.

But to return from this digression. After Jamie Dawson and Andrew Gibb had completed their arrangements, the latter set off to his bed, advising his companion to follow him as soon as he was 'through wi' the wife'. Jamie accordingly hurried down to the kitchen to receive the mistress's orders, which were of a peculiarly important and confidential character. Her eldest girl was at school, and was becoming an exceedingly accomplished young lady; she had sewn a number of samplers full of unique-looking trees and fruit, and stiffly shaped dogs and peacocks. Two gorgeous specimens of her handiwork had been framed, and now graced the walls of the chief room. Miss in short was become proficient at this sort of work. And now she was to be allowed scope for her genius in a new line. At a convivial party at Mains's, the mistress had observed that the gentlemen's punch tumblers were placed on 'little holipie towellies', as she described them to her daughter next day, manufactured by Mains's own gudewife. By a piece of finesse (to avoid showing her own ignorance), she had lately learnt that the name for this sort of article was a wine rubber; and wine rubbers she would have. Yea! and a gorgeously large cloth to lay on the bread basket to boot; for why, Eliza could knit them in the finest style of workwomanship, if she were but learned. But here a dilemma arose: an instrument was needed wherewith to do the knitting, and where would it be got? The shopkeeper who had generally a supply of almost every conceivable commodity under the sun had been applied to in vain. The smith was next urged to make one, but the worthy man shook his head; he was more at home hammering and welding shoulder picks and plough irons. Now at the port of —, where Jamie was to be next day, there were shops at which the gudewife had no doubt the desiderated article could be got. Jamie, therefore, received not a few instructions as to how he was to conduct the search; what amount of coppers the wished for crochet needle should cost; and specially to tell wherever he went that the article was for Mrs Sheepshank of Wardend, the gudewife seeming to think that her name should have some weight.

When Jamie had received all his orders, and undertaken to fulfil them, the mistress commenced, or rather re-commenced, quizzing him on his greenness and want of knowledge of far away places; and, truth to tell, the young man had never been far out of his native district, his life from childhood having been a same, unceasing round of servitude, he had never even been in sight of the sea. Knowing this, his mistress sagaciously informed him that 'he wudna think it was water ava to see't, it luiket liker a blue hill wi' sheep upon't.' Much more highly useful information would Jamie have got, interspersed with anecdotes of Mrs Sheepshank's own experience, for she had seen wondrous things by land and sea, having once, when a young 'quean', actually been nearly out of sight of land in a fishing-boat; but as the gudewife, being in a talkative humour that day, had treated the lad to a resumé of a great part of the same facts and collateral observations at the dinner hour, Jamie took the opportunity of a pause in the conversation, caused by her going into the milk closet for a jug of milk to a favourite cat, to slip off to bed.[7]

6

It was on a beautiful summer evening near the end of June, that two young men might have been seen coming slowly down the back avenue from the farm buildings of an extensive landed proprietor. They had evidently been talking, or were about to talk, on some subject on which both parties felt embarrassed, and they walked on for some distance in almost complete silence. By a turning in the avenue, an old gentleman and two or three young ladies came in view, at some distance before them.

'That's some o' yer gentry,' said one of the young men, looking round as if he would have gladly avoided meeting them, had there been a possibility of doing so.

It was Geordie Brown who spoke, and he directed his words to Jamie Dawson, his former friend and companion.

'Never min',' was the quiet answer to Geordie's abrupt address, 'it's but the laird an' ane or twa o' the young ladies.'

They walked on, and while Jamie's lifted bonnet was acknowledged by a nod of the head from the ladies and a brief sentence of recognition from their father, Geordie moved on with half-averted look. As soon as they were so far past as to run no risk of being overheard, Geordie made some remarks on the 'braw life' led by 'folk like that', alluding to the gentry. This led to a short desultory conversation, but there was evidently something weighing on Geordie's mind, for he again relapsed into silence, as they strolled across the fields.

Some years had passed away, during which the young men had seldom met but at the half-yearly terms of Whitsunday and Martinmas. Geordie was now known among his companions as a 'first rate han'', and a 'fine spreein' chiel', while Jamie Dawson had plodded on in comparative obscurity – he could not boast, like his companion, of having served a number of the principal farmers in a wide district of country. Though compelled to change his master at times from the wretched system of estrangement that exists between our farmers and their servants, he had generally done so with something like a feeling of regret, and while his companions went to the feeing market shouting in uproarious glee, he felt deeply the degradation of his position. In pursuing his own method of reading and study, he had borne the sneers and raillery of unthinking and profligate companions, till such sneers and raillery were beginning, per force, to be turned occasionally into something like words of admiration. 'He was a clever, deep chiel,' that was admitted; and as he had never allowed his pursuit of knowledge to interfere with his duties as a servant, every master he had served would willingly have given him a certificate of character and ability, and it was sometimes prophesied that as he was 'kent for a steady chap', and was moreover 'sairn' wi' the laird', he would come to something.

The two friends at last came to a halt, and a long and apparently serious conversation took place. Geordie had got his mind relieved. He was about to be married; and though aware that Jamie had some previous knowledge of this, he had felt considerable difficulty in announcing officially the happy event to him. Geordie, as already remarked, had obtained the character of a 'spreein chiel', and as such he had been involved in a number of love adventures; and though never absolutely 'untrue' to his first love, it was somewhat wonderful the number of sweethearts he had had in his short career. He had now, however, run the length of his tether, and had been brought up in a manner not particularly creditable to himself. To Jamie's question as to 'whaur he intended to keep his wife', he answered that his intended bride 'was livin' at her mither's enoo, an' wud bide there for a whilie'.

'Hoot, man,' exclaimed Jamie, 'if I war' gettin' a wife, I sud hae a house o' my ain, though it michtna be a vera big ane.'

'We'll maybe get that shortly,' answered Geordie, attempting to look gay – rather ineffectually, for he now felt that marriage was a serious matter.

Geordie had of late ceased to make Jamie his confidant, and had not seldom twitted him on his want of spirit – wherefore did he now feel such an impulse to rely on his advice? Could not some one of his hearty boon companions be a more fitting 'young man'[8] at the forthcoming marriage? And could he not consult with them regarding the necessary arrangements? Alas! Geordie now discovered that those who were the very best of company for a spree by day or night were ill-suited indeed for giving advice when about to take an important step in life. He laid his case fully open to his sympathising friend, and the blush of shame rose to his cheek when forced to ask the loan of some money to defray the expense of the marriage festivities. This was a request Jamie might well have been excused for refusing to grant, seeing he had an aged grandmother almost entirely dependent on him for support; and Geordie, beyond giving his parents a trifle at the half-yearly terms, had never been a pound out of pocket save for his own proper use. He however immediately promised to supply the necessary funds, and they parted – the one to return to his master's, the other to carry the tidings of his approaching marriage to his father and mother.

Geordie had not proceeded far when he observed a sturdy fellow coming across the corner of a field with a spade over his shoulder. On a nearer approach the pedestrian turned out to be his old acquaintance, Rob. The surprise on meeting was mutual. They had not seen each other for about a year, and Rob, now a married man, was on his way to his own home, it being Saturday night. After the salutation was over, they tramped on, talking of bygone days. After skirting along the edge of a plantation of straggling firs a few hundred yards, they came upon a couple of rickety straw-thatched cottages that stood end to end at the northern extremity of a large turnip field which stretched upward in dreary uniformity before them, there being no passable carriage-way by which they might be approached saving through the middle of said field. These were a specimen of the cottages erected by some large farmers for the accommodation of their married servants. The farmer to whom they belonged had some years previously, in a philanthropic mood, resolved to provide houses for his married servants; and houses accordingly were built, of the cheapest materials, and at the spot where they would be least in the way of anything else. Somehow the experiment had failed in making the persons thus benefited one whit more attached to him, and, finding his benevolence entirely thrown away, the worthy man was now in the habit of letting the huts indifferently to such parties as offered the highest rents. One of the cottages was Rob's dwelling, and Geordie was now invited to enter. As the door opened, their ears were greeted by the discordant sounds of a child crying bitterly and a woman's voice shouting, 'That's a bisness! but little to me wud ca' aff yer head, ye creatur – there never was a bodie try't as I am wi' a confoun'et littl' ane.'

The words proceeded from Betty Tapp, otherwise Mrs Robert —. How it should have come to pass that Rob had taken a woman to be his wife he had formerly made a point of rendering ridiculous at every available opportunity must be left for the reader to conjecture. But so it was, and things not very dissimilar have come to pass with wiser people, which certainly ought to act as a check on the wit of bachelors and young ladies in particular cases. Rob and Betty had been man and wife for six or seven months, and the child that was now undergoing such a terrible scolding was one of Rob's children that had been taken home to live with them. The child, while at its supper, had allowed the dish of milk and bread to roll on the floor, scattering its contents hither and thither, and after receiving a cuff or two about the head, it was comforted by the intelligence that it 'sud get nae supper the nicht'. Betty was removing the fragments of the bread and milk as her husband and Geordie entered, and as she did so she continued to move a cradle that stood in one corner by a string across almost the entire breadth of the house. Her voice was lowered for a little to welcome the folk, but as the child – a timid-looking flaxen-haired girl about three years of age – continued to blubber piteously, she commenced afresh: 'Haud yer tongue this minute, ye little smatchet, or I'se pit ye to the ootside o' the door – hard 'at a bodie wouldna hear their ain word for ye.'

'Hoot, pit her till her bed, an' stop that yelpin',' interrupted Rob, authoritatively.

'Tak' the string an' rock the cradle twa three minutes than.'

'Na, sang, I've something ither adee nor come here an' rock your cradle,' was the answer.

Betty retorted with some bitterness, but the matter was set at rest by Geordie undertaking the task of rocking, and the unhappy child was bundled off to bed by the judicious stepmother, with a sweetie in her hand as an inducement to 'haud her tongue.' Geordie looked round on his friends' dwelling. The walls were rough and unplastered, and the not very transparent panes of the two pigmy windows had rather a superfluous number of 'bull's eyes' amongst them. There was no ceiling to hinder the eye from ranging at will among the sooty couple bauks. The stock of furniture was but scanty; a couple of clothes' chests, which had formerly belonged to the master and mistress respectively, and which were now their joint property, forming rather prominent features in the display. Perhaps Geordie thought of his own future home and what it would contain; but, notwithstanding all the intimacy that had formerly existed between him and Rob, and notwithstanding all Betty's pertinent inquiries, he left without having given them any hint of his intended marriage.[9]

NOTES

1. A settle. It is surprising what activities take place on Gushetneuk's 'deece' in *Johnny Gibb of Gushetneuk*.
2. Chapter 1, *North of Scotland Gazette*, 31 December 1852.
3. Chapter 6, *North of Scotland Gazette*, 4 February 1853.
4. Chapter 10, *North of Scotland Gazette*, 18 March 1853.
5. Chapter 7, *North of Scotland Gazette*, 11 February 1853.
6. The diminutive crane for hanging a cooking pot or kettle over the kitchen fire. Called different names in different parts of north-east Scotland, but 'swing' is most descriptive: for the crane was pivoted, allowing a pot to be attached to the hook away from the fire, then swung into the flames.
7. Chapter 16, *Aberdeen Free Press*, 13 May 1853.
8. Best man, in current usage.
9. Chapter 21, *Aberdeen Free Press*, 8 July 1853.

4   *The Aberdeenshire Crofter*

1

The position of the crofters in the region which may perhaps be best described, in a loose way, as the Highland crofter area,[1] has for a good many years been a theme of prominent public discussion. The wrongs of the crofter population within that area, and the miseries of their social condition, have been amply and variously expatiated upon. When premonitions of the acute stage of 'No rent' had became discernible in certain acts of rebellion against landlord domination, a government Commission of Inquiry was appointed;[2] and now, when the attitude of those Celtic small cultivators has stiffened up in a way that few seemed to anticipate as possible, we have no fewer than three Crofter Bills in parliament. One of the three, promoted by the government, and with a very fair chance of passing into law, embodies proposals in the crofters' interest which, although they fall short of the provisions of the other two bills, would have been denounced ten years ago as utterly revolutionary and subversive of the rights of property. At such pace do we go in these times. We have no intention, however, of discussing the Highland crofter question. But possessing, as we do, some slight knowledge of the crofter as he exists nearer home, we have a distinct conviction that, though in sundry ways a very different man from his Highland compeer, as found, for example, in Sutherlandshire and the western seaboard and island parts of Inverness-shire — he too not only has his own individual merits, but has suffered his due share of wrong and injustice. And of him too we would speak. Our remarks will be confined to Aberdeenshire, and the statements, both as general facts and individual instances, are to be taken as typical rather than exhaustive. They will be based throughout on personal knowledge and the information supplied by reliable correspondents.

Before, however, coming directly to our subject, it may not be without interest to cast the briefest glance backward at the rural economy of Scotland in byegone centuries, as bearing on the case of the small cultivator generally. In his description of the state of things on the lands belonging to the Monastery of Kelso, based on the Monastery Rental of 1290, the late Mr Cosmo Innes tells us that of the inhabitants of the grange or mains the lowest of the scale was the nativus, neyf or villein of the English law, who was transferred like the land which he laboured, and might be caught and brought back if he attempted to escape, like a runaway ox or sheep. Outside the grange, but near it, dwelt the cottarii, a class a good deal above that which we call cottars, for each occupant had from one to nine acres of land along with his cottage for which they paid rent, a considerable part of that rent consisting of services in seed time and harvest, in addition to a small amount in money. Beyond the mains and the hamlet or cottar town lived, each in his separate farm-stead, the husbandii or husbandmen. Each husbandus held a definite amount of land, generally two 'oxgates' of thirteen acres each, that being the extent effeiring to the cultivation of one ox, 'where pleuch and scythe may gang'. The husband-land of twenty-six acres could keep two oxen; but the plough required a team of eight; so four husbandii joined to work the common plough on their joint occupancy or 'plough-gate' of 104 acres or thereby, all under the rules of 'good neighbourhood', duly laid down.

The interest attaching to all this lies in the fact, firstly, that 600 years ago there was, in the more fertile parts of Scotland at least, as good cultivation as was witnessed during the succeeding 500 years; and secondly, that the social condition of the small cultivators, particularly those who held of the religious houses – whose rulers were better landlords than the reiving, ignorant brutal barons – was one of greater comfort than it frequently was in later times. And, in the third place, we find traces of the old arrangement as to the common plough, the division of land, common pasture and so on, in Aberdeenshire, not only down to the end of last century, but during the first quarter, at least, of the present one.

When, in 1794, Dr James Anderson drew up his Report for the Board of Agriculture on the state of farming in Aberdeenshire,[3] the era of agricultural improvement, in which the notable feature was the introduction of the turnip husbandry, had commenced; but up to its date, improvements of all sorts had been carried out mainly by the proprietors, the body of the tenants, great and small alike, being lacking at once in capital, enterprise, and skill as cultivators. Not many years of the present century had passed when this state of things had undergone something in the nature of a radical change. Partly through a new light, leading to the principle of a fixed rotation of crops; partly through the increased prices for 'horn and corn', consequent upon the long-continued Peninsular War, for which we are all paying the piper today, tenant enterprise got largely developed; and during the first half of the present century the arable area of the county was enormously increased. Putting together land reclaimed from heather, broom, and whins; and land drained and converted from bog, rough moss, and clay puddle, into corn-growing fields, it were hardly too much to say that something like a third was added to the cultivated acreage of the county. And in all this the lairds had but a limited share. In many cases where forty to fifty years ago they professed to assist the tenants by enabling them to participate in government loans, they took care amply to recoup themselves by charging six per cent, or more, against the tenants for money for which they paid only three or three and a half per cent. The loan,in short, was over three-fourths paid by the tenant during his nineteen years' lease; and then at the end of the lease the laird felt no shame in adding to his exorbitant greed by exacting as much of an increased rent as could be got by virtually exposing the tenant's improvements to public competition.

About this time, if not exactly through this very process, the crofter and small farmer suffered conspicuously, for the double reason that it not seldom was their part to do the 'rivin' in' of the roughest bits of hill-foot places, and the like; while no sooner was the lease out than they were apt to fall a prey to some grasping large farmer, if their little holdings were of a nature to tempt his cupidity. Or perhaps the laird or his factor concluded that it would be less trouble in management, and save cost in keeping up buildings, to extinguish the croft and let its occupants go elsewhere.

Before entering upon details, we may glance at the general state of present occupancy in the county of Aberdeen, which we are enabled to do through a careful analysis and abstract of the valuation roll, made in 1868 by Mr Alexander Fraser, Inspector, Stamps and Taxes Office, Edinburgh, at that time one of the assessors for the county. At the date mentioned the total number of holdings of all sizes in the county was 11,462; and of these no fewer than 8,022 showed a valued rental of under £50. Deducting the number of small farms with rents of £20 and under £50 – 2,497 – the number of holdings with rentals ranging from £4 and upwards, but under £20, was 5,525. The proportion of both small farms and crofts shown in this abstract is, as will be seen, very large; and the proportion has not since changed in an appreciable degree. A statement given in evidence before the Scotch Agricultural Commission of 1867, by Mr Hannay, factor for the Earl of Fife, of the approximate number of farmers and crofters in his district of Aberdeenshire and Banffshire corresponds, to its extent, with the figures for the county of Aberdeen as a whole. Out of a total of 742 tenants, 589 paid rents not exceeding £50; and of these 440 paid rents under £10.[4] As can thus be seen, the proportion of small holdings in the county of Aberdeen is still large; and the proportion of really large farms is very small. In Mr Fraser's abstract, the number of farms of over £500 valuation is only sixteen; and the total number over £300 only sixty six.[5]

2

We have already indicated that during the first half of the present century tenant enterprise became largely developed, and that a great increase was made in the acreage of the arable land of the county by the industry and perseverance of the tenant farmers and crofters. As time wore on, and when most of the improvable land had been reclaimed, a re-arrangement of marches naturally followed. And in this re-arrangement it frequently happened that the smaller holding was incorporated in its bigger neighbour. At this point came the limitation to crofter enterprise and further settlement. While the prosperous time lasted, people imagined that they could not get too much land; farmers became veritable land-grabbers; and in many cases they were not scrupulous as to the methods they adopted to 'influence' the laird or his factor,[6] in order that their covetous and selfish desires to add to their acreage and get rid of troublesome neighbours, as they deemed them, by taking possession of the crofter's small holding, and turning the cottar off the land, might have effect; while prosperous shopkeepers and other townspeople flocked to the country and offered exorbitant rents – rents which the land was barely fit to pay under any circumstances, and rents which even yet serve as the standard by which the proprietor fixes the value of the farms. The latter set of people flew at the higher game, and bade for farms which would justify their employing a 'grieve;' and in the scramble the crofter and small holder fell a prey to the larger farmer, who knowing that the croft contained soil which, having been well looked after, could be made to produce abundant crops, seldom hesitated about doing his part in the eviction process. The crofter, it might be, had spent the best part of his life in the reclamation of the little spot on the hillside where he had been allowed to make his home, and where he had done his honest part laboriously as cultivator, making a bare living without being able to put past anything for a rainy day, and in the expectation that his nest would not be disturbed. Yet the proprietor, in his need or his greed could not afford to give heed to sentimental associations nor even to the claims of justice and fair-dealing. If an advanced rent could be got, and no legal obstacle intervened, the crofter had to go to the wall. It was in vain to appeal to abstract principles of justice and equity, or to urge that property had its obligations as well as its rights; for until very recently the 'rights', so-called, of landed property were regarded with an almost superstitious reverence by the very class who had most reason to complain of their abuse. Latterly, in most districts of Aberdeenshire there has not been a rapid decrease in the number of small holdings. Yet on many estates 'the oldest inhabitant' can stand upon the knowe overlooking his house and point to the sites of dozens of homes which at one time were the life centres of holdings now merged in larger farms.

In the evidence taken by the Scottish Agricultural Commission of 1867, several of the Aberdeenshire witnesses make incidental reference to the subject of crofts; and it is instructive to note the diversity of view expressed. The late Dr Garden of Alford, who was a bank agent and farmer, expressed the opinion that a farm-servant who had continuous employment was in a better position than any occupier of less than a pair-horsed farm; and, if farm-labourers were to be occupiers at all, their holdings, he held, should not, as a rule, exceed five or six acres, as in that case they might hope to give personal services to some neighbouring farmer for the working of their land, which could not be the case if the holding were larger. He further held that, though probably not more than one in fifty farm-servants saved money, they had ample opportunity to do so before marriage; and in proof of the soundness of this doctrine, in addition to memorandum of bank deposits made by a number of male and female servants in Alford, said, '"I knew one farm-servant named George Smith, who died at the age of seventy, and left nearly £1,100. I was his executor; he was never married. He was very thrifty, and continued to work as a farm-labourer until within a few weeks of his death."'[7]

Colonel Innes of Learney, in his evidence, said: '"I have a considerable number of crofters upon my property. Labourers are very anxious to have crofts, particularly for the purpose of enabling them to keep a cow; I think it is important to maintain crofters in order that their families may keep up the supply of labourers well instructed in farm work."'[8] The late William Leslie, Esq of Warthill, and formerly member of parliament for the county, said, '"I have on my property as many crofts as I have farms. I consider the crofts of great value for the purpose of supplying the country with a class of respectable servants; and constituted to bring up families of a lower, but respectable class in habits of self-respect and independence."'[9] Mr Leslie also considered that the most profitable size of holding for a crofter was six acres of good land. The late Mr Andrew Boyd, who stated that he had the management of estates in Buchan yielding a rental altogether of nearly £30,000, said there were a great many crofts on these estates; '"We give,"' he said, '"all countenance to the crofts where they exist, and are properly managed; we think them very useful as the producers of labour. They have all leases. I think that a croft should rarely exceed ten acres . . . They think they are better off with a croft than working as labourers without one, and I think so too; it is a great thing for the family to have milk."'[10] Mr John Sleigh, factor to Mr Baird of Strichen, stated that '"There were formerly a great number of crofts in the neighbourhood, but, of late years, since the price of labour and manure has increased as much as it has, it has been impossible for the small crofters to live, and they have been simply breeding up a race of paupers, and consequently a great many of the crofts have been consolidated; a great many new steadings and farm-houses have been built, and some of the old crofters' houses have been left standing for the accommodation of the farm-servants."'[11]

A current story, for the authenticity of which we do not absolutely vouch, was that, when the purchaser of the Strichen estate from the Fraser family was carrying out the 'consolidation' referred to, the parish minister, a man, as it happened, exceptionally conversant, practically, with the style of life common to the crofter and the agricultural labourer, ventured to remonstrate with him on the ruthlessness of the proceeding, adding, 'Where are the poor people to go?'

'They may go to hell for me,' was, it is said, the polite rejoinder.

'If you really want to put them permanently out of your way,' said the minister, 'I think you had better send them in the opposite direction.'

The story is one which, if not literally true, ought to be.

Leaving the pages of the Blue Book, to which we may take occasion again to refer, we shall now endeavour to get a glimpse of the crofter himself as he was wont to figure in bodily presence and daily action fifty years ago, and later on. The first example of the class we light upon, though various others are in retentis, is Donald Jack. Not of Highland patronymic, perhaps, but of veritable Highland stamina – one of the class who, as youngish men little accustomed to systematic labour, descended from 'up throu' and 'the wast' to become indefatigable stonebreakers and makers of turnpike roads. Tough and thrifty, Donald about 1835 found himself in Udny; a married man with no particular outlook, but owning a grand capacity for patient, plodding industry. He obtained as a sub-let from the then tenant of Hillbrae a piece of rough, hilly ground extending to some eight to ten acres; and which, up to that time, had produced little or nothing but whins and heather. Donald's first care was to build himself a dwelling-house. This he did on a very cheap scale, the walls being mostly of turf, and the roof 'divots'. He trenched some of the land himself with pick and spade; and he wrought hard and willingly to his neighbours who had horses, in return for 'yokings' of their ploughs to enable him to conquer the more reclaimable bits with greater speed. By such means he formed a croft that enabled him to keep a cow and stirk, which he contrived to buy. He was now paying his way and bringing up a family; but the farmer under whom he sat unfortunately failed, and was sold out. The result was that Donald was ejected, and, of course, without any compensation for all his hard labour and hardly-earned outlay.

It was now about 1840, and Donald made another similar venture on a small 'possession', partly hill and partly moss, on the estate of Ardo, in the parish of Belhelvie, and although this was his second speculation he either was not careful, or was unable, to get any better security of tenure than in his first venture. Again he built and improved at his own cost; and he was only fairly begun to reap the fruits of his labour when he was unceremoniously turned out and his improvements confiscated by the laird. It may be noted in passing that in this his second misfortune Donald had several neighbours who shared a similar fate. Donald, not yet quite worn out but much failed in strength, next embarked in a new undertaking on the side of the Red Moss of Belhelvie on the estate of Millden. In this his third adventure he did obtain a nineteen years' lease; but was left to work entirely on his own resources, the laird incurring no obligation in the way of expenditure for improvements. By this time Donald's family were partly grown up; and assisted by them he soon reclaimed out of black, mossy, heather land as much as enabled him to yoke a plough. Whether the land was worth a shilling an acre when he got possession of it we know not, but at the end of his lease, when the whole improvement fell into the hand of the laird, a yearly rent of £26 was obtained for the 'placie'. In other words, taking it at the very moderate rate, for the time, of twenty years' purchase, Donald had added to the capital value of the estate fully £500. He made for himself the barest of livings, and had to leave all that of 'unearned increment' with the laird.

Our next example, J C, succeeded his father as tenant of a small farm, also in Belhelvie, though not on the same property. About 1841 he entered on a new lease at a rent of £40. At his own cost he built a substantial dwelling-house and stable, and also roofed the barn and byres. He trenched about seven acres of whins; put in many stone-filled drains; and 'blasted' rock heads and boulders, and grubbed up earth-fast stones to an extent that nearly enabled him to fence his fields with the results. By the end of his lease in 1860 he was getting old and much used up with hard work. At the date mentioned he was offered a renewal of his lease at a rental of £63, being over fifty per cent of an advance on the previous rent. The poor tenant hesitated; demurred; declined to accept the holding on such exorbitant terms; but after he and his wife had spent several sleepless nights over the, to them, serious situation, he returned to the unrelenting factor, and reluctantly consented to the hard terms insisted upon. He lived a few years after; and his son, as successor in the lease, came bound under the unfair bargain. He, too, had a wife and children; and by the end of the lease, though all sober and industrious, the family were in poverty.

Such are examples of a class of cases that might be almost indefinitely multiplied; and by lairds, lawyer factors, and others, the victims were held to have suffered no legal injustice![12]

3

One of the witnesses whose evidence is recorded by Assistant-Commissioner Norman in the Blue Book of 1867 was the late Rev John Middleton, minister of Glenmuick, who in speaking of the Ballater district, said: '"There are few crofts, and the tendency is rather to diminish the number that still remain. A circumstance, in my opinion, much to be regretted, inasmuch as families reared about a holding where something is produced, even though the production be small, are always trained to more careful and thrifty habits than about a household where the expending of

earnings is the only school for training to habits of caretaking."' Most wise
and weighty words these in their immediate application. And in continuing
his statement Mr Middleton added: '"A portion of land in the higher
districts of the parish which had been under cultivation fifty or sixty years
ago, has passed again into pasture land. This has occurred in cases where
there had been a number of small holdings with a common right to hill
pasturage. Those common rights have generally been abolished, and large
grazings substituted."'[13] Though probably not within the period of Mr
Middleton's ministry it is of considerable interest to know that up to a time
less than fifty years ago there existed in the region between Ballater and
Braemar, a system of holdings, which, if not practically identical with, closely
resembled the present West Highland crofter townships. Up to that time,
and even later, Gaelic was very commonly spoken among the natives of the
district, though English was also understood by them. Passing up the public
road between the two places named, the centres of more than half a dozen of
these townships could be pointed out, Coilacreich being the first. Taking one
of these, though not perhaps the one named as typical of the others, there
were in it five tenants who paid rent to the laird; and six cottars, each
occupying a house and a kail-yard. These paid rent, mostly in service, to the
tenants, who in turn saw to their comfort in the most neighbourly way, by
bringing home their fuel, and supplying them with milk and whatever else
could be spared. The cottars were generally, but not always poor and old
people; and the able-bodied amongst them were wont to take service, often
at a distance, during summer, and then come home to lie idle during the
winter, and live upon their earnings. The rents paid by the tenants ranged
from £10 to about £30. The arable acreage was small, the township
depending chiefly upon the hill pasture, which was held as a commonty for
both sheep and cattle, as was also the case with the arable land as soon as the
crops were harvested. As regards cultivation the arable land was in great part
held on the system of 'run-rig,' i.e., a ridge of from six to twelve yards in
width, cultivated, with a 'baulk', on which was heaped all the stones gathered
off the arable land intervening between it and the next cultivated ridge; and
so on, rig and baulk alternately.

It is worth note in passing that the region of Crathie and Braemar was the
scene of several spirited movements in the direction of agricultural reform
and improvement before the end of last century. Mr Farquharson of
Invercauld and some other proprietors planted very extensively. Lady
Sinclair, Mr Farquharson's first wife, as we learn from the writer in the Old
Statistical Account – Rev C M'Hardy, minister of the parish – established a
dairy in 1755, 'under the proper regulations, which was attended with the
greatest success. The butter and cheese made in this dairy were of the best
quality;' and though this was owing in a great measure to 'good old pasture,'
it was also, we are told, due 'principally to the attention paid to the breed of

cows'.[14] Her ladyship at some date established a spinning school, under a
properly qualified spinning mistress, who taught the women, previously
ignorant of the art, how to spin with both hands 'on the little wheel'. The
animal statistics of the combined parish in 1795 included '995 horses, 1,846
black cattle, and 14,591 sheep'. And, besides these, there were 'about 800 or
900 black cattle grazed in the summer season, and about 2,000 of the above
number of sheep sent to other places to be pastured through the winter.' At
the date last mentioned we read that 'the language generally spoken is the
Gaelic. Most of the people, however, understand so much of the English as
to be able to transact ordinary business with their neighbours of the Low
Country.'[15]

The system we have generally described had prevailed time out of mind.
It was a system not compatible with what might be termed the rules of good
husbandry under modern conditions. As to the precise course adopted in
bringing about a change our information is not sufficiently specific or
comprehensive to warrant going into minute details of individual cases.
Generally, the bad times experienced about 1838, when the heaviest
snowstorm of the present century occurred, led to a readjustment of
holdings; and with that view all the leases were made to expire at the same
time, viz 1846. Up to that date very little improvement had been effected. In
view of reletting, Invercauld's factor mapped out the new farms. A few of the
old possessions had previously become vacant through the death of the
tenants, and had been absorbed in the adjoining ones; and a further reduction
was now made, the factor selecting the tenants. The hardship experienced, or
complained of, was almost wholly on the increase of rent asked; and rather
submit to that increase some of the tenants emigrated, though most of the
industrious amongst them were, one way and another, accommodated on
the estate. The tenants under the new leases set to work vigorously to
improve their holdings, and the whole face of the district underwent a
marked change. Baulks were cleared away, while the old arable was freed of
boulders; fences (little known before) were built; trenching of heather land
was carried out, and bogs and morasses drained and improved, and all
without a single penny of outlay by the proprietor, or a penny of
compensation to the tenant. Yet, curious to say, it was during this lease only,
that almost any savings were made by the industrious occupier. Prior to
1846, the life led by the people was one of native contentment, if the
expression may be allowed, but at the same time a life which by its
meagreness was fast becoming intolerable – a mere hand-to-mouth existence
under conditions, as to food, and it might be clothing and housing too,
which implied hardships that would not be deemed endurable now. The rent
was little, but the means of raising it were equally deficient till old modes got
changed. Then, after renewal of the leases in 1865 – about which time crofts
on various of the Upper Deeside properties got reduced in number – the

fresh increase of rent asked checked the well-doing of tenants, and even led to some industrious occupiers losing all, or the greater part of what they had previously been able to save.

It is the opinion of those well qualified to speak that while a change from the old state of things had become absolutely necessary, the point where the proprietors, even the best of them, were in error was in practically confiscating the tenant's improvements by raising the rent whenever the lease expired. It was not that he did not get an offer of renewal of lease at the proprietor's valuation; but that the valuation, by allowing nothing for 'tenant right', was frequently too high, leading many tenants to decline renewal of leases. And this very practice has been a chief bane of our agriculture in other regions than Upper Deeside. Its first result was to deprive the capable and industrious tenant of the due reward for his industry; and in the second place, from the simple circumstance that it has made the body of tenants a much poorer class as a whole than they ought to have been, it has brought Nemesis on the lairds more speedily, and in a more relentless guise than would have happened if the tenants had been a prosperous, well to do class, and so fitter to do the best with the land, to weather a run of 'ill years', and to face extended competition with heart and hope. Had the provisions of the Agricultural Holdings Act of 1883, moderate as they are, and inadequate as they are now deemed by farmers to be, been in operation a quarter of a century ago, their effect would undoubtedly have been highly beneficial as regards the interests of both laird and tenant.

As regards crofts scattered about among large farms in various districts of Deeside, these seem to be rapidly disappearing, owing to the difficulty, in not a few cases, of getting them laboured so as to make them pay. We shall, however, revert to that point in another connection.

Before proceeding to present a remarkable example on Lower Deeside of indomitable crofter energy and perseverance in reclamation of land, the following 'instance' in an upland locality at some distance off may be briefly given in the words of a correspondent, who vouches for the exact accuracy of the facts stated:

> In the year 1805, the father of an old neighbour of ours entered a farm in — on a lease of nineteen years, the rent consisting of £15 in money, eight bolls of meal, two bolls of bere, and two reek hens. The farm was what is called a hill run place, with about thirty acres arable, on poor land, and in very bad order. During the lease the arable was considerably improved, and part of the hill land reclaimed by the tenant. In 1824, the lease was renewed, the rent being raised to £30, eight bolls of meal, and two bolls of bere. During this lease, the tenant built at his own cost a new dwelling-house and steading, and reclaimed more of the hill land. In 1843 the lease

was again renewed, the rent being £60. During this lease the farm was
enclosed with stone dykes, the landlord contributing twopence halfpenny
per yard towards the expense of said dykes, the tenant meanwhile
continuing to reclaim part of the hill land. In 1862 the lease was once more
renewed, at which date the arable land amounted to about a hundred acres,
the rent being £90. But during this lease another farm of nearly sixty acres
was added at a rent of £67, the rent of the two together being £157. In
1881 the lease was once more renewed, the rent being reduced to £147, at
which it stands at this hour.'

What to be noted here is that, with the exception of limited help given in
building dykes – which added to value and became his own property – the
laird, or several successive lairds rather, did not expend a single farthing on
the farm from 1805 up to 1881; and yet the rent was twice doubled, and fifty
per cent added in course of less than sixty years, largely through the skill,
energy, and direct expenditure of an improving tenant, who reclaimed
seventy acres, and built a dwelling-house and steading at his own charge.[16]

4

The remark has been previously made that the Aberdeenshire crofter is, in
certain respects, a wholly different man from his contemporary crofter in the
Highlands and Islands of Scotland. It is, in our view, doing no injustice to the
Highland crofter to say that the Aberdeenshire man is a vastly more efficient
and capable cultivator than his Highland counterpart. We have seen both at
work, and we have seen the results of their cultivation; and, undoubtedly,
without the slightest desire to disparage the Highlander – and making all
due allowance for climatic drawbacks – the Aberdeenshire Crofter takes the
foremost place by a long way as a competent and industrious tiller of the
soil. And as bearing directly on the point, which is one of considerable
importance at the present juncture, we may be permitted to say that when
the Duke of Sutherland was carrying out his scheme of land reclamations at
Kinbrace some years ago, crofters from both the east and west side of the
county were freely employed during the summer months; and the statement
made to us by one who had the best opportunity of judging of their faculty
and capabilities was that 'a stout chiel from Aberdeenshire accustomed to
handle the pick and spade would do as much work as three of them on an
average.' In course of the discussion for going into Committee on the
Crofters Bill, on Monday evening last, Mr J W Barclay[17] made a statement in
accordance with the view just indicated, to the effect that 'the crofters in the
Lowlands had done more for the improvement of their holdings than the
crofters in the West Highlands and Islands,' upon which the honourable

member was met with a cry of 'No.' That this cry was based on pure ignorance of the facts, and a sort of false sentiment evoked in behalf of the Highland crofter as a monopolist of all the virtues that can belong to the class, we need have no hesitation in saying. But as facts are of more importance than mere general assertions can be, we go on to give the facts in a case of crofter enterprise and industry in Aberdeenshire, leaving it to whoever cares to make the attempt to produce a parallel instance, or one that shall eclipse it, in the whole of the Highlands of Scotland.

The crofter of whose career as a cultivator we shall give an account is Mr George Carr, Westhill of Park, whose holding is on Lower Deeside, about ten miles from Aberdeen, and some distance up from the north bank of the river, in a region of bare hillocks, and abounding with 'rock heads' and boulder stones, great and small. George was a farm-servant originally, and had been so employed in various districts for about twenty years, when he formed the idea that the time had come to carry out his strong desire to obtain a holding of his own. His balance at the bank – about £180 – though not large for the purpose in hand, was highly creditable to a man in his position. And with confidence in his own stock of energy and indomitable pluck, he did not shrink from facing an undertaking, which, even at the time, would have dismayed all but the most resolute, and which, as matters now stand, we venture to believe, no sane man would attempt. The work he deliberately set himself to was that of reclaiming rather over thirty imperial acres of barren heath which he got on a lease of twenty-one years from the late Mr A J Kinloch of Park. This was in the year 1863. The 'subject' to be operated upon was of a very unpromising character. It had been planted, but the trees did not thrive upon it; and probably this fact may have influenced the owner in placing it at the disposal of the stout-hearted little man who had the courage to attempt to subdue the bit of stubborn-looking glebe.[18] The land had a good southern exposure, almost the only thing to recommend it as a fit subject for agricultural enterprise. The conditions of occupancy were that the tenant should for the first seven years sit free, then pay five shillings per acre for the next seven years, and ten shillings per acre for the succeeding seven years; but not a stone was to be put upon another in the way of building at the proprietor's expense. George Carr started under an 'improving' lease – a sort of tenure which may in certain cases have had its advantages to the tenant, but was in nearly every case a much greater advantage to the proprietor, who, as a rule, stepped in at the end of the lease to claim the whole of the tenant's improvement as his own. Proprietors in this way, at very small or no expense got their waste land brought under cultivation; whereas if it had been done at their own charge the work of reclamation would have cost them from £15 to £20 an acre, at least. And this value practically represented the amount in manual labour and money which the poor struggling crofter in those times expended for the ultimate benefit of the lord of the manor. The ordinary argument in reply is that the crofter repaid, or ought to have repaid, himself during the lease; but with the strong 'yird hunger' upon him, and the presumption of law all on the landlord's side, the crofter, little qualified to make a strict business calculation at best, had no fair chance.

But to return to the subject of these remarks. At the outset of George's operations a dwelling-house had to be erected, which, including personal labour, cost well on to £80. Stones for the building were found in abundance on a portion of the ground on which reclamation operations had been first begun. And not only that; the enormous number of huge boulder stones that were encountered would have led a man with less courage than George Carr to discontinue further attempts to bring the land under cultivation. Instead, however, of flagging at his work, trenching was steadily continued, and at the end of the first year he had the satisfaction of seeing no less than eight acres of the land under crop. His original capital was soon all exhausted; and participation in a government loan had become necessary. He obtained the money — between £300 and £400, we believe — in the usual way through the gentleman who, at that time, acted as local Loan Commissioner, but at the usurious rate of seven and a half per cent to enable him to carry on his improvements. This of itself was equal to a considerable rent on the holding — the cost of trenching being about £11 an acre, while the additional cost of clearing off the extraordinary number of stones and roots dug up could not be calculated at less than £5 per acre. The stones, some of which weighed as much as half a ton, were disposed of in huge 'consumption' dykes, which, as they now stand, and, for generations to come, are likely to remain, a striking monument of George's splendid energy and courageous perseverance, while they serve to remind the country what it owes to a class whose treatment in the past has not been always in strict accordance with justice.

The dykes which surround the Westhill croft measure in their own length some 1,900 yards; they are from five to fifteen feet in width, and from five to eight feet in height. The stones, some of which, as we have said, are of great weight, were nearly all lifted, or sledged, into their present position by the tenant himself. No proper idea could, however, be formed of the magnitude of the labour involved without visiting the place itself. The dykes are more like a great military rampart than anything else, and the visitor is disposed to be incredulous when he is told that they were all built by one man, who, with the aid of his tough and hardy 'horsie', that seemed to get nearly as well accustomed to the work as himself, had actually lifted the whole material of these huge fences off the land, and no limited part of it after a stiff 'pilget' with pick and pinch to get the individual boulders out of their earth-fast beds. Yet such was the case. Under the conditions of tenancy it was important, of course, that the reclamation should be accomplished as early as possible, and the whole place was actually brought under cultivation by the end of the first seven years.

The soil of the little farm is of a light loam, with open subsoil, and required little draining; but where needed the drains were put in three and a half feet deep, and filled with stones to within two feet of the surface. At first the subsoil, which had been turned up and mixed with the loam, militated against the crops which were very poor; but by liming, and applying a large quantity of bones and farm-yard manure, the productiveness of the land was greatly increased. At the end of the first seven years the tenant was able to report upon the Westhill reclamations, then accomplished, in the *Transactions of the Highland and Agricultural Society*, for which George Carr received a silver medal. In this report it was said: 'I think there is a reasonable prospect that the improvements will yield me a fair return; and I have great satisfaction in seeing comparatively fertile fields, where a few years ago there was nothing but barren heath.'[19]

At the same date suitable offices had been erected comprising a barn, with a two-horse threshing machine, a byre to accommodate about a dozen cattle, and a stable for two horses. These have since been further extended by a turnip shed and a new stable, which have been erected recently, the total cost for the whole being not less than £50.

Twenty-three years have gone since George Carr entered upon the croft where we still found him only the other day. He has brought up a family of eight who have gone into the world to earn an honest livelihood for themselves. Sixty years, by far the greater part of them spent in hard unremitting toil, have left the tenant of Westhill less robust than he was in 1863; but he is still young in the buoyancy of his hopes and in his unabated perseverance and industry. He says he has spent more upon the place than would have bought it; and anyone who has seen the results of the Herculean labours he has accomplished will believe him. He is contented with his lot, and three years ago entered on a new lease of the holding, which, with recent additions, extends now to nearly forty acres. His new lease is for nineteen years, and the rent is £35, or seventeen and sixpence per acre. The times of late have been hard, and the income from the croft not what could have been wished; but nothing is paid for hired labour, and this most deserving tenant, by strict economy and close attention to his business, is likely to surmount difficulties which have already brought financial ruin to not a few who have held their heads higher. He has kept the land in good 'heart' by occasional applications of lime and heavy doses of farmyard manure. He places no reliance on artificial manures. '"Keep your farm well stocked, and the farm will keep you"' is his maxim. It is upon the returns for his cattle that he feels the depression most. Four quarters per acre would be over the average for his yield of oats, and instead of selling these, he often finds it more profitable to feed them to his stock. In some years he has got as much as £30 for a single animal; and though the prices at last Christmas markets were very low he realised nearly £26 for a fat beast sold off the croft.

Such then is a sample of the Aberdeenshire crofter at his best. George Carr is no doubt a man of somewhat exceptional energy and determination; yet he is only a true type of a class of which Aberdeenshire has produced hundreds. We do not assert that examples of equal industry and capacity may not be found amongst Highland crofters; we only say we have never yet seen such an example.

In concluding the present paper, we may add that most of the crofts which, twenty to thirty years ago, were found scattered round the Loch of Park, in the locality of Westhills, have disappeared, being absorbed into adjoining farms. And of the original crofters many have left the country. Was their flight voluntary, or had they been subjected to conditions which they knew they could never fulfil, and so had to leave after they had brought the barren heath under the dominion of the plough? That question we do not meanwhile stay to answer, though it need not be assumed that the Park crofters were treated with exceptional stringency.[20]

5

Passing from Deeside into the lower part of Aberdeenshire for the present, we find in the district of Monquitter, including the estates of Greeness, Hatton, Greens, Teuchar, &c, a region presenting an exceptionally large number of crofts, the greater part of which have been formed by the reclamation of waste land within the last forty to fifty years. And while the number of crofts has on the whole increased, a great many changes have been made during the period indicated through the absorption of crofts into larger holdings. This has happened notably on the estate of Greens, and on Sealscrook, where an entire hamlet was extinguished, or rather reduced to a single holding, as many as five or six crofts going into one farm. The reason for this course being adopted here, as in other parts of Aberdeenshire, was the absurd and short-sighted idea entertained by proprietors of keeping down pauperism by the extinction of crofters and cottars on the passing of the Poor Law Act of 1845; the actual result being to diminish the supply of agricultural labour, to deteriorate its quality, and to enhance its cost; a result which both lairds and tenant farmers have had good cause to deplore, but which was directly due to their own grasping and selfish conduct.

The remark must here be made that, while the Monquitter crofts of the present day are not less in number than they were thirty to forty years ago, the crofts of today are not to be compared with those that existed before the changes referred to had taken place. The crofts of fifty years ago were, as a rule, formed on the lower lying and naturally fertile portions of the land, whereas those desirous of obtaining small holdings more recently have too commonly had either to be content with leasing a bit of the bare hillside, or want. And if the query were asked, 'Why come there at all to sit down on a cold, bleak, shelterless and barren-looking spot?' the answer – and a suggestive enough one in its way – would most probably be, 'Jist for a hame.' And so indeed it has been. After toiling for years with the 'frem't' the prospect of a 'hame' of his own, in which he might hope to pass the 'gloamin'' of life, has forced itself strongly upon many an honest, industrious day labourer and farm-servant, with wife and family to provide for; and who would far rather face the struggle of life under very hard conditions on a small holding of his own than entertain the idea of going into a town, with its sense of grimy and irksome confinement and its unaccustomed ways. And little wonder 'tis that, to one born and brought up in the pure air and out-door life of the country, the thought conveyed in the expressive words, 'I cudna suffer the idea o' gyaun till a toon,' should naturally arise. And yet, in almost every case, the crofter, as we find him here, is fain to confess that, but for the assistance rendered by his family, he could not have struggled on, even with the most rigid economy. For his rent has not been an easy one, nor the conditions favourable, all things considered. As his sons and daughters have grown up, they have in many cases given him substantial aid, the former in his reclaiming operations, the latter in housework, at least, if not also upon the 'grun'; keeping out hired hands; and all the while receiving no remuneration, save it might be, bare food and clothing. And he has deemed himself lucky if, with all this, he could get ends to meet, and avoid running into debt. The houses are by no means ambitious structures, being, for the most part, built of 'feals' and 'thackit'. Though erected by the occupiers, and without such assistance fron skilled artificers, there is about them internally an astonishing air of comfort and tidiness generally, while the old-fashioned 'hingin' lum', still prevailing in the ben end, seems to allow the peat fire to diffuse its warmth about the ingle cheek far more effectually than many fire-places of more modern construction.

As indicating the thrifty and self-helpful style of the class of crofters of whom we are just now speaking, it may be stated that it is a very common thing to 'trace' (that is, to train) the cows to go in the plough and harrows, to draw the turnip sowing machine, and even to do the necessary carting. An intelligent and industrious crofter was proud to show our commissioner a cart of his own particular invention, and which, though furnished with what is proverbially regarded as a superfluity in the shape of a 'third wheel', seemed exceedingly well adapted to its purpose. It was in use at the time for the purpose of driving home turnips from the field, the team consisting of the owner's two cows; and a more tractable or docile team it would have been difficult to imagine; indeed the assurance was given by a neighbour that not only did they obey their owner readily and efficiently in the draught, but that one of them, in particular, would come from the most distant part of the holding whenever he chose to call and wave his hat as a signal that her presence was wanted for business! There is a good deal of 'clubbing' of forces amongst the crofters in this district in the working of their land; one giving to his neighbour the loan of his horse or 'wark steer' to do his ploughing, and in turn receiving the use of his neighbour's beast for his own work.

The average extent reclaimed by crofters on the different estates mentioned varies from seven or eight acres to over double that extent. The work of reclamation has been done partly by ploughing, partly by trenching. The average cost if paid in coin would have been £15 to £20 an acre. As to conditions of occupancy, the rule has been very small rents at outset of lease – say, half a crown per acre first seven years, then a rise to five shillings for a similar period, and a further rise for the remaining years of the lease, with either no allowance or a limited one for buildings, and no payment for improvements. On asking a crofter of considerable experience his opinion, we find it in brief to be that, in place of being asked to pay half a crown an acre for the first seven years' occupancy of a bit of barren heather land, the occupant ought to have some assistance from the laird in reclaiming it, as well as fair compensation for improvements at the end of the lease.

His own experience was as follows: he took ten acres of land in the centre of a heather hill on a twenty-one years' lease. It was expected that the whole of it would be under cultivation by the end of that period, but there was no bondage to do so. He got £1 per acre to assist in building houses, or £10 in all. The terms were half a crown per acre for the first seven years, five shillings per acre for the next seven years, and fifteen shillings till the end of the lease, but only ten shillings per acre was exacted. At first a feal house was erected, afterwards a more substantial one of stone and clay. It was stipulated that the value of £10 was to be left in houses at the end of the lease, or else be made good by the tenant. Nothing was allowed for improvements. Through the kind aid of friendly neighbours some five acres were 'riven' in in course of the first year, and the whole croft was brought under cultivation in eight years. About half the acreage had to be reclaimed by the spade. He wrought to neighbours during the day, and trenched his croft in the evenings. All the money he earned was spent on the 'placie', and as his family grew up they rendered great assistance. The reclamations would have cost about £20 per acre, or £200 in all. The houses are now worth £30 or £40; and had he required to leave at the end of his lease he would have had a very heavy loss. But his landlord, who takes a warm interest in the welfare of his tenants, and wishes to 'live and let live,' has given him a new lease without asking any increase, and has, moreover, added a 'bittie' of land to the holding.

Another crofter adjoining, but on a different estate, had a croft of twenty acres, of which he improved fully twelve acres, and built the necessary houses at his own expense – some £20. He paid no rent for the first ten years, a mere nominal rent for the next five years, and now he is charged ten shillings per acre, or double the amount for the first fifteen years. The reason 'or the increase, he says, is 'because I farmed well.' Not very encouraging to an enterprising farmer or crofter, certainly. He laboured apart from the croft, and brought everything he earned and put it into his holding in the shape of manure, lime, &c. One year he spent as much as £11 in this way, and had only one boll of meal in return.

Mr C, another small farmer, acquired twenty seven acres of heather, all of which he reclaimed, and built the necessary houses without any assistance from the proprietor. Most of the land had to be trenched, and the subject being 'main coorse', was given for the first lease at the nominal rent of one shilling per acre. The second lease was entered upon at £7 per annum, but only eleven years of it had run when the property changed owners, and having no 'tack', the tenant had to pay £12 per annum, or flit. His improvements cost some £10 per acre, and all the compensation he would get upon quitting would be £7 for houses. The place in his experience is worth just about £5 of rent per annum, and he would not have a great living even supposing he got it for nothing. In proof of this the whole of the crop sold this season was two and a half quarters of oats of thirty nine pounds per bushel, price £1. 18s., and the year before he sold three and a half quarters. He rears two stirks. With the corn and cattle he has to pay the £12 of rent, labour, manure, &c. The profits cannot be much! This is a case of 'sticking in' for the sake of his family, and no desire for the 'gay life' of a town. It is only fair to add that on this property, although the industrious crofter who has spent all his time and money in improving the soil, is now, as he believes, rack-rented for his trouble, there are no instances of putting away tenants who wished to stay. The only case indeed of eviction [quoted] in this house was that of a crofter, who, some thirty years ago, reclaimed twelve to fifteen acres of a 'perfect bog', or quagmire, and had to leave his 'placie' much against his will; and all because, as was alleged, a near relative of the factor's wished it added to his farm. The 'peer' crofter got no compensation for his improvements.

Keeping still among the class of crofts held on improving leases, we might next find material for remark in the case of an estate in the vicinity of Peterhead, the greater portion of which has been reclaimed within the last twenty-four years. The predecessor of the present proprietor gave crofts to improving tenants on the following conditions: five or six years' free, on the understanding that so much area should be made arable; the tenant erecting the out-houses himself and getting £5 or £6 to assist in building a dwelling-house. The second five years the rent to be five shillings per acre, and for the balance of the lease eight to ten shillings per acre at the discretion of the laird, by which time it was calculated the ground would be worth that rent, provided the tenant had been moderately diligent.

Let us see how the thing has worked. Here is a sample out of several: J W got a croft of sixteen acres of heather on the hill. His bargain was that he should take in the land and build the houses, receiving compensation for the latter at the end of the lease. He required some help to build the houses, and the proprietor kindlily gave him a few pounds, the capital to be repaid, with interest at five per cent, within a certain number of years. The man would probably have had some difficulty in getting the money otherwise than through the laird, and he accepted it, and duly repaid it within the specified time. The laird's kindness was not, however, restricted to this one act. In view of the fact that the tenant had put up substantial houses (he had spent about £60 on them), he was allowed to sit another year rent free. J W, by dint of great perseverence, reclaimed all the land within the lease, mostly by trenching; at the same time earning daily wages for his own and his family's support by ditching and working 'day's warks' for neighbouring farmers. He spent about £8 per acre in reclamation; about one pound an acre for lime, and later on about £38 for dung and manure. At the end of his lease he found that he had put into the ground about £240, besides paying about £80 of rent − total, £320. Having been a hard-working and saving farm-servant in his younger days, he entered the holding with some little capital, but it had all gone for the benefit of the croft, in the expectation that as he had been good to the land during the first nineteen years it would repay him during the coming lease. He went to the laird in the full expectation that he would be granted a renewal of the lease on the same terms; but alas! there had arisen a king who knew not Joseph! The rent of the place was now to be £1 per acre; take it or want it. In vain the man tried to explain his position; the heart of the laird was adamantine. He could get £16 of rent were he to advertise the croft to let, and it was his duty to take the best offer. Rather than leave all his capital and labour in the ground, J W offered sixteen shillings per acre, but the offer was not accepted, and he got a week wherein to make up his mind. It is the old story; he promised to try and pay the rent demanded, and up till now has managed to do so. But he has to struggle for a bare existence; and with prices of produce so low as they are at present, he can never expect to recoup himself for his outlay, let alone getting a fair wage for his own labour. Our informant adds that, as if to make the oppression complete, he was told that the proprietor having advanced part of the money to build the houses, and the tenant having sat rent free for an additional year, he now has no claim on the inventories.[21] It will be observed that by this sleight of hand performance on the part of the proprietor he lost only the sixth year's rent, equal to £4, while he gained a high interest for his money and a substantial steading. The land is worth about ten shillings per acre − not more.[22]

6

Lighting down for the nonce at Udny station on the Buchan and Formartine Railway, we plod our way inward with the feeling of being near the centre of a large and excellent agricultural district; and putting ourselves alongside an intelligent and well-informed resident, we proceed to get his ideas of how the crofter has fared generally in the region.

'Has the number of crofts increased or decreased within living recollection?'

'Decreased,' is the unhesitating reply.

'And as to causes?'

'Oh, the causes! Well, unwillingness on the part of the proprietors to renew buildings; a wish on the part of factors to save trouble in management; and readiness on the part of the farmer to get "a bit mair", and to square his march.[23] In fact, most of the large farms in the district were made out of crofts and small holdings; but chiefly at a time anterior to living recollection. Here, for instance, is the farm of Cultercullen, not far from the railway station, which, since the year 1824, has extinguished no fewer than twenty-two fires.' A crofter, still alive in the district, we are told, remembers the last four of these small holdings, and can give the names of their tenants. And running over what has happened within a radius of two miles, the said crofter can enumerate an additional eleven crofts and small holdings which have been absorbed in larger farms during the past fifty years. It is right, however, to say that two crofts have been formed, one being for the blacksmith. Of the more recent changes in the parish of Udny, some seven crofts in all have disappeared without any others being formed. Taking a short excursion outside the parish, we come on the estate of Disblair, in the parish of Fintray, on which some fourteen crofts have been absorbed in neighbouring farms.

As to the question of rental now, compared with what it was formerly in the case of crofts and small holdings; our present informant states that, generally speaking, rents are higher than of old; but that, where the tenant or his father built the houses, the rent has not been raised much, if any – at any rate on the Haddo House property in the district.[24] And passing on to Tarves parish, where a couple of calls are made, we find two specially well-informed tenant farmers agreeing in the statement that the rents of small holdings are much higher than formerly. In the words of one, 'Rents have risen enormously within the last forty years.' The other puts it that, while in a good many cases a comparison cannot be made, he would be inclined to say that the rents of crofts and small holdings had increased fully fifty per cent compared with what they were twenty-five years ago. As to the cause of decrease in the number of crofts, both agree that the worn-out state of the houses and the disinclination of landlords to be at the cost of renewing buildings – a cost which, keeping in with the extent of the holding, is often felt to be disproportionately large – is a main cause. 'I have in my mind's eye,' says one of our informants, 'the case of a small crofter who pays a rent per acre considerably in excess of the rent paid per acre on the neighbouring farm. The dwelling-house and out-houses on this croft are in a very wretched condition; not fit, in fact, for habitation. Nevertheless, when this poor crofter goes to the factor to ask for better houses, he is told that, unless he is content to sit with the houses as they are, his croft will be taken from him and added to the next farm; and this, be it said, is no uncommon case.'

On the point just touched – that, namely, of extinguishing crofts – it will not be out of place here to insert the remarks of a correspondent dealing with the matter in another of its aspects. He says:

> I have directly before me a comparatively recent case of the addition of a croft of considerable extent to a comparatively large adjoining farm. In this instance the croft broke up the regularity of the farm; the houses on it were done; and the occupier was leaving for a larger possession. Now, while I hold that crofts should be increased in number, it ought to be done on system; and that they in many cases should be done away with and added to farms, if they were so situated as to spoil in a measure the farm. As I write I can look out of my window and see a large croft, which I hold should be added to a neighbour's farm. At the same time I have before me several cases where outlying portions of farms should be turned into crofts. In supporting the movement for a Land Court, I have always had in view that its function would not be merely to settle a fair rent for the crofter or farmer, but also to take land from or add it to farms as might be deemed necessary for the general well being of the community.

From Tarves we cross the Ythan, and, after surveying bits of the intervening region, find ourselves in the district of Savock of Deer, where we have the benefit of a consensus of opinion drawn out by the inquiries and conversation of an intelligent tenant farmer. It is generally to the effect that hereabouts, as in other districts, crofts and small farms have been decreasing. 'There are several pretty extensive farms in my neighbourhood,' says our informant, who is a Haddo House tenant, 'and two-thirds of these have at different times within living recollection been augmented by having crofts or small farms added to them.' We give the continuation of our informant's statement in his own words:

> Although this policy of reducing the number of small farms for the purpose, it has been said, of adding to the respectability of an estate, has been carried into effect to a greater or less extent on most estates, still there are exceptions to this rule. If you look back for five and twenty years you will find that crofts and small holdings have been rather on the increase, as they are being reclaimed from the heather – the Hill of Dudwick is an example. The reason for this isn't far to seek. It never could have paid a farmer to reclaim these lands, the nature of the soil being so wretchedly poor. It is only the poor plodding earth-worm, who, by manual

slavery – I can call it by no other name – and indefatigable perseverance, can accomplish this sort of work with his own hands and the hands of his wife and daughters – the labour of removing by hand, and barrow, stones large and small, turning over the heather land, building their humble dwellings, and spending on those uninviting plots a sum not less than £15 per acre. Should the proprietor burn down all those houses, and turn the crofts into larger farms, it would not pay him. The rack-rents of today can only be extracted from the man who is prepared to slave himself from early morning to late at night to secure bare existence. I have known some of these tenants at different times going some six or eight miles for a cart-load of 'neeps' or a few bushels of 'taties', to put them round a corner. On the Haddo House property the principal causes that have led to decrease of small holdings are (1) Tenant dying and leaving no direct heir, or, if he had, his sons might either have emigrated or been in service, and would perhaps find difficulty in obtaining the means to enter the place. (2) Tenant falling behind with his rent and having to be removed to a smaller holding – it has been in the past a proverbial rule with the Aberdeen family that they never evict a tenant, although they may occasionally have to remove one to a smaller holding. (3) Tenant securing in some way a little additional capital and moving into a larger croft or farm. (4) Tenant leaving on account of houses being done.

Thus far of Savock, where we are told that, in addition to the somewhat general reason for reduction of crofts found in the natural reluctance on the part of the proprietor to put out money on buildings, instances of other and less excusable methods being adopted have occasionally occurred, such as that of letting off a piece of barren land to a tenant, who was allowed to sub-let, naturally on harder conditions than those under which he himself sat; and then, when the struggling sub-tenants had improved or partially improved their little holdings, and, their resources giving out, failed in being able to go on longer, the sub-let was obliterated as a distinct holding and came back into the hands of the first tenant, either he or the laird getting the full benefit of what the sub-tenant had done in the way of reclamation of the barren waste.

We shall conclude our present paper by summary report of a 'crack' with an octogenarian small holder near Clola. Interviewed by our Commissioner, the shrewd old man proceeded in this wise:

> Aboot craft – have they increased or decreased? Oh weel, there wus mair o' them fifty year syne than there are noo. The proprietors preferr't muckle fairms, an' the fairmers coveted the weel ta'en in-aboot little bits. Fewer hooses were requar't, and there was less wark to the factor. I cud point oot sax or saiven crafts, aboot twa kye's maet the piece, pitt'n in tae bigger fairms. In former days some o' the crafts were sub-lets fae the fairmers, the

crafters payin' their rent chiefly by wark; an' lots o' the fairmers sat as life-
renters. I've kent crafters crap their lan' year aifter year, without devall, an'
for the hinmost ten year pit naething into the lan'. My father cam' to this
pairt aboot the beginnin' o' the century. The place was boggy, an' aboot
fifty Scots awcres o't. He drain't it a', an' it grew splendid craps at first. The
rent for the first two nineteens wus sma' — twalve or fourteen pund, with
four bows o' meal in name o' victual, to be deliver't atween Yule an'
Can'lemas — an' syne, for the neist tack, it was doobl't. For the fourt
nineteen the laird said he wud gie't at the aul' rent if we would big a
steadin'; an' this was deen. The rent noo is £1 the acre, an' we get
inventory for the wa's, but nae for the reefs. I consider fairms o' eighty to a
hundred acres to be the best size for fairmers an' for the countra. Lots o'
placies o' forty acres or mair used to be wrocht wi' a horse an' a steer; an' a
fine thrifty method it was; but they're a' sae uppish noo 'at they canna pit
up wi' that, but maun hae their pair o' horse beasts, an' their fine blaicket
graith; an' that paysa sair wi' some o' them. A' the best fairm-servants were
brocht up on crafts an' sma' placies under their pawrents trainin'. I dinna
like the haibit that fairm-servants hae noo o' nae gaen to the kirk. I'm nae
sayin' that there mayna be gweed aneuch men that disna atten' the kirk,
but its nae a gweed sign fan a man, be he fairn-servan' or fatever else, mak's
nae mair ootward acknowledgement o' a God abeen him nor the brutes i'
the field. At hame the loons an' lassies were learn't to be thrifty an' to dee
honest wark. The aul' fashion't crafters lived sober, an' there was naething
hin'erin' them to mak' siller in a sma' wye. There's a hankerin' noo amo'
young lads to be aff into the toons raither than be at fairm wark: an' wi'
mony, there's sic a cry aboot education. Noo, the Education Act[25] may be
a' gweed aneuch, but it was better fan the boys cud be keppit herdin', or
workin', a' summer, and gae to the skweel in winter. The fairm-servan's
noo-a-days hae nae richt trainin' ava, and they dinna ken their wark, an' as
little do they care foo they dee't. I forgot to mention that, in addition to
the rent in siller an' meal, my father paid half a steen o' butter, twal hens,
an' sax dizzen o' eggs, wi' some capons to the laird's table. An' he had to
cairry sax bows o' lime an' cairt peats to the laird, besides gi'en wark in
hairst. A gey cheenge in maist things fae fat it was than-a-days; an' nae a'
for the better.

And we could not but agree with our shrewd octogenarian friend.[26]

7

In our last paper, the Hill of Dudwick and its crofts received brief notice.
Before passing from that locality, we may give the opinion of a local
resident, to the effect that there are still a hundred acres on the hill

unreclaimed, which, if cultivated, would yield good fair crops, 'only the laird put a stop to takin' in, cause they were encroachin' on his sheetin'.' An original notion of the principle adopted by a certain well-known valuator in assessing his valuations, found acceptance here. It was expressed thus, 'His rowle, in a general wye, is to add a third to the aul' rent; and he is little guidet by ony ither preenciple.'[27] Our informant added that the advances of rent on his own place had been by lease and bounds that considerably transcended the one-third rule.

Taking now the north-eastward quarter of the parish of Ellon, the proportion of crofts, we are told, has greatly decreased; the causes assigned being precisely the same as elsewhere. Selecting six farms of considerable size, we find that in the course of the past forty years thirteen small holdings have been absorbed into these six farms, and two new crofts formed; the net number of crofts extinguished being thus eleven. One or two of the extinct holdings were of sufficient size to keep a pair of small horses; the other crofters depended on some adjoining farmer for having their horse work performed, the crofter giving labour in harvest or at other times in return. Most of the crofters could keep two or three cows and a stirk or two. The crofter buildings have all disappeared, save three of the dwelling-houses, which have no land attached, and are occupied by labourers. As to the comparative rents, we are told the rent of one of the farms, which was £140 forty years ago, is now £365; and the rent of another, which was £85 forty years ago, is now £211. 10s.. Reckoning the other farms in the same proportion, which it is believed may safely be done, it would seem that, for every £10 of rent paid forty years ago, £28, or nearly three times as much, is paid now. The amount of produce from these farms forty years ago would, our informant believes, have been quite equal to what they are now.

Extending our perambulations farther inward, we call another witness, also from Ellon parish, into court. In his district crofts had decreased considerably at an early period, and not so rapidly during the past twenty to thirty years. The causes have been those prevailing elsewhere – the landlord's desire to economise in the expenditure on buildings, straightening the marches of farms, and so forth. In the case of crofts long under cultivation on select patches, rents have been increased twenty- five to thirty per cent during the past forty or fifty years; while, in the case of those reclaimed from the bare hillsides and bleak moorlands, the rents have been increased from fifty to a hundred and fifty per cent, and in some cases even more. And our present interlocutor cannot recall to mind a single case where an improving tenant has not had his rent raised upon him. Two instances may be given. A B reclaimed sixteen acres of hilly land, building houses and dykes at his own expense, and paying a rent of £4 per annum for nineteen years prior to 1875, when the lease ran out. Being now an infirm old man, his landlord allowed him to continue to occupy the holding from year to year, till his death in

1884, at the yearly rent of £14. A B having no direct heirs likely to succeed him, the holding, charged at same rent, was joined to a somewhat larger one adjoining it, on which a modern dwelling-house and steading have recently been erected. The advantage to the landlord, as will be seen, is that he obtains the same rent, gets the land equally well farmed, and saves the cost of one dwelling-house, and half the cost of a suitable steading for one of the crofts; in short, the interest charge for buildings is only three-fifths of what it would have been had the crofts remained separate.

In the other case, A C got a nineteen years' lease of twenty acres of moorland, wholly unreclaimed, and without habitation of any kind. He undertook to pay one shilling an acre during the first five years; five shillings an acre during the next five years, and ten shillings an acre during the remaining nine years of the lease. He also bound himself to erect, at his own expense, a dwelling-house, byre, &c, and have the whole twenty acres under cultivation at the end of the first five years; for all which, by way of encouragement, the landlord agreed to remit the last year's rent – ten pounds – as the unexhausted value of the improvements made, at the end of the lease! Well, now, let us see how the thing ran. A C set stoutly to work, and by-and-by had thirteen to fourteen acres reclaimed, partly by trenching, partly by 'fauching,' bringing the land ultimately into a state of high cuitivation. Including liming and other preparation for first crop the cost at a moderate computation was not under £10 an acre – equal to say £130 in all. The buildings, which, at the end of twenty-one years, give evidence of economical construction, may be put at £20, making £150 in all of capital expenditure by the tenant. The rents paid, as per receipts shown, have been £5 during the first five years, £25 during the second five years, and £90 during the remaining nine years of the lease – £120. The lease expired in 1884, and A C has made repeated applications to the factor for renewal of lease, with assistance to rebuild his houses in a more substantial way, but up to date of visit this had led to nothing beyond promises of visits of inquiry by the factor or the laird. Since expiry of his lease A C has been sitting as a tenant at will, paying the old rent of £10, with the assurance given in a way that 'if he goes on as he is doing he will not be disturbed.' Had he broken the connection, at the end of his lease he would have been entitled to a single payment of £10 against his capital expenditure of £150 and rent payment of £120. But he has continued to sit on, and the last year's rent under the old lease for improvement has not been remitted; albeit A C had acted fairly up to bargain, while he freely owns that he is a poorer man now than when the lease began.

Bending our steps in a north-easterly direction now, by way of Bog of Ardallie, we drop in upon a well-known resident, whose opinion, frankly expressed, is that, though latterly there has not been any diminution in the number of crofts, the tendency amongst big farmers up to a recent date was to grab the crofter's land whenever they could. 'A'thing was payin' fine at that time, ye ken; and fairmers didna' see faur they war to lan'.' The system of renting in the locality, we are told, has been too prevailingly 'the screw' all along, and upon one or two estates some of the rents have been doubled.

About the crofters, particular instances are not the least effective in the way of illustration, and our present instructor gave his examples thus:

A character came from —, a carter or something sic like, and bade for a croft. His bade was so very good that the factor saw he was to be a useful man. A number of crofts were out at the same time and were advertised. When this man applied for one of the crofts (the rent was then £12) he offered £27 or £28 for it. The factor told him to offer for 'the puckle' and he might get one of them. Some of the houses were miserable shielings. In one case the man was living alone without any woman body, washing his own shirt, the house about tumbling down, the place entirely away from growing anything but weeds. It was not cultivated, you see, yet when it came into the market there were five or six candidates for it. The best farm in the locality came into the market last year, I may say, and there were only two offerers for it, which shows that big farms are not wanted, but that folk want something in the way of shelter to hap their heads. Men are anxious about crofts, but, in my opinion, the difficulty is quite as much about getting decent houses for labourers and such like on reasonable terms.

However, to proceed. Take one of the crofters in the lot referred to, B say. He has twenty three acres of ground, and he entered upon it forty years ago, when it was a wilderness of gorse and heather. He paid £11 of rent, and put up houses for himself. The man was naturally anxious to better his position in the world, if he could. At the end of the first nineteen years, he had it all under the plough and then got his lease renewed, the rent being fixed at £18, with the land in fair working order. He goes on his weary pilgrimage, till the close of the second nineteen years, when this interloping old carter comes on the carpet, and bids £28 for the croft. And this follows: the factor, having got similarly exorbitant bids, in the way indicated, for over half a dozen of the crofts, goes round the poor characters and says to one after another, 'Now I've been bidden such and such for your place; I would not like to see you shift, but you could not expect that I could let it at less money than I have been bidden. Will you give me a pound more than the offer I have mentioned?' The result of what on the factor's part it would need one or two profane words properly to describe was that, rather than flit, the crofters gave rents out of all proportion to their bits of land; that they lost all the little money they had made, and have never since been able to hold their heads properly above water. B, whom I have mentioned, bid £23 for his placie, but the factor says, 'I would like to be fair with you, Jeems, so if you will split the difference, and say twenty five pun' ten, you will get it.' James, after a great deal of deliberation, comes up to £25. 'It's cheap, Jeems,' says the factor,

'and you'll manage the other ten shillings.' And that ten shillings James B
had to pay, and does pay to this day. The man is seventy-six years of age,
and during fifty years has continued in a course of the hardest industry and
perseverence, bringing his land under the plough, and continuously
cultivating it – practically making the place – for which he pays twenty-
two shillings an acre. It was, I need hardly say, a lawyer factor; a man weel
kent in Buchan and its capital in mair capacities than one. 'Pawky!' aye,
wasna he pawky; but, oh, man, it was damnably cruel – as cruel as maist
that even the Highland crafter ever thol't, only it was thol't wi' greater
helpfu'ness an' faculty. It only needs to be said further that the person who
was the tool used in forcing up the poor crofters' rents was literally hoist
with his own petard. He got one of the crofts, and in less than nineteen
years spent all his means upon it, and ended in bankruptcy.[28]

The fate of the crofter within the range of my observation has been a
hard one. In a general way, the Aberdeenshire crofter, meaning thereby all
small holders up to about fifty acres, has reclaimed, probably, a third of the
cultivated soil. And, in many instances, as soon as it is well taken in, and
made fertile by careful cultivation, and such manuring as an industrious
crofter could give it, it was added to the larger farm, and the man kicked
about his business. As for improvements, the crofter was allowed the
privilege of leaving them to the laird. No doubt many of the houses were
not really worth much; and partly because the man, seeing no likelihood of
his being able to take his place again, suffered them to get into a tumble-
down state; and of course the laird could not think of spending money on
buildings; it was a much easier process to swamp the croft in the next
adjoining farm. In the case of improving leases, the croft land, taking the
expense of reclamation into account, would, as a pretty general rule, have
been worth nothing in the shape of rent for the first nineteen years; and,
generally, the rents are much too high. Some of the croft land here,
honestly worth about ten shillings an acre, is rented at from twenty-five to
twenty-eight shillings an acre; and so on in proportion. On the whole
there is a want of straightforward outspokenness; and too great a
veneration for big folks among agricultural people; and a deal of toadyism
still goes on, which does mischief to all concerned. Give a certain class the
right of land-holding and they are only too ready to put down their foot
so as to make it felt. An idle, debt-ridden laird never fulfils the first
conditions of his right to live; he is often a scourge to the country, and
ought to be swept out of existence, as he is likely soon to be."[29]

8

From the point last reached we 'take' round by Cruden, in which parish the
improving crofter is found struggling on in various quarters. His class has,

we are told, decreased considerably; fifty crofts and small holdings, of which the names are volunteered, have been extinguished and added to larger farms, the reasons for their extinction being the same as we find prevailing elsewhere. Rents of crofts and small holdings had up till lately been increased by probably not much less than fifty per cent on an average. The names of three small holders on the estate of L— are given who have been increased fifty per cent, eighty per cent, and 120 per cent respectively – 'or flit;' and three others are named who, it is said, had all their holdings taken over their heads by outsiders, after having erected buildings and made other substantial improvements. Many cases, it is added, can be given on different estates in the parish where the tenants have erected buildings at their own cost. And, before leaving the locality, we may be permitted here to insert as nearly as possible verbatim et literatim, an epistle handed to us by a former resident, inviting a second visit and more minute inspection.

As I am a constant reader of the *Free Press* I am very much taken up at the present with your Crofter's Commission, and more so when I read about such men as George Carr; but if you would take a turn down by the estate of—, in the parish of Cruden, you will find scores of Carrs there; and more so. I think they have done more, as a good many of them that were old farm-servants had nothing but one half-year's wages to make a start with. I think I am right in saying that the one half of the estate mentioned has been reclaimed by crofters of this kind; and that they never received one penny from their laird. They got five years free, and other five for five shillings,[30] and the next nine years for ten shillings. They built all their houses and reclaimed the waste land, and the most of them when their leases were out got their rent raised to £1 or else 'flit.' I may mention one case to you. J A reclaimed his croft out of solid rock, nearly. I may say it was about twenty acres, and at the end of his time he offered the laird £17 for his croft, but the laird told him if he did not give twenty it would go to the market. But he was obliged to let it for £18, and put the poor man out for the sake of a pound. An honester man never lived, I think on earth. I may tell you a little about his honesty. He was at one time grieve to Mr — of —, and at that time they had to drive their grain to Peterhead. There was no station nearer them, and Mr — was in the way of giving the men money to pay their expenses along with them. So J A starts for Peterhead in the morning, and pays all expenses out of his money that he gets. But he had one halfpenny over. Now, he thinks, 'What can I do with this mite? Will I offer it back again? No, it is not worth while.' But he thinks again, 'It is not my own.' So the next day he offered Mr — the halfpenny back; and he took it. How many will you get, so honest men? I may say that the gentleman mentioned was the proprietor of the estate at one time, but he died, and a new Pharoah sprang up, which knew not J A, and he got the worst of it. I could give you a good deal of information about crofters, but

I am afraid to live in Rome and strive with the Pope; and that's why I don't want my name put down.

On Strichen estate the decrease of small holdings since the estate was acquired by the late Mr Baird has, we are told, been over a hundred. Whole farms were made out of crofts, from which the previous occupiers had to remove; many of these having reclaimed their land from the side of Mormond Hill; and now there are only about twenty crofts remaining in the whole parish. No compensation was given for reclaiming the land, half a year's rent, merely, being allowed for the value of the houses built. Generally speaking, the rents of crofts are one-third higher in proportion than those of adjoining farms. When the property belonged to the Lovat family, the conditions for an improving small tenancy were a nominal rent of £1 for twenty-one years, with a rise at the end of that term. After that family ceased to own the property it was year-to-year tenancy until the crofts were joined into farms.

The statement of a Strichen small holder was to this effect:

This place was just a moor when I took it from the Lovat folk. There was no house. I built the houses, being promised a year's rent therefore when I got a new lease. I am entered upon my third lease since Whitsunday. My first rent was £7 for nineteen years. I have spent at a very moderate estimate £10 an acre, and have improved sixty-four acres. I was then raised to £21 for the second lease. I called back and fore for years asking my year's rent for the houses, but never got it. The factor stav't aff an' stav't aff, and then latterly told me I would not get it. I pay interest on the drains. My place might be worth £30, but I pay £40. I get nothing for inventories. I have put in 1,500 ell[31] of drains at my own expense. There was a promise to pay so much for drainage to a neighbour, but when the time came the factor said they had not been put in according to the style he wanted, and he asked a bit here an' there to be taken up so that he might see them. The crap was on the ground, and the tenant, raither than destroy growin' stuff, thought he would let sic chance as he had of getting money from the laird go.

Another resident adds to the history of the Strichen crofters, of whom 120 were cleared out, that from the time they began to settle on the sides of the hill, they doubtless 'made' their land with more or less success, but they mostly were living in miserable hovels; not a few of them little better than semi-barbarians, and apt to merge into pauperism, adding materially to the burdens of rates. And thus a certain clearance was needed. Mr Baird spent a good many thousands in the erection of farm buildings, on which the tenants pay four per cent, doing also the cartages and maintaining the buildings. On the estates of New Pitsligo, Boyndlie, and Brucklay, the croft system has been kept up, only the rents are, it is said, by far too high. At the end of the lease there is always a rise of rent expected, whether the place be dear or cheap. But on these estates the old tenants always have the preference. Taking a round by New Pitsligo village, with its lotted lands[32] and its numerous peat stacks, we find the complaint to be that the feuars have more grievances than the crofters. Fifteen years ago, a great rise of rent was put on by the proprietor, when the feuars went to the Court of Session in defence of their rights. The feuars offered to abide by mutual valuation, which was, however, refused. What they complain of is that the land, the whole of which has been reclaimed by them at great cost, is rented at a rate equal to twice the amount paid by the neighbouring farmers and crofters, while in addition to this, the feuar pays a heavy assessment on the houses he occupies; whereas, the crofters and farmers pay only on their land.

In the northern part of the parish of New Deer, and within a space which embraces less than a third part of the parish, twenty seven crofts have, we are assured, been extinguished during the past forty or fifty years; rents have been increased three-fold, and, in some cases, much more, within the time some can remember. Here is the case of one small tenant, who has occupied his holding now, fifty acres in extent, for thirty one years. At entry it was unenclosed, and thirteen acres unreclaimed; rental £28. During the first lease of nineteen years he reclaimed the thirteen acres, and erected dykes and sunk fences at the cost of £30. He sank his inventories to the value of £120. After this he sat for nine years at a rental of £30, and during that time he spent £160 in building and repairing houses. At the end of the nine years he renewed his lease, and his present rental is £53. 8s. He has put in 7,000 yards of drains, and all the help he got from the laird was tiles for 3,000 yards. We are assured by several informants that something like one half of the land in this district has within their recollection been reclaimed by the tenants without any aid from the proprietor; and yet rents have been forced up in the proportion indicated. The statement of one is, that on the holding he occupies, and within his own recollection, ten miles of drains have been put in without assistance from the proprietor; and that until about twenty years ago tenants got no assistance in building, in draining, or reclaiming land; their rents were systematically raised on their own improvements.

Before taking a glance at the Philorth estate we pass Techmuiry, where we are told as many as seven crofts have been absorbed into one farm, three into another, and two into another. In the case of some of the crofts the rents at the expiry of the first lease were quadrupled, and more. On Philorth, from various sources, we hear of extensive improvements carried out under conditions which the tenant seems to consider 'stiff'; but all, apparently, according to bargain. But it is with the crofter, specially, that we have to do; and we are told that his class has decreased by a long way.

'From where I stand (the spot is near Greenburn), I can see the sites of four crofts that were made into a farm of seventy acres; of five made into another; two into another; three into another, the same way; two into another; five into another; two others joined into one small possession; and three into another – in all twenty six crofts transformed into eight farms.' And our cicerone for the time being allowed the index finger of his right hand again to drop by his side as he proceeded: 'And that is all within a radius of two miles or thereby, as you can see, and all on the same estate.'

'What were the operative reasons?'

'Oh: simple enough, and common enough. In prosperous times the proprietor or his factor were inclined to disannul tenants and set good, biggish tenants. It was much less trouble; and the proprietor saved on necessary buildings and the like. There was less chance of a number of these old and worn-out crofter people becoming ultimately a burden on the parish, while the laird had a better chance of getting his rent from the big farmer. Five crofters continually complainin' were waur to deal wi' than a single fairmer, d'ye see. About rents? We'll tak' a case where four crofts were put into one farm. The croft rents were £26. 10s.; £26; £2. 10s.; and £17. 10s.– total, £72. 10s.; but a shop was taken off at £6. 5s.; leaving a rental of £66. 5s. The tenant of the combined farm pays a hundred and twenty eight pounds; but doubtless the siller, and more, could have been got out of the crofts let separately. As regards the old state of matters generally, the crofts had been all taken out of the heather, and the rents always raised at second taking. The crofters did not lay out much money – they had not it to lay out, in fact – but they laboured on, struggling to make ends meet; nearly all bringing up big families; while they mostly died penniless. The crofts were from six to fifteen acres in extent, and the crofters generally took 'day's warks', coming home at night – sometimes a good long tramp – and in their spare time trenching and making the land, which produced wonderful crops in a dry year. The crofters expected payment for buildings at the end of their lease, but the houses not being in accordance with the estate regulations, they did not get it, which caused sore disappointment; only they could not afford to fight it at law with the proprietor. I know one amalgamation of crofts, in particular where the proprietor has gained increased rent by the process. The rent of the original farm was £42. 10s.; and there were added five crofts, rented respectively at £12, £24. 10s., £17. 10s., £16, and £5; total, £117. 10s. Well, the rent of the farm during last lease was £165, and it is now £180. The crofters' houses were all knocked down, and they got no compensation, though some of the crofts certainly were the best manured and best kept bits on the estate; and, during last lease, the present tenant put up a steading, at a cost of £600, which he leaves to the laird. The 'unearned increment' a' to the laird,' said ye? Weel, I ken little aboot ootlandish words o' the dish there, an' if't dinna leave the tenant wi' a sober aneuch morsel to fill's crap, I'm nae judge; that's a'.'[33]

9

From the point reached in last paper we hold on to north-westward, and take a glance at New Byth district in passing. The proportion of crofts and small holdings in the district is much about the same as it was fifty years ago. A great number of crofts have been added to the cultivated area by reclamation; while about an equal number have been absorbed in adjoining farms or two or three put together into larger holdings when the crofts were fully improved, and the cheaply constructed habitations of the original crofters were getting delapidated. Rents at the present day of single crofts and of several added together, have increased 'in some cases threefold within the last forty years.' On the estate of Byth there are forty six farms and crofts, exclusive of the home farm, and three of the largest farms are in the proprietor's possession.[34] During the last twenty-five years there have been upwards of fifty removals. Among the causes have been: (1) bankruptcies – seventeen, three of which occurred during the last year; (2) means exhausted in other cases; (3) would not let at rent which either sitting tenant or strangers would offer. Within the period indicated the arable area on this estate has been much extended by reclaiming and draining waste land, in no inconsiderable part by the tenants, though within the past five or six years at least £2,000 has been spent by the proprietor in deepening the Burn of Byth and erecting new buildings.

In the way of individual examples, two brothers, we are told, were let crofts of heather land for nineteen years, rent free. At the end of their leases their land, mostly reclaimed, was added to a neighbouring croft a few years older. The tenant of this croft had been paying £5; but when the other two tenants were ejected, and their crofts added to his, the rent was raised to £21. In another case two crofts of heather land, which were rented at about two pounds each, were, at the expiry of their leases, added together, and, with ten acres from a neighbouring farm to make up its extent, the holding is now rented at £52. In yet another case an improving crofter had trenched about three acres, and got four acres ploughed within a very few years. He believed himself to be sitting on nineteen years' tenure, but at the end of twelve he was served with a notice of removal or pay £7 a year of rent. Having nowhere to go, the crofter accepted the latter alternative for nineteen years, at the expiry of which the rent was raised to £13. 4s. for seventeen acres. At that rent he has struggled on, but has recently obtained consent to quit on equitable terms. Various similar cases could be given.

Complaints on the score of increased rental on this estate seem to apply chiefly to a period a good many years byegone, when – and in the case of the village lands, perhaps, as much as any – the increase appears to have been unduly great. These village lands extend to about 206 acres, and the rental in 1860 was about £330. In 1880 it stood at 460, and it is now £425. The present factor has, moreover, introduced new conditions some years ago, giving compensation for draining, liming, and boning. These conditions were favourably commented upon in our columns at the time; but hardly a single tenant has, we are informed, taken advantage of them.

From New Byth we pass on to take a look at the lotted lands on the property of the Earl of Fife, which, being of considerable extent, merit something more than a passing notice. We find them at three centres — Macduff, Turriff and Aberchirder. And, through the courtesy of Mr Hannay, factor to Lord Fife, we are able to give an exact statement of the acreage, rental, and number of tenants in each case, as follows, viz:

	Acres	R	P	Rental (£. s. d.)			Tenants
Macduff lotted lands	927	3	3	1,162	4	9	154
Turriff lotted lands	675	3	8	1,042	2	0	110
Aberchirder lotted lands	400	0	0	420	0	0	88

Aberchirder being in the county of Banff, need not be further dwelt upon here. In the case of Macduff[35] the land economy that obtains has for long seemed to us to present features worthy of careful attention. The population of the town, amounting, in all, to about 3,600, is a mixed one, including fishers and other seafaring folks, as well as a considerable proportion of people engaged in commercial pursuits and various industrial occupations. And out of this population 154 feuars hold lots of land, averaging about six acres in extent, for which they pay at the average rate of about twenty-four shillings an acre. Taking the average number in a family at six persons, it may thus be said that not fewer than 924 persons within the burgh — almost a fourth of the population — are directly interested in the land and its cultivation. That the effect of this arrangement is a thoroughly wholesome one can hardly be doubted. For a town of its size it would be difficult to find any similar place with more of the appearance of homely comfort, honest industry, and almost entire absence of squalid misery than Macduff presents. And nothing is more evident than that, from long use and wont, its good people generally both know the value of a bit of land and have acquired, or inherited, an adaptability in its cultivation to useful ends, be it garden plot or feuar's croft, not by any means general in urban communities.

The lotted lands, though let in connection with the feus, are not held in perpetuity, but simply during the pleasure of the proprietor. And this is deemed essential in the interest of the community, inasmuch as a good many of the feuars sub-let large portions of the land they rent without the superior's consent, asked or given, at rents perhaps twice or three times the rate they pay to the superior. And were the land not held from year to year it might lead to very considerable abuses, while preventing many who might wish to keep a cow or two from obtaining the necessary acreage to enable them to do so. There is no fear of the land ever being taken from those who care to keep it and who attend to its proper cultivation. And the rents, being for what may be regarded as town lands, are very moderate. In the case of any lots set free by some not caring to have land in connection with their feus, and the like, these are always given to other residents, who may desire to keep one or two cows. The same arrangements, practically, obtain in the case of the lotted lands at Turriff, where, as will be observed, the average rent per acre is higher than at Macduff; and the quality of the land is also superior.

In the matter of horse labour, the holders of the lotted lands depend chiefly upon the town carters for ploughing, laying down their crops, and so on, payment being made either at so much per acre or per day. Ploughing is also done occasionally by neighbouring farmers (though this remark applies more to Turriff), either as a favour or for payment, which, not unfrequently, assumes the form of a few days' labour at turnip-hoeing, or at harvest work. The harvest work on the lotted lands is accomplished chiefly by 'acres,' that is to say, a band of two or three scythes with the necessary uptakers working under a contractor, who contracts to do the reaping at so much per acre.[36] About Turriff, however, a good deal of the crop is sold on the ground by public roup a few weeks before the harvest. Formerly the threshing of the crop was at times a rather serious job, the owner of the adjacent horse or water-mill who undertook the work being often scarcely able to accommodate his customers so rapidly as they required. But nowadays the produce of three, four, or more crofts, or feuars' holdings is stacked in some convenient place and rapidly threshed out by the peripatetic steam threshing mill of the district.

In the Fishrie district, King Edward, where Lord Fife owns a large crofter colony, the number of crofts has increased considerably during the past thirty years. In no instance has there been a putting of two or more holdings together. The rule on the estate is to make openings for the sons of those who already occupy crofts if possible. The cause of the increase therefore, is principally due to this fact. The practice of extinguishing crofts and small holdings by adding them to larger farms, etc, is practically unknown on the Fife estates. On the whole, the rents for the small crofts are at present rather down than up as compared with former years. In cases where a man takes a piece of hill ground, cultivates it, builds a house, and puts on a slated roof, he is paid for the value of the roof, doors and windows at the end of his lease. For the first nineteen years the crofter gets the land for a few shillings of formal rent, and if he has brought, say ten acres, properly under cultivation, he gets another lease of it for about fifteen or twenty shillings an acre, more or less, according to the situation and quality of the soil. A good many of the crofters who take off ten acres of prairie land at from half a crown to seven and six per acre, as the case may be, bind themselves to cultivate the whole of it perhaps during the first ten years. It often happens, however, that at the end of that period, or at the end of even the nineteen years, the man has not improved two acres of it, and sometimes none. They not unfrequently employ themselves as farm servants, the man leaving his wife to make the best of the place, and she breaks up a spot here and there of the best of it for growing potatoes and such like. There are many instances, however, of tenants possessing such holdings for more than a lease, and never improving so much as two acres, although the arrangement had been that, if they did not bring it under cultivation, it would be given to the adjoining tenant, who was farming well. There are scarcely any instances, however, of this being carried out, as the original tenant generally gets a second chance by the granting of another term of nineteen years. Evictions or the taking of a holding over the improving tenant's head are unknown on the Fife estate.

In reference to the statement by a Strichen crofter embodied in last paper, we have been furnished with documentary evidence which goes distinctly to show that the crofter's particulars as to his own case were on various points inaccurate. Briefly put the facts are that on Mr Baird buying the property, statements were submitted showing that payment had to be made to the respective tenants for walls of houses, fences, and drains. Any draining done in Mr Baird's time was done by the proprietor, interest being paid by the tenant. The crofter in question, who held under a lease granted by Lord Lovat, was under its terms entitled to a year's rent for walls of houses if of that value at reletting. On the place being valued at reletting, for the usual term on the estate of fourteen years, the rent was reduced as much as would buy up the value of the houses and more. At last letting in 1884, being under trustees the tenants were asked to offer. This one did so, offering £30, and the valuation being £28, he got renewal at that figure, the difference between rent stated by him (£40) and £28 fixed, being made up of interest on outlays by the proprietor for draining and building a new dwelling-house – the rate for the former being five per cent and for the latter four per cent. The character and substantiality of the previous dwelling-house are indicated by the fact that it got to be uninhabitable in about thirty years. The holding is some fifty-two acres in extent, and the plan shows that about a fourth was arable at the tenant's entry, and the part drained by the proprietor was brought under cultivation mostly by ploughing. As regards the tenant's estimated expenditure of £10 an acre in reclaiming, that is held to be purely mythical; and as to payment for houses, the thing resolves itself into a question of paying the tenant twice over for the same subject. Then as regards drains the sole and intelligible condition of payment is that they shall be kept clear and in good working order.

So far of the individual case. It will be of interest to add that the total number of holdings reduced since Mr Baird bought the property has been eighty eight. There are, however, only about forty five fewer 'fire houses' on the estate; and up to last year a sum of about £34,483 had been expended on buildings on the property since it was bought by Mr Baird. A few of the old buildings that yet remain show what they were like, but it may be stated that at date of purchase there were only seven slated houses on the whole property, and now there are only about twenty that have not been substantially rebuilt, with slated roof, &c.[37]

10

At the point now reached, and in view of the probable necessity of, for a time, intermitting this series of papers, we may not unfittingly offer a few remarks of a more or less general kind based on the statements that have already appeared in print, and on other information – not less interesting – applicable to other parts of the county. Upon one point there is no doubt or difference of opinion. It is that, in the agrarian economy of Aberdeenshire, the crofter, or improving small holder, generally, has filled a most useful part in the past. To them it is due that many hundreds of acres of barren moor have been brought under the plough within the last fifty or sixty years; and from his class, trained up in habits of industry, thrift, and self-reliance, there have continued to go forth into various walks of life men and women fitted to act well their part under any circumstances; the main cause of regret without doubt being that in such limited proportion of numbers have these men and women been retained in connection with the soil as settled labourers, cottars, crofters, and farmers, from the smallest tenant upward. But while it will be readily admitted that the existence of crofts in a county like Aberdeen – and, indeed, in any agricultural county – is in the highest degree desirable; and while one may assert, without much fear of contradiction, that a judicious blending of farm and croft is greatly preferable to either a community of crofters apart from farms, or a collection of farms without a mixture of the crofter element, we are not blind to the difficulties that attend the successful perpetuation of the crofter system, as we have been wont to view it, under the changed conditions that now obtain. Speaking on the subject on a comparatively recent occasion, the Marquis of Breadalbane said:

> The crofter question was one of the very greatest importance, and he did not think anybody would venture to say that the crofter system, properly worked out, was not of great advantage to the country at large, as well as to the particular districts, because the crofters were the backbone of the country. But crofters must not be huddled together; they must be mixed up with large farmers; and were this done, he felt confident that the crofter would be a very great benefit to the farmer in supplying him with labour,

while the farmer would be a considerable benefit to the crofter in giving him the means of earning a livelihood. Many of the proprietors had made a very great mistake in throwing their small farms and crofts into large farms, but he did not think that in all cases the proprietors had been entirely to blame. The factors in many cases preferred to have a few large tenants to deal with rather than a number of smaller ones, which gave them more trouble in management. Many of the proprietors were considerably to blame in leaving a great deal too much of the management of their estates in the hands af their factors, and being too little in touch with their tenants.

That there is a great deal of sound common sense in these remarks is undeniable; and it is a lamentable fact, as well as a forcible comment upon the civilisation of the latter end of the nineteenth century, that the breach between the landlord and the tenant, and between the tenant and the cottar, has been, and still is, becoming wider and wider.

It is not so very long ago [writes one correspondent, well acquainted with the state of matters] that in Aberdeenshire a sort of family interdependence existed between the laird and the farmer, and between the farmer and his cottar; but during the last quarter of a century, or little more, we have drifted from that position, to the advantage of neither the one nor the other. A very good example of this might be found in the annual gathering on rent day, when the tenant, be his holding large or small, was kindlily received and entertained by the laird; difficulties were talked over and, mayhap, adjusted; and even where the proprietor was unable to accede to all the tenant's requests, the latter found some consolation in having treated directly with his principal. Factors are officials, and cannot be expected to put themselves completely in the landlord's shoes in dealing with tenants. The same feeling of interdependence existed between the farmer and the cottar. The farmer knew that in the cottar he had a workman of a superior caste to the chance day-labourer, while the cottar looked to the farmer for his daily bread. The rent day at the 'Hoose' had its parallel at the 'fairm' at Auld Yule, when the cottars had a 'fore-nicht' playing 'catch the ten', their refreshment being 'sowens' and their conversation a rehearsal of events that had occurred years and years previously.

About the time to which these remarks apply it was not unusual for the laird to allow a tenant to sub-let a portion or portions of his farm. The sub-tenant, in general an able-bodied man with a wife and family, had modest ideas as to the structural character and capacities of his habitation, and, with the assistance of the farmer, a 'but and ben' were erected at small outlay in cash. The man at once set to work on his 'bittie', the rent being frequently paid, not in coin but in labour, and not only so, for the sub-tenant in many cases exceeded his contract by earning wages of the farmer, or at any rate establishing his claim to a 'yokin'' or two of the plough to till his croft, or the service of the tenant's horses and carts to drive home his peats, and the like. As already indicated, a large extent of land has been reclaimed in Aberdeenshire by crofters holding in this way.

An individual example may, however, be given from the parish of Aberdour, a part of the county where this reciprocity was much practised.

> — was a servant to a large farmer in the parish. Seeing that he was an industrious man, the farmer sub-let him a small croft of unreclaimed land, for which he was to pay a comparatively nominal rent. — built a house and continued to work his day's work for wages, returning home at night and rising in the morning to trench odd corners and places difficult to take in by the plough. The farmer gave him an occasional yokin' and thus by and by he got as much land improved as enabled him to make a comfortable home and living. He brought up his family certainly in a different and better manner than is done now by the majority of farm servants. He lived and died in that croft, having brought up a family of three sons and a daughter – all of whom became farm-servants. In the meantime, however, a rearrangement had to be made between the farmer and the proprietor, who allowed the widow to possess the croft until she was unable to look after it. None of the sons got a chance of succeeding their father, however, as the land, being in a good state of cultivation, had become a titbit to both tenant and proprietor, the former being willing to pay a high rent to the latter for possession of the little holding, in which the family were regarded as having no unexhausted right whatever.

The principle of the crofter giving labour in return for the service of the farmer's horses in tilling his croft was not, however, confined to cases of sub-letting, but was in very general operation, even where the small crofter who could yoke no kind of plough held directly of the proprietor. And where the holdings were a little larger, it was the practice in many cases either to 'neeper' by two crofters lending the single draught animal either possessed to the other alternately, or having a side of the plough taken by the stoutest growing ox in the crofter's possession, or, it might be, by one of his cows. And undoubtedly the more rigidly commercial spirit of the times, which leads the modern farmer to demand full payment in cash for the service of his horses in ploughing in place of an easy equivalence in labour, constitutes one of the difficulties to be faced in working small crofts advantageously. Then, in the case of those with holdings of what may be styled the second degree, there is, we imagine, less of a disposition to make a shift, and scheme, in a humble thrifty way, by training an ox or cow to do its part in the ploughing, the animal suffering nothing all the while either as a marketable subject or for dairy purposes. And the more advanced social ideas which lead the crofter to feel that, in place of the old but and ben erected at the cost of a few pounds, he must have a house to dwell in costing £100 to £150, with suitable out-houses, constitute another formidable difficulty, inasmuch as the charge for interest on buildings becomes in the case of a croft of a few acres, almost equivalent to a full rent for the land attached. We do not profess, meanwhile, to discuss the question of how far these difficulties that face the small cultivator are to be solved, but quote with pleasure the opinion on the crofter's position generally of a well-known Buchan farmer, who, although he has exceeded the allotted span of three score years and ten, and is 'sitting his third nineteen' on his farm, is as shrewd and clear-headed as most men in their prime. His scheme for solution of the question is as follows:

I would have every farm that is worked by two pairs of horses to have a croft on it of such a size as would keep two cows, so as to have always the command of a good labouring man. That would be a great benefit to the country. In the case of four pairs of horses I would have two crofts, and so on. I do not believe in the principle of sub-letting by farmers, because farmers are like lairds in that respect – only human – and they would screw the cottar. He would have a less severe taskmaster in the laird than the farmer. The croft should be let direct from the proprietor; and if the land be equal in quality to that on the farm, the rent should be in proportion. The crofter would be under no obligation to the farmer, but should be taken bound by the proprietor to give his labour, if required, on the estate. I would not restrict him in selling his labour in the highest market on the estate; and the rate on the estate would be regulated by the rate outside it. The farmer would get far better labour from such a man than from a tramp darger,[38] and it would pay him to give the crofter better day's wages, or to pay him partly in money and partly in horse work. Such a crofter would be anxious to get ploughing, etc, from the farmer, and the farmer would prefer giving labour at odd times to paying him in hard cash, and this could be done to mutual advantage. The farmer would get the man's labour when he wanted it, and very likely he would thus be saved a servant. The man would be earning wages as a ditcher, a dyker, or the like during the day, and would go home and do his orra jobs at night. It might be said that this is taking it out of the cottar. So it is; but it is for his own benefit. He is earning his daily wage, and he is in his own time preparing his croft land to yield him a supplementary income. A while ago there were plenty labourers; when the prosperous times were on us they were not to be had; and now again we have an overflow, because there is not much work in the country, farmers being inclined to let everything lie just now in order to see whether the present depression will pass over. A few more years like this will bring a large number of farmers to ruin.'[39]

APPENDIX: CORRESPONDENCE ARISING FROM
THE ABERDEENSHIRE CROFTER

Sir – I have read with much interest the papers in your columns on the Aberdeenshire crofter. I have no doubt that the writer wishes to draw a faithful portrait of him, and no one has greater skill.

I was specially interested in the charming picture he sketched yesterday of old Donald Jack, who apparently was foolish enough to make a present of £500 to his laird, while earning only 'the barest of livings' for himself. Your contributor's information is, however, not very accurate. If he had taken the trouble to verify the facts, I would willingly have given him a true account from the documents now before me. Donald Jack's 'placie' has not been let for £20, and the £500 is a myth.

About forty years ago, when the peat began to fail in the moss of Millden, the late Mr Still, the proprietor, marked the ground off into sections, to be let as crofts from time to time as the peat was removed. The soil was well worth improving, and, when improved and equipped with buildings, it would at that time have brought in the market a rent of from twenty to thirty shillings per acre.

A fifteen-acre section was let to Donald Jack at Martinmas, 1846, on a nineteen years' lease. It was then worth about £4 a year as pasture. The tenant built a very humble but comfortable dwelling of 'feal and divot', and he added 'offices' to match. These buildings were very unlike the slated houses erected nowadays, but they cost little and served their purpose. Donald brought up his family respectably, and by degrees he brought the land under the plough, except about two acres of worthless outlying ground not worth improving.

For this holding he began with a yearly rent of £1, or nine pence per acre, which was about one-fourth of what would now be called its 'prairie value'. After five years the rent rose to fifty shillings or three and fourpence per acre; and after five years more it rose to £5 per annum, or six and eightpence per acre, at which it continued for the remaining nine years of the lease.

I cannot, of course, tell what the buildings cost the tenant, nor what was the value of his labour in improving the place, which must be distinguished from the labour of ordinary tillage; but I am safe to say the cost was less than one half of what the improvement might have been if the whole had been effected by the landlord by contract according to modern ideas and in modern fashion. On this plan the expenditure on building, fencing, trenching, and draining, even at the prices ruling forty years ago, could not have been less than £300; and in order to maintain the previous value of £4 and to get a fair return for such outlay he would have required to obtain a rent of £19, or twenty five shillings per acre, which would have been no more than a fair rent. On this footing, in the course of a nineteen years' lease the tenant would have paid £350 in rent. As it was, he paid in all during that period only £62. 10s. Out of the surplus he remunerated hinself for his outlay and his labour in building the houses and reclaiming the land. It is not difficult to prove what was the actual fact – that at the end of his lease the tenant found himself considerably richer than when he began, while the landlord got back his holding worth, on the basis of calculation adopted by your contributor, £220. Its original 'prairie value' was £80, the 'increment' was £140, and if this 'increment' was 'earned' by the tenant he was well paid for it during the lease.

When the lease expired in 1865, Donald, who had reached a good old age, retired in favour of his son George, who obtained a fresh lease of nineteen years. The croft was slightly reduced in size, the most worthless outlying ground having been detached, and for the holding of twelve arable acres as thus arranged, a rent of £11 was amicably agreed upon. Seven years ago, when the adjoining croft of fifteen acres, on which there are no buildings, fell out of lease, George asked and obtained a nineteen years of it, and at the same time he got an extension of the then current lease of his original 'placie'. The fresh lease of his combined croft is now current. The rent of £26 of which someone has told you, is made up of the rent of £11 for the 'placie' and £15 for the adjoining croft, which the tenant did not improve.

In short, during the last forty years Donald Jack lived and thrived, and finally retired in favour of his son, who has since more than doubled his holding in the moss of Millden. I am, &c,

J Murray Garden.

7 Union Terrace, Aberdeen, 23rd March, 1886.

(The writer of the crofter article has only to say that the correspondent who supplied him with information about the case referred to no doubt omitted, inadvertently, to specify acreage; and the writer accordingly erred in assuming that at renewal of lease the extent remained as before. For the rest of it, he must hold substantially to his opinion that Donald was simply one of the class of men who expended indomitable industry upon the land, and lived a life of the most rigid economy, without sharing in the results to the extent he ought. The writer freely owns that he is no match for Mr Garden in handling figures, but he claims to have had a good deal more experience of peat land, and he has never once encountered a sample of it worth anything like the rent Mr Garden mentions, even when fully improved. It is possible some blockhead might have rented an exhausted peat moss brought under cultivation, at twenty to thirty shillings an acre, during the heat of competition for farms a quarter of a century ago; but forty years ago it is not easy to believe that anybody would have done so; and in most cases half the amount would have been enough with buildings fully provided.)[40]

Sir – Might it not be worth the while of your correspondent who is writing about the Aberdeenshire crofters to take some pains to verify the gossip which he parades as reliable facts? I am in circumstances to say, without fear of contradiction, that the whole statement about Cruden is a tissue of falsehoods. The spirit of that statement is most malicious, and the averments are utterly baseless. The general statements can only be generally contradicted, but he has given a model case – a morsel very sweet to his taste, which may be examined and tested. The case of 'J A' cannot be mistaken by those in the L— district. The facts of that case are diametrically opposite to the slanderous assertions of the correspondent. Thus J A did not build his own house at his own expense; did not offer £17 of rent for his place; was not asked to give £20 for it; and was not put out of the place for £1. On the contrary, his house was paid for to him in full, partly at its erection and partly on his leaving. He was offered a renewal of his lease again and again for several pounds less than its present rent, but he refused it. After irrevocable steps had been taken, he repented, acknowledged that he had been misled by a neighbour, and offered the sum previously asked from him for the place. By that time, however, another offer had been accepted, and J A, the dupe likely of the party who furnished this mendacious letter to your correspondent, left his croft. If the other instances of landlord tyranny detailed by your correspondent are as false as the above, as I fear most of them are, your space might be better occupied than by publishing such gross slanders. I am, &c,
A Residenter.
5th May, 1886.

('A Residenter' is evidently very angry and somewhat needlessly abusive. Our Crofter Commissioner has only to state, in reply, that the case of J A, as appeared on the face of it, was printed as sent to him by a respectable resident, who did not say that the case occurred in the L— district. 'A Residenter' seems, however, to have found enough in it to make him fix it down there – if not also to attempt pulling on the cap on his individual head. As to the general denunciation to which he has been subjected, it is enough to remark that our Commissioner has taken pains to verify his information; and that even as regards the district of L— he has no fear of any impartial inquirer who may visit the locality making such charges as the person who signs himself 'A Residenter' does, to say the least of it – OUR CROFTER COMMISSIONER.)[41]

Sir – I have read with interest your papers on the Aberdeenshire crofters, and was not a little surprised to find your Commissioner so far at sea with regard to the crofts on the Fife estates in King Edward. He says: 'The practice of extinguishing crofts and small holdings by adding them to larger farms is practically unknown on the Fife estates.' His stay in King Edward must have been short, or his information defective, before he could have made such a statement. Within three miles as the crow flies of King Edward Station no less than ten crofts and small holdings have been added to larger farms within the last twenty or twenty five years. In the case of one of the farms, to which three small holdings are added, every one of the tenants kept a horse, and either wrought with his neighbour, or had an ox or cow that took the side of the plough. Some of these ten holdings have been absorbed quite recently by the larger farms, and at less rent than the crofters were paying. Within cry of the lotted lands of Macduff a nice little farm is being added to a large one at present. I am not finding fault with the management of the estates, but let facts speak for themselves. I am &c, A Farmer on the Fife Estates.

(The expression used by our Commissioner was no doubt too loose, and required to be taken in connection with what was said in a previous paper on the subject of adhibiting and detaching crofts, generally. Editor, *Free Press*.)[42]

NOTES

1. The area that was about to be defined as 'the crofting counties': Argyll, Inverness, Ross and Cromarty, Sutherland, Caithness, Orkney and Shetland.
2. Royal Commission on the Condition of the Crofters and Cottars of the Highlands and Islands of Scotland, *Report and Minutes of Evidence*. Parliamentary Papers, 1884, XXXII–XXXVI, C3980.
3. J. Anderson, *General View of the Agriculture of the County of Aberdeen* (Edinburgh, no publisher stated, 1794).
4. Royal Commission on the Employment of Children, Young Persons and Women in Agriculture, *Fourth Report*, Appendix Part II, Parliamentary Papers, 1870, XIII, C221.
5. *Aberdeen Free Press*, 17 March 1886.
6. Many readers would recall the mixture of bribery and flattery which the appalling Mrs Birse applied to Dawvid Hadden, the petty tyrant who acted as the laird's ground officer, in an attempt to have Gushetneuk engrossed in Clinkstyle. See W Alexander, *Johnny Gibb of Gushetneuk* (Turriff, Heritage Press, reprint of 8th edn, 1979), pp 235-41.
7. R C Employment of Children etc, p 7.
8. Ibid, p 11. The milk cow held a central position in the croft's internal economy. See M Gray, 'North-East Agriculture and the Labour Force, 1790–1875,' in *Social Class in Scotland: Past and Present* ed A A Maclaren (Edinburgh, John Donald, 1976), p 94.
9. R C Employment of Children, op cit, p 12.
10. Ibid, pp 10-11.
11. Ibid, p 13.
12. *Aberdeen Free Press*, 22 March 1886.
13. R C Employment of Children, p 7.
14. J. Sinclair (ed), *Statistical Account of Scotland* (Edinburgh, Creech, 1791–9), vol 14, p 341 footnote.
15. Ibid, pp 339, 343. The flavour of this Highland Aberdeenshire, Gaelic speaking

farming community, with its strong reliance on seasonal movement of stock between upland and lowland pastures, comes through a detailed study of parallel arrangements in Highland Perthshire: A Bil, *The Shieling* (Edinburgh, John Donald, 1989).

16. *Aberdeen Free Press*, 29 March 1886.

17. Barclay was the radical Liberal member for Forfarshire, and parliamentary spokesman for the SLRA. He was vice-president of the parallel body in England and Wales, the Farmers' Alliance. That he also farmed in a very big way on Deeside shows how compromised he must have felt when required to press the SLRA's radical demands, which threatened the interests of both large tenants and landlords.

18. An irony which the reader may care to contemplate is that George Carr's unremitting labour turned the land in a full circle. Today Westhill of Park lies under pine plantations, the trees drawing up George's fossil sweat.

19. G. Carr, 'On Improvements on the Farm of Westhill of Park', *Transactions of the Highland and Agricultural Society*, 4th series, 1870–1, vol 3, pp 407-8.

20. *Aberdeen Free Press*, 5 April 1886.

21. By sitting rent free for one year the tenant had forfeited his right to claim compensation for his own improvements to the farm, under the 1883 Agricultural Holdings Act.

22. *Aberdeen Free Press*, 12 May 1886.

23. To straighten the boundary of his farm.

24. The Haddo House estate was held by the Gordons of Haddo, the premier Liberal family in the county. Under successive Earls (later Marquesses) of Aberdeen, Haddo dealt generously with tenants, whether large or small. In the 1770s this raised the contemptuous fury of that flint-hard East Lothian farmer, Andrew Wight (*Present State of Agriculture in Scotland* (Edinburgh, Creech, 1783), vol. 4, p 608), with his single-minded attachment to the bottom line in profit and loss accounts. 'It is a great misfortune to be too rich,' he thundered; 'for it makes many men negligent as to the improvement of their estates.' The Gordons reaped the fruit of this benevolence a century later. As rent arrears rocketed on neighbouring rack-rented estates in 'the great depression', arrears remained negligible on Haddo. See *Expenditure and Outgoings on Certain Estates in Great Britain, and Farm Accounts*. Parliamentary Papers 1896 XVI, C8125, pp 48-9.

25. The 1872 Education Act (Scotland) made full-time primary education compulsory for all children, and thus took child farm labour out of the market. Very few children under ten had been full-time hired farm-workers in the decades immediately before this, though many had worked as herds in summer and gone to school in winter. Multitudes had combined elementary education with part-time labour on the family holding. It was dad who defined what was 'part-time labour', of course.

26. *Aberdeen Free Press*, 19 April 1886.

27. This 'well-known valuator' could be G J Walker, who had acted as the Assistant Commissioner to the Richmond Commission in 1881 for the whole of northern Scotland. In 1886 Walker was attacked for his method of valuing the Cushnie estate, on grounds very like those set down here.

28. This horror story comes from Lenabo, a crofting colony on the Aden estate. A letter from A Bath in the *Free Press* (2 February 1886) attests to the truth of the report, based on personal inquiries.

29. *Aberdeen Free Press*, 26 April 1886.

30. Rent per annum for each acre of the holding.

31. For those of a mathematical cast of mind, an ell equals 37.059 inches or 94.130cm.
32. Lotted lands were to be found around many Aberdeenshire towns and villages. They were small parcels of land let along with village houses, often for grazing milk cows. Lotted lands always attracted very high rents. See Select Committee (House of Commons) on Small Holdings, *Report*, Parliamentary Papers, 1889, XII, C313 questions 9041-57.
33. *Aberdeen Free Press*, 3 May 1886.
34. Because the laird had not been able to let them profitably as cash crop prices fell in 'the great depression'.
35. Macduff was also in Banffshire, of course. A modestly thriving spa in the early nineteenth century, Alexander seems to have had a soft spot for the town. See the early chapters of *Johnny Gibb of Gushetneuk*, with their charming description of getting the Gibb family to 'the Walls' in the farm cart.
36. For more information about harvest methods see A Fenton, 'Sickle, Scythe and Reaping Machine: Innovation Patterns in Scotland', *Ethnologia Europeae*, 1974, vol 7 pp 35-47.
37. *Aberdeen Free Press*, 10 May 1886.
38. A travelling day labourer.
39. *Aberdeen Free Press*, 17 May 1886.
40. *Aberdeen Free Press*, 25 March 1886. J Murray Garden was a leading local lawyer factor.
41. *Aberdeen Free Press*, 7 May 1886. William Alexander's skilful wrong-footing of 'A Residenter', with his hint that the man was the laird of L— and had evicting propensities, brought another letter from the fuming residenter. The *Free Press* acknowledged receipt of the second letter, but declined to publish on the grounds that it was malicious and used language 'that are not the terms that come naturally to the lips of a gentleman'.
42. *Aberdeen Free Press*, 17 May 1886. Note that in this case the comment comes from the *Free Press*'s editor, Henry Alexander, rather than from his radical brother William. The Earl of Fife was an important local Liberal, and William Alexander must be kept from taking pot shots at him.

PART 3 FICTION

5 A Career in Farm Service[1]

Tam Meerison flits

When the Martinmas term of 1840 was drawing near, Johnny Gibb wanted to know of Tam Meerison whether he was disposed to remain as his servant through the winter. Tam's answer to this question, addressed to him while he was busy currying the bay mare,[2] was not decisive either way.

'Aw cudna say,' quoth Tam drily; 'aw wudna care a great heap, gin we can 'gree aboot the waages, an' a' ither thing confeerin.'

'Confeerin or no confeerin,' said Johnny testily, 'I wunt a mair direck answer – fat siller are ye seekin'?'

'It depen's a gweed hantle on a body's neebors tee,' continued Tam.

'Ou ay, I ken the loon an' you's been aye haein bits o' sharries noo and than; but he's a weel-workin', weel-conduckit loon, an' ye winna pit an aul' heid upo' young shou'ders.'

'Will he be bidin?' asked Tam.

'Lickly, though he hasna been speer't at yet; an' Jinse's bidin – hae ye ony faut to fin' wi' her?'

'I've naething adee wi' women's wark, an' never meddles wi't,' said Tam, pursuing his grooming very industriously. 'Roun', Jess – wo – still, you thing.' The latter part of the sentence was of course addressed to the animal then undergoing its daily trimming.

'Weel, weel, but tell me, ay or no, an' fat fee yer seekin',' insisted Johnny Gibb.

'I cudna say foo the fees'll be rinnin this term; an' aw wudna like to name siller till the mornin' o' the market.'[3]

'A puddin' lug, min,' exclaimed Johnny. 'That's aye the gate wi' you chiels; tum'le aboot a haill kwintra side, sax month or so here, sax month or so there, for half o' your life-time, an' never save a saxpence to bless yoursel's wi'!'

'I cudna dee't though,' said Tam, who still carried in his mind Johnny's demand to know what fee he wanted.

Johnny at once turned him about and left the stable.

Now the truth of the matter was that Tam Meerison did not wish to leave Gushetneuk. The loon, Tam's fellow servant, was just a little of a thorn in his side occasionally, by his lack of reticence in speech on certain subjects;[4] but then there was much seemingly to balance this very partial grievance. If

Johnny Gibb was occasionally a little hasty, he was on the whole a kind and indulgent master. The horses Tam drove were handsome, well appointed and well fed — an important consideration, and properly so, with every man in Tam's position. Tam admitted that the servants were 'weel ees't' in the way of food; and then the presence of Jinse Deans had come to be something that seemed to be essential to Tam's perfect serenity of mind. But for all that Tam was so far the slave of habit that he could not clearly see his way to departing one jot from what, among his compeers, had come to be considered the correct mode of bargain-making in convenanting for their services; he had a kind of general idea that it was on the whole an effeminate sort of thing to 'bide owre lang i' the same place', and he had now been eighteen months at Gushetneuk.

On the morning of the feeing market day, Johnny Gibb no doubt asked, once more, what wages Tam required, but evidently Johnny was in a decidedly more indifferent mood than when he had previously mooted the subject. And, accordingly, when Tam, who by that time had begun seriously to doubt his previous policy, 'socht,' he somewhat curtly 'bade' ten shillings less than the sum Tam mentioned. With few more words they separated, and each went away to the market in his own interest, but with a vague notion on Tam's part that they 'wud lickly meet afore they were lang there'. Early in the day, however, Johnny had a stoot gudge, anxious to 'work a pair o' horse', pressed on his notice, and easily arranged with him. Tam hung in the market for good part of the day receiving only indifferent offers, and the upshot was, that he at last, reluctantly enough, engaged himself to be foreman at Clinkstyle. Peter Birse, as was not an unusual case with him, was about to make what is understood by 'a clean toon' of his servants, and, according to his invariable practice, had been endeavouring to fill up the vacancies in his establishment at the cheapest rate; so he managed to pick up Tam Meerison at an advanced period of the market, at a crown less fee than Johnny Gibb had offered Tam on the morning of the same day.

The change from Gushetneuk to Clinkstyle was one that Tam Meerison did not find exactly conducive to his comfort. In explaining his reasons for making the change, Tam, to put the best face upon it, told his friends that he was desirous of getting to a 'muckler toon' than Gushetneuk, where he would have more 'company' and so on. But, poor lad, the company he got were a cause of no little trouble to him. It so happened that Mrs Birse's notions about the proper mode of feeding servants were not such as to command the approval of those servants who had had practical experience of them, or to procure for Mrs Birse herself a favourable reputation among that class where she was known. The new servants — second horseman, orra man, and cow baillie — were disposed not merely to grumble but to break out into open insurrection, on the ground of the unsatisfactory character of the victuals supplied to them. And they expected Tam to vindicate their rights in the matter; a duty which he found by no means easy or pleasant. So far as mere inarticulate growling, or the utterance of an incidental anathema against the victuals in the hearing of the servant maid went, Tam found no difficulty in going fully along with his companions. But a crisis came by and by. The gudewife, in her thrifty way, had for a good many nights in succession supplied boiled turnips and turnip brose to the lads as the staple of their supper. And in testimony of their appreciation of the fare thus furnished, they latterly had no sooner smelt the odour thereof as they entered the kitchen night after night, than they duly commenced to low like as many oxen. Then it was that Mrs Birse seized the occasion to catch them flagrante delicto, by bursting into the kitchen as they were bellowing away; and a very stiff onset she gave them about this unbecoming behaviour.

'An' fat hae ye to say against gweed sweet neeps to yer sipper, I sud like to ken?' demanded the irate matron.

'Oh weel, it's owre af'en to hae them ilka night 'cep Sunday for a haill ouk,' said Tam.

'Owre af'en! Birst the stamacks o' ye; fat wud ye hae!'

'A cheenge files.'

'For fat, no? There's fowk maybe't kens their place better nor set their servan's doon at the same table wi' themsel's; and gin ye hinna leern't that muckle gweed breedin' yet, the seener ye're taucht it the better; fat sorra div ye wunt?'

'We wunt naething but a fair diet,' answered Tam.

'A fair diet! An' weel't sets ye — aw wud thank ye to tell me fan your fader, the roch dyker,' and here Mrs Birse looked directly in Tam Meerison's face, 'was able to gi'e 's faimily aneuch o' onything to ate. But that's aye the gate; them that's brocht up like beggars 's aye warst to please.'

This outburst took the wind so considerably out of Tam that he utterly failed to make any reply; and Mrs Birse, after a brief pause, went on, 'Deed, they're but owre gweed for ye — wi' weel hir't brose, an' plenty o' as gweed milk to yer kyaaks as ever cam' oot o' a byre.'

'Sang, it needs't a' — near aucht days aul', an' as blue as blaeworts; but it's nae the milk't we're compleenin o' eenoo,' said the second horseman, after another pause.

'Na, an' ye wud be baul' to compleen, ye ill-menner't pack; but ye'll jist tak' yer neeps there, an' nae anither cheep oot o' the heids o' ye; or gin ye dinna, we'll ken fat wye to tak' an order o' ye.'

'Tak' an order o' the aul' Smith,[5] an' ye like; neeps sax nichts oot o' the seyven winna stan' law at ony rate,' said the former speaker.

'An' it's muckle ye ken aboot law,' replied the gudewife scornfully. 'Jist gae ye on till I need to gar yer maister tak' ye afore the Shirra, an ye'll maybe hae some diffeekwalty in stannin yer grun for refeesin a gweed halesome diet.'

With this deliverance, and unheeding the rejoinder, 'Aweel, aw daursay

ye've hed the chance o' hearin' the Shirra afore noo,' Mrs Birse turned, and
bounced away 'ben' to the parlour, where she proceeded to make tea for her
husband and hopeful progeny, now gathered round the table, at the same
time letting the unspent balance of her wrath blow off in a general way, to
ease her mind; the head of the household getting a slight incidental
scorching, when he happened to come in the way.

'I'm sure, man, I'm jist keepit in a fry wi' ae coorse pack aifter anither; ye
seerly wile the vera warst that ye can get fan ye gae to the market.'

'Hoot, 'oman, ye sudna vex yersel' aboot them.'

'Easy to ye; but an' ye hed the maetin o' them's I hae, ye wud tell anither
story. A vulgar, ill-fashion't set.'

'Fat's been adee eeno?'

'Adee! refeesin their neeps, an' makin' a din like as mony nowte fan they
cam' in.'

'Hoot awa'.'

'Yes,' interjected Miss Eliza Birse, 'an' I heard the second horseman cursin'
aboot the kitchie cakes.'

'An' fat did he say, my dear?' asked Mrs Birse.

'He bann't at Betty, an' said they werena fit for swine to eat.'

'An' fat did Betty say, 'Liza?'

'She said't hoo't she cudna help it; that it was your orders to mak' them
weet i' the hert to keep the men fae eatin' owre muckle.'

'The dooble limmer!' exclaimed Mrs Birse. 'An' her leukin a' the time't a
bodie speaks till 'er as gin butter wudna melt in her cheek.'

'Weel, I heard 'er at ony rate; for I was jist gaen up the stair, an' stoppit and
hearken't at the back o' the inner kitchie door.'

'The oongrateful ill-menner't jaud't she is,' continued Mrs Birse. 'But I'll
sort 'er for that. She'll be expeckin to get some leavin's i' the teapot, to be a
cup till 'er fan the men gaes oot to sipper the beasts, as esswal; but she'll luik
wi' clear een ere she see that again, I doot. That's the reward't fowk gets for
their kin'ness to the like o' 'er.'

While this conversation was going on, the tea was proceeding apace. The
three young Masters Birse and Miss Birse, with their respected parents, were
seated round a somewhat clumsily set out table, containing in the way of
solids, an ample store of bread, oatcakes, cheese, and butter. The olive plants
were all at school, except Peter junior, who, being designed for agriculture,
was understood to have the literary part of his education about finished, and
was taking to farming operations, including some minor attempts at cattle-
dealing at which he had been allowed to try his hand, very kindly. Suddenly
Peter senior called across the table to his youngest born, Benjamin: 'Benjie!
fat are ye deein pirlin aboot at yer breid that gate?'

'Weel,' answered Benjie, sulkily, "Liza's gi'en a nae gweed bit, an winna
hae't 'ersel'.'

'The breid's a' perfeckly gweed – ate it this moment, sir!' said Peter Birse senior, severely.

Benjie put on a look more dour and dolorous than before, but failed to fulfil the parental mandate.

'Fat is't, my pet?' asked Mrs Birse, in her most sympathising tones, addressing Master Benjamin.

'Weel, it's nae gweed,' answered Benjie, proffering his mamma the unacceptable bit of cake – a thick, rather sodden-looking 'piece'.

The worthy lady examined it for a second, and said, "Liza: that's a bit o' the kitchie kyaaks – fat wye has that come here?'

'I dinna know,' answered Miss Birse; 'it was upo' the truncher.'

'Is there mair o' 't? Eh ay – here's twa korters! Betty cudna but 'a kent that she was pittin 't upo' oor maun. I sudna won'er nor she's stown as muckle o' the parlour breid till hersel'. Sic creatures wi' oonhonesty. Lay that twa korters by, 'Liza, till we see better in till't. I'se be at the boddom o' that, though it sud cost her 'er place.' The careful mother added, 'There's a better bittie to ye, my dautie,' and as she said this, she handed to Benjie a full half of one of the quarters of parlour cakes, which bore about the same relation to the 'kitchie kyaaks' that a well-browned biscuit does to a lump of dough.

'Hoot, 'om-an,' Peter Birse had commenced to utter, in the way of deprecation of this proceeding, when Mrs Birse cut him short by tossing the lump of 'kitchie kyaaks' towards him, and exclaiming: 'Weel, weel, try't yersel', gin ye hae onything to say. But ye canna expeck the bairn's stamackie to be able to disjeest the like'o' that.'

'Humph, I cud ate it brawly,' said Peter Birse senior; and in proof of the truth of his assertion he did eat it. Only his next helping was taken, not from the remaining bit of 'kitchie kyaaks', but from the parlour cakes.

The result of the turnip controversy was that Tam Meerison and his companions did get an occasional supper of 'kail', very purely prepared with salt and water; only as the three lads coincided in holding decidedly that Tam ought to have 'stuck'n up better to the aul' soo,' his influence and authority as foreman were correspondingly diminished. And the less Tam was disposed to renew the quarrel with his mistress, the more did the others swear 'at lairge' when they happened to be about the kitchen. Not seldom was this done, with the evident intention of provoking warfare, as well as of manifesting the slight degree of respect they entertained for Tam, and for everybody else connected with Clinkstyle; the general result being that Tam would sit, mainly dumb, a good part of the evening, hearing no end of jibes indirectly launched at himself; while Betty, the hardworked bedraggled kitchen damsel, would at one time giggle and laugh with the rough fellows, and be at next turn coarsely tormented till she was in a state of the highest wrath; or be made the butt of their oaths and obscene allusions. As for Mrs Birse, 'bauld' woman as she was, even she found it to her comfort to make as few errands to the kitchen as might be, while 'the boys', as her husband termed them, were about.

And here, good reader, I bethought me of giving utterance to a few moral reflections on the degraded character of our farm-servant class; and how blameworthy they are for being such immoral and unmannerly boors. But somehow my line of vision came always to be obstructed by a full-figure image of Mrs Birse of Clinkstyle, who, you will perceive, is a very particular and intimate acquaintance of mine. Mrs Birse would come into the forefront, and her husband, Peter, was vaguely discernible in the background. So I gave up the attempt. You may make it on your own account; but I doubt whether you will be able to search thoroughly into the causes of this social evil without being also troubled with the image of Mrs Birse of Clinkstyle.

Tam Meerison's private affairs

Six months after the date of his removal from Gushetneuk, Tam Meerison had once more to decide on the question of renewing his engagement with his master, or seeking a new one. His experiences at Clinkstyle had not been altogether of the most pleasant sort, whether as regards his master or mistress or his fellow-servants, and the natural conclusion would have been that Tam certainly would not stay longer there. But conclusions in such cases are sometimes affected by circumstances which it is not so easy to guess at. A day or two before the feeing market day it had leaked out that Tam was 'bidin'', and the fact considerably intensified the feeling of contempt which his fellow servants had been in the habit of occasionally exhibiting towards him. They had hoped to leave Clinkstyle with a clean toon again, and they were angry at being disappointed. While Peter Birse manifested his satisfaction by talking more than usual to Tam, or stalking along for a bit with him at the plough, the lads lost no opportunity of throwing out a taunt at his craven resolution; or reminding him of those bygone interludes when Mrs Birse had chosen to express her private opinion of him and his. Doubtless these taunts were not pleasant; but I don't know that they weighed most on Tam's mind at that particular juncture. In point of fact, the state of Tam's affections, combined with the adverse influences that seemed to be arraying themselves against him, kept him in a condition of no little anxiety. Tam now bitterly regretted that pig-headed sense of self-importance on his part, which had made him, without the shadow of a valid reason, decline Johnny Gibb's first overture to re-engage him at the previous term; and thus had earned for him a bad situation in place of a good one – precisely the course that I have seen many more of Tam's class follow, to reach exactly the same end. But this was not all. Tam was seriously in love with Jinse Deans. Whether Jinse had hitherto reciprocated his passion in any true sense, I would be loth to venture an opinion. It was certain she received Tam as a suitor; but it was equally certain that Tam was not the only person so favoured. Tam knew this. Nay more, while he had over and over again met with what he reckoned 'slichts' at the hands of his enchantress, he had an agonising suspicion that Johnny Gibb's new man, his own successor, and whom Johnny had described as a 'stoot gudge an' a gatefarrin', was also 'stickin' up' to Jinse. Ah! poor Tam, thou wert truly out of the frying-pan into the fire! Tam had writhed under and sought to resent the slight scorchings he had to endure from the youth Willy M'Aul on the subject of his courtship; next he had assumed the high horse with Johnny Gibb, and then left Gushetneuk a half-repentant man, allowing his successor to come in and court his sweetheart at leisure. Whereas, had he remained there still, he would have had opportunities for baulking competitors which none other could have had. It was like abandoning a strongly defensive position in face of the enemy.

So thought Tam Meerison, and his meditations were not sweet. When the next term approached, Tam accordingly contrived to get early information about Johnny Gibb's arrangements. Unhappily for him, his successor at Gushetneuk was 'bidin''. 'Jist like 'im; inhaudin scoonrel,' thought Tam. However that might be, Tam had got a little 'bocht wit' on the subject; and he felt that, if he stood at a certain disadvantage with Johnny Gibb's 'stoot gudge', inasmuch as the gudge, being at Gushetneuk, had so much readier access to Jinse than he had, being at Clinkstyle; then if he left Clinkstyle, and ran the risk of having to transport himself several miles farther off, his position and prospects would be yet further damaged in proportion to the increased distance.

Therefore it was that Tam Meerison made up his mind to bear the ills he had, and to remain at Clinkstyle.

Another six months had passed and left his courtship much in the same state; but by that time Tam had put his foot in it, by talking disrespectfully of Master Benjamin Birse. It was in the kitchen, and, though Tam was not aware of it, Miss Birse was behind the 'inner door', where we have heard of her being before. What Tam had said was to the effect that 'Benjie was an orpiet, peeakin, little sinner'; and that 'he was fitter to be a dog-dirder, or a flunkey, nor to gae to the college;' sentiments which – although they seemed to meet with a rather hearty response from the audience immediately before him – when retailed to Benjie's mother, were productive of a storm, that thereafter burst with no little fury about Tam's ears. Tam's mood, I fear, had been desperate at any rate, and he now retorted on Mrs Birse by somewhat bluntly telling her she 'mith be prood to see 'er loon wi' a pair o' yalla breeks an' a strippet waistcoat on; it wud be ten faul better nor be a muckle goodman, wi' a wife that wudna lat 'im ca' 's niz his ain.' Mrs Birse took this as personal. And when the term came, Tam left Clinkstyle, half reckless, as it seemed, of his fate; for surely Jinse's heart was too hard to win, and what else need he care for!

Tam Meerison had gone off to a distance of over a dozen miles, and for the next twelve months the region of Pyketillim saw nothing, and I really believe heard very little of and still less from, him. For Tam was not a man of the pen. He had, indeed, learnt to write a sort of decent small text at school, but the accomplishment was of wondrous little use to him. He never wrote letters, except on very pressing emergencies, and not more than three or four of these had occurred since he became a man. It was not the mere writing that dismayed him; it was the composition – 'foo to begin' – and the 'backin''. These were the grand obstacles; and Tam's chief exercise in penmanship had been the occasional copying of some approved receipt for the composition of blacking for horse harness, in the way of friendly interchange with a cronie.[6]

At the Martinmas of 1841, Johnny Gibb changed his principal man-servant. The gudge, whose ambition it was to rise, was leaving on a friendly understanding, with a view to go to school for a quarter with Sandy Peterkin, to rub the rust off his literary and arithmetical acquirements, and then learn the business of a mole-catcher when spring came, and Johnny promoted Willy M'Aul, now grown a stout lad of over nineteen, to his place. The gudge had been at the feeing market, from which he came home at a pretty late hour, and in high spirits, with sweeties in his pockets, not merely for Jinse, but for Mrs Gibb as well, when fit opportunity should occur for presenting them.

'An' fat's the news o' the market, min?' asked Jinse of the gudge, who had seated himself at the top of the 'deece' to eat his supper.

'Little o't; slack feein'; an' plenty o' drunk fowk.'

'The waages doon?'

'Doon! Ay are they. Gweed men feein' at seyven-pun-ten; an' women for oot-wark hardly winnin abeen a poun' note. An' dizzens never got an offer.'

'It's braw wardles wi' them't disna need to fee,' said Jinse, with a sly reference to the gudge's hopeful prospects.

'Weel, Jinse, fat encouragement is there to the like o' me to bide on an' loss my time at fairm wark? Ye may be the best han' 't ever gaed atween the pleuch stilts, but ye can never get an ondependent or sattlet wye o' deein.'

'Div ye mean a place o' yer nain?'

'Weel, gin a body cud hae the chance o' gettin' a bit craftie. But I'll appel to yersel', Jinse – Fat comes o' maist ilka fairm servan' 't gets a wife?' – (and the gudge looked sweetly on Jinse) – 'they're forc't to tak' to the dargin, an' gae awa' an' bide aboot the Broch, or some gate siclike.'

'But hinna ye nae mair news?' said Jinse, desirous of turning the conversation.

'In fack, there's nae chance but slave on to the en' o' the chapter; oonless ye win in to some ither wye o' deein in time,' continued the gudge, whose own scheme naturally occupied a favaurable place in his thoughts at the time.

'Hoot, min, gi'e 's the news o' the market,' said Jinse.

'Weel, fat news wud ye like?'

'Fa's bidin' or flittin'?'

'Weel, I didna hear particular. Ye see I was oot o' the throng a gey file arreengin some things o' my nain.'

'Gweeshtens, ye've seerly been sair ta'en up. Didna ye traffike neen wi' common fowk the day?'

'Ou weel, ye see, fan a body has some buzness o' their nain to atten' till they're nae sae sair ta'en up wi' fat's gaen on in general.'

'Sawna ye nae bargains made ava?'

'Weel, the only bargain't aw cud say't aw saw was Mains o' Yawal feein' a third horseman. I was in 'o Kirkie's tent gettin' a share o' a gill wi' a cheelie't I was ance aboot the toon wi', fan Mains cam' in, skirpit wi' dubs to the vera neck o' 's kwite. I didna ken the chap, naething aboot 'im, but fan they war jist aboot bargain't Mains luiks owre an' refars to me. 'That's an aul' servan' o' mine,' says he to the chap, 'an' ye can speir at him aboot the place.' They hed threepit on a lang time; but an coorse wus comin' nearer't afore Mains socht the drink, an' at length he bargain't wi' 'im for a croon oot o' seyven poun' to ca's third pair; an' that was the only bargain't I saw.'

'Did ye see ony o' oor fowk – or hear onything aboot them?'

'I didna see neen o' yer breeders.'

'I wud like richt to ken gin they be flittin' or no. Neen o' Clinkstyle's fowk bidin', aw reckon?' asked Jinse.

'That's weel min'et,' exclaimed the gudge, with some vivacity. 'Bidin'! na, nae lickly; but fa div ye think's comin' there again?'

'Comin' there again? Fa cud tell that – somebody hard up for a place, seerly?'

'Jist guess.'

'Ha! fa cud guess that? Like aneuch somebody't I min' naething aboot – fowk 't's cheengin the feck't they hae at ilka term.'

'Weel,' said the gudge deliberately, 'it's jist Tam Meerison!'

The light of Johnny Gibb's old iron lamp, with its one rush wick, was not brilliant at best; and it had been getting worse in consequence of the protracted sederunt in which the gudge had indulged. Therefore, though I rather think Jinse did start slightly, and colour a little at the intimation just made by the gudge, I don't think the gudge observed it; and, truth to say, the gudge himself was a very little agitated.

'Gae 'wa' to yer bed, than, this minit,' said Jinse; 'see, ye've keepit me sittin' wytein ye till the vera nethmost shall o' the lamp's dry.'

And the gudge went to bed accordingly.

A start in life

On a certain afternoon, about a week before the Whitsunday term of 1842, Johnny Gibb, who had been busy afield, came toddling home when the afternoon was wearing on, and went into the 'mid house', to look out sundry blue-checked cotton bags with turnip seed, for he meditated sowing of that valued root. He was hot and tired, and his spouse invited him to rest for a little on the deece. Would he take a drink of ale?

'Ay will aw, 'oman,' said Johnny, 'an' ye hae't at han'. Lat's see the caup there.'

Mrs Gibb obeyed the command, and Johnny drank of the reaming liquor with evident satisfaction.

'Rest ye a minit than, an' drink oot the drap; for ye've never devall't the haill day,' said Mrs Gibb; and saying so, she 'lean't her doon', with some intention apparently of entering on a confab with her husband.

'Are ye thinkin' o' gyaun doon to the market on Wednesday?' asked she, with that kind of air which seems directly to provoke an interrogatory answer; and Johnny at once exclaimed: 'No; foo are ye speerin that? Ye ken't baith the boys is bidin: I've nae erran'.'

'Ye never think o' speerin aboot Jinse,' replied Mrs Gibb, still in the key that suggested the necessity for an explanatory note.

'Jinse Deans!' exclaimed Johnny. 'Fat's the eese o' speerin at her? An' she binna pleas't wi' 'er waages, she wud seerly 'a tell't ye lang ere noo.'

'I doot it's nae the waages a'thegither, peer 'oman. But Jinse's needin' awa'.'

Mrs Gibb had evidently made up her mind now to give some farther explanation about this new movement, when, as Fate would have it, the colloquy was broken in upon by Jinse (who had been unaware of her master's presence there) herself at the moment stumbling into the kitchen, from which she had been temporarily absent.

'Fat haiver's this't ye've taen i' yer heid noo?' demanded Johnny, addressing Jinse. 'Are ye gyaun clean gyte to speak o' leavin' yer place; and it only an ouk fae the term tee? Faur wud ye gae till?'

'Hame to my mither's,' answered Jinse, exhibiting somewhat of discomposure at Johnny's vehemence.

Jinse's mother lived not far off Benachie, in a very unpretentious residence. 'An' fat on the face o' the creation wud ye dee gyaun hame? Yer mither's but a peer 'oman; she has little need o' you wi' 'er,' said Johnny.

Jinse, who was making, on the whole, an uneasy defence, averred that her mother 'wasna vera stoot.'

'But is she wuntin you hame?' was Johnny's demand. 'Tell me that.'

Here Jinse gave symptoms of breaking into tears, and Mrs Gibb interposed with a 'Hoot, man: ye're aye sae ramsh wi' fowk.'

'Weel, weel,' quoth Johnny, as he seized his bonnet and marched toward the door; 'ye're a' alike. Fa wud ken fat ye wud be at!'

I don't know that Johnny Gibb meant to include his wife. The reference was rather to the class to which Jinse belonged, though, no doubt, he went away with the conviction that women-kind in general are absurdly impracticable in their ways. But be that as it may, Johnny found that he had to provide a new servant lass.

In private audience Jinse Deans had revealed to Mrs Gibb, with many sighs and tears, that Tam Meerison had 'promis't to mairry her'.

What more I don't know; but the worthy gudewife, after scolding Jinse as severely as it was in her nature to do, told her to 'wash her face, an' nae mair o' that snifterin. An' gae awa' and get ready the sowens. I'se say naething mair aboot it till the term day's by. Nae doot ye'll be i' yer tribbles seen aneuch wuntin that.'

Poor Jinse, the prospect of marriage did not seem a cheerful one to her, notwithstanding the number of candidates there had been for her hand. Of her reputed sweethearts Tam Meerison was the one for whom she had at any rate affected to care the least; and since the time Tam had begun seriously to court her, his jealousy had been again and again roused by the undisguised preference given to others, his rivals. And yet Tam Meerison was to have her to wife. It would be wrong to say that Tam had not a certain feeling of satisfaction in the thought of this; for, notwithstanding his adoption latterly of a more seeming-reckless style, Tam had been from an early date severely smitten by Jinse's charms. Indeed his satisfaction was presumably considerable, else he had probably not formed the laudable resolution to marry. But then there were counter-balancing considerations. The idea of marriage as an actual event had been forced upon him with a kind of staggering suddenness, which caused the approach of the reality itself to awaken a rather uncomfortable feeling of responsibility. Tam began to see that it would be troublesome to go about and he had but a dim notion of the indispensable technicalities. Then there was the question of a house and home for his wife; and here Tam's case no doubt merited commiseration. There was no house whatever available within a circuit of several miles; for the lairds in the locality, in the plenitude of their wisdom, and forseeing the incidence of a Poor Law, had, as a rule, determined that there should be no possibility of paupers seeing the light on their properties. They would rather pull down every cottage on their estates. What could poor Tam do? Jinse said she would go to her mother's. Where Jinse's mother lived was three miles off; and with her mother Jinse could only get what share she might of a hovel that very barely afforded room for two beds in its dark and diminutive 'but and ben'. And there also an unmarried sister and two brothers, all in farm service, claimed to have the only home they possessed. It was not greatly to be wondered at if Tam felt perplexed, and began to consider marrying really a stiff business. It was under this feeling of perplexity that he succumbed once again to Clinkstyle's offer of a renewed engagement, and in order to get one foot at least planted down without more trouble, agreed to bide with Peter Birse for another six months.

Tam had ventured across to Gushetneuk at a suitable hour on the night of which we have been speaking, to talk over with his affianced what most nearly concerned him and her. The two sat on the deece again; and this time nobody disturbed them.[7] Jinse was sobbing. Tam put his arm about her; and there was genuine feeling in the poor chap's words, I have not the least doubt, as he said in his tenderest tones, 'Dinna noo, Jinse. Ye'se never wunt a peck o' meal nor a pun' o' butter as lang 's I'm able to work for 't.'

By-and-by Jinse's emotion moderated, and they got into a more business strain; and then Tam asked: 'Does Gushets ken yet?'

'Eh, aw dinna ken richt; aw never got sic a gast's aw got the nicht i' the aifterneen, fan aw haumer't into the kitchie upo' the mistress an' him speakin' something or anither aboot me gyaun awa'.'

'But an' coorse she kent aboot it afore?'

'She jist kent the streen't I wudna be here aifter the term; I gyauna 'er muckle audiscence fan she speir't foo I was leavin'. But an' ye hed heard the maister fan he brak oot — I cudna 'a haud'n up my heid, Tam, nor been ongrutt'n, deen fat I hed liket!'

'An' did ye tell him onything mair, than?'

'Geyan lickly! Fa wud 'a deen that, noo? But I tell't her aifter he was awa' — it was rael sair, Tam,' and Jinse threatened greetin again.

'Did she say ony ill upo' me?' asked Tam.

'No; but though the maister was in a terrible ill teen, jist aboot's gyaun awa' an' that, I was waur, gin waur cud wun, fan she scault's an' gya's sae muckle gweed advice, tee.'

'Ou weel, Jinse, we're nae waur nor ither fowk, nor yet sae ill's plenty.' With this comforting reflection the conversation turned, and Jinse asked, 'But fat are ye gyaun to dee a' simmer?'

'I'm bidin' again.'

'Bidin' at Clinkstyle?'

'Aye.'

'But it's a coorse place to bide in, isnin't?'

'Weel,' answered Tam, slowly, and not quite willing, in the circumstances, to make that admission, 'the wife's some roch an' near b'gyaun, but there's little tribble wi' the maister 'imsel'.'

'Didna ye hear o' nae ither place at the market?'

'But I wasna there. I bargain't the day afore, and didna seek to gyang. Ye see I taul' the maister't I wud tak' a day for't fan the neeps is laid doon.'

Tam evidently considered this a stroke of management, and Jinse, brightening up a little, asked, 'An' fan wud it need to be?'

'Jist as seen's things can be sattl't. We maun be cried on twa Sundays,[8] at ony rate.'

'Twa Sundays?'

'Ay, there's nane but puckles o' the gentry gets't deen in ae Sunday, aw b'lieve.'

'Weel, ye maun come up to my mither's on Saiturday's nicht.'

'Ou ay, an' we can speak aboot it better than. Your mither'll ken a' aboot the wye, o' 't, I'se warran'. But I doot she'll be pitt'n aboot wi's bidin' there. I wuss we cud 'a gotten a hoose ony wye.'

'Weel, we maun jist pit up wi' things like ither fowk, I suppose.'

'But it'll mak' sic a steer in her hoose, ye ken.'

'Oh, we'll manage fine for that maitter. There's her but bed, it's nae vera sair in order eenoo; but I've twa fedder pillows o' my nain, an' a patch't coverin', forbye a pair o' blankets 't the mistress helpit's to spin, an' gya's the feck o' the 'oo'.[9] There'll be plenty o' room for my kist i' the but, an' ye maun hae yer ain kist aside ye, ye ken.'

'But yer mither winna hae gweed sparin' 'er room constant, it's nae's gin't war only a fyou ouks. She winna get nae eese o' 't hersel'.'

'Ou, but ye ken there's nane o' oor fowk comes hame eenoo, 'cep Rob an' Nelly at an antrin time; Jamie's owre far awa'. An' ony nicht 't Rob's there, gin ye chanc't to be the same nicht, you twa cud sleep thegither,[10] seerly; an' I cud sleep wi' my mither, an' Nelly tee, for that maitter.'

'Foo af'en does Rob come?'

'Aboot ance i' the fortnicht or three ouks.'

'I think I'll win near as af'en 's that mysel',' said Tam, upon whose mind the general effect of this conversation had been rather exhilarating than otherwise. His sweetheart had not merely contrivance; she had also foresight and thrift, evidently, as the general inventory given of her 'providin'' testified. Still he hankered after a house that he could call his own. It was not that Tam's ambition on this point was extravagant. If he could get one end of a 'but an' a ben' cottage, about such a place as Smiddyward, with a 'cannas-breid' of a garden, and the chance of going to see his wife once a week, he would have been well content.

But this Tam found to be impracticable. He made full inquiry; and even invoked the aid of his acquaintance the smith, whose banter was turned into hearty sympathy with the statement of the case now laid before him. The smith tackled Dawvid Hadden, the ground-officer, and urged the reparation of part of the old erections of which Sandy Peterkin's school formed the main wing, as a dwelling for Tam. As the manner of sycophants dressed in a little delegated authority is, Dawvid's answer was a kind of echo of what he imagined Sir Simon would have said, 'Na, na, smith, it's a very fallawshus prenciple in fat they ca' poleetical economy to encourage the doon-sittin' o' the like o' them in a place. Ou, it's nae the expense. Na, na; the biggin o' a score o' hooses wud be a mere triffle, gin Sir Simon thocht it richt in prenciple – a mere triffle. But there they sit doon, an' fesh up faimilies till they wud thraten to full a destrick wi' peer fowk – the brod[11] cud never keep the tae half o' them. No; I'm weel seer they'll get nae hoose i' the pairis' o' Pyketillim.'

It was not a kindly speech that of Dawvid Hadden; albeit it expressed, firstly, the newest view of political economy in the locality, which was just then beginning to be practically carried out; and, secondly, an accurate statement of Tam Meerison's chances of getting a house within the parish. In this particular, Tam had his strong wish and reasonable desire completely defeated. It may be difficult for the man who lives in a comfortable home with his family about him to estimate with precision either the keenness of feeling, or the deteriorating effects involved in such disappointment. I don't think it should be difficult for any man to make up his mind as to giving a hearty condemnation to the too common land policy which has entailed the like cruel hardship upon hundreds of honest hard-working men in the class to which Tam belonged.

But my business is not to moralise, I daresay; and I have only to add to this chapter that, as better could not be, Tam Meerison and Jinse Deans had no help for it but get married, and commence their career of wedded bliss under the slenderly equipped conditions already indicated.

NOTES

1. Excerpted from W Alexander, *Johnny Gibb of Gushetneuk* (Turriff, Heritage Press, reprint of 8th edn, 1979), pp 46-52, 83-7, 93-8.
2. Tam was combing the mare's coat, not cooking it.
3. The feeing market set the wage rate for the next six months. Tam will have cause to regret not closing a bargain to continue working for Johnny Gibb, but it could make sense to be cautious if there was a chance that wages would be up at the market.
4. Notably Tam's designs on Jinse Deans, the kitchen maid.
5. The devil. With their strong submerged witchcraft heritage nineteenth century Aberdeenshire folk feared him, but 'auld Nick' was more of a cantankerous and untrustworthy neighbour than Calvinist theology's embodiment of absolute evil.
6. An interesting comment. Several Aberdeenshire horsemen's books still exist. They do contain recipes for harness blacking, but they usually contain something else as well: ceremonial details of the secret Society of the Horseman's Word. This primitive trade union was built around an initiation ceremony culminating in the initiate 'shakin' the aul' chiel's han'' – making a pact with the devil. Ubiquitous as it was among nineteenth century Aberdeenshire horsemen, it is quite likely that the youthful Alexander himself had joined the society by 'gyaun thru the c'affhoose door'. He drops the slightest hint here, with his reference to exchanged blacking recipes, but many of his country readers would have been able to decode the message.
7. Much earlier in the novel Jinse and Tam sit courting on the kitchen deece at Gushetneuk one night, when they are disturbed by the arrival of two more of Jinse's

suitors. Tam is forced to spent uncomfortable hours on the floor below the deece, hearing Jinse romanced above him.

8. Have the banns read in kirk.

9. Hand spinning and weaving survives in Pyketillim, evidently. We should not assume Alexander simply to be describing life in the Garioch of the 1840s. Mrs Gibb's textile work matches her husband's sturdy attachment to effective but rather outmoded farming methods.

10. This may outrage late twentieth century sensibilities, but Tam would have thought nothing of it. Male farm servants habitually slept two to a chaff bed in chaumer or bothy.

11. The parish's Poor Law board, comprising local landowners.

The Rise of Couper Sandy[1]

His undergraduate career

It was in his schoolboy time that my acquaintance with Sandy Mutch began. We two sat, with several others, on the same form, and had our sympathies stirred in common against what we deemed the harsh and unfeeling spirit that animated the pedagogue to whose rule we were subjected. Not that Sandy and his immediate companions were in all things precisely alike as it concerned their tastes and capacities, or that their dread of an application of the tawse sprang always from similar causes. The dominie himself would make a distinction. Against certain of us his complaint mainly was that of indulgence in too frequent fits of trifling (alas! poor man, he never fully found out the extent to which that habit was carried), and consequent failure to do the work one might easily have done. So said the dominie, and doubtless with perfect truth. His unvarying allegation against Sandy was that he was simply an incorrigible dunce, who neither could nor would learn his tasks – a condition of things that was to the dominie a real afflication; for somewhat slovenly and unscientific as his methods were, it grieved him to train up a lad who could not even make a decent show of concealing his ignorance.

And how far soever the dominie's opinion regarding the one set of his pupils may have been correct, or the opposite, there really seemed to be substantial grounds for believing that his conclusions concerning Sandy Mutch's capacity as a pupil were essentially sound. Sandy had no clerkly tastes or leanings whatever. As a reader he was fearfully deficient, and his efforts at spelling reduced the dominie to despair. In arithmetic it was just a case of absolute propulsion through some of the simpler rules; but even at his most mature stage he got hopelessly aground at the 'Rule of Three', and there lay high and dry, without once obtaining a glimmering of what it was all about. Writing he did moderately well, as far as fashioning the mere letters went, but there his old habit came in again. He could not but mis-spell, even with the copy line before him; when it was absent, the grotesque violence done to the recognised orthography was bewildering to look at, and caused the 'Maister' frequent paroxysms of anger and disgust.

Curiously enough, Sandy Mutch had a sort of faculty in the way of technical memory. And thus in answering questions in the Catechism, if too strict inquisition were not made after a distinct and literal rendering, he would occasionally rattle off a sort of vague paraphrase that in its rough contour and likeness to the sound of the characteristic words bore a strong general resemblance to the real answer. Any analysis that demanded 'meanings' of course threw him completely out, to say nothing of the 'proofs,' which the dominie prided himself on having been the first in our Presbytery to compel his scholars to tackle, and which Sandy Mutch found utterly beyond his powers.[2]

Well, there could be no doubt of it; Sandy Mutch, on the scholastic side of him, was certainly a dunce. Outside the school he seemed to possess no very striking characteristics. His temperament would, I imagine, have been deemed phlegmatic. A lumbering, uncouth sort of lad; willing enough to take a share, more or less, in any rough or mischievous enterprise going on, but without sufficient energy or recklessness to be a leader. His tendencies were, on the whole, toward those occupations that could be carried on without much physical effort; and, in particular, he had a decided taste for bargain-making, as it went on among a certain section of his schoolfellows. In this connection Sandy was the subject of some envious talk occasionally. It was known that, by a system of judicious barter, he had become the possessor of almost the finest set of 'bools' going amongst his contemporaries; and then, not to speak of other and minor transactions, while he had come to school with merely a 'Life-knife' – cost fourpence-halfpenny, as all the world knew – supplied to him by paternal outlay, the winter 'raith' was not half over when there was in his possession, in exchange for the Life-knife and sundry other very inconsiderable articles, a real 'Jockteleg gullie', erstwhile owned by one of the bigger loons; and it was a patent fact that a gullie like it could not have been bought under eighteenpence.

Robbie Mutch, the village souter, was a talkative, intelligent, outspoken little man, as village souters often are; not devoid of intellectual keenness, and much given to political and theological discussion when he found suitable companionship. His wife was a large flabby woman, the reverse rather of intelligent – only she had a power of incessant talk of a gossiping, credulous, and even superstitious sort. And in virtue of her mere physical bulk, and this power of uttering herself with a kind of irrepressible clangour, she dominated the souter in a much greater degree than could have been expected on any grounds of reason. The souter's family took mainly after their mother, not after the souter himself; and in the case of Sandy, their only son, this was quite marked. He had his mother's physique very distinctly, and also his mother's aptitude for hearsay. Beyond that, his capacity, in the direction of any of the arts by which man's life is sustained, and still more, as indicated, of literary acquirement, had not hitherto shown itself to any good purpose whatever.

The souter was disappointed. He had early concluded that Sandy's lack of manual dexterity, not to speak of his lack of interest in the craft, unfitted him for successful application to the awl and lapstone. And though he would have willingly stretched a considerable point to give him as ample a share of schooling as he possibly could, and so push him forward into some of the learned professions, he saw that that too was utterly hopeless. 'Our Sawney winna brak' the clergy ony wye,' was the somewhat bitter remark addressed by Robbie Mutch to his wife, when the point occasionally came up.

But the time had come when Sandy must do something for himself in the way of earning a livelihood.

'Aw'm seer, man, ye mith hae patience wi' the laddie; he's but a bairn yet,' argued Mrs Mutch when the souter had raised the question.

'Patience, 'oman! Fat for? Fat gweed's he deein'? A nickum that thinks naething o' truein' the skweel ilka ither day, an' gyaun awa' takin' minnons i' the burn wi' an aul' creel, or colleaugin' wi' idle company, instead o' leernin 's lessons?'

'Hoot, that dominie has nae boun's wi' 'im! Fat for wud he gar creaturs gae on wi' nae deval till they war blin' and dottl't wi' leernin'? Sawney badena awa' fae the skweel a' last ouk, 'cep on Tyesday an' Saiturday; an' aw'm seer, man, he wud hae nae gryte miss for a' the time.'

'He's nae the best judge o' that; and he kent weel aneuch 't he ocht till 'a been at the skweel, fan the maister taul' 'im that he hedna ae single word o' 's lessons.'

'An' him lickin' the creatur till 's very fingers wus neerhan' peel't! Fatna a laddie cud get lessons an' 's gardies stounin' wi' aiven doan ill-essage like that? It's aneuch to gi'e 'im a mischief, I'm seer.'

'Buff an' nonsense, 'oman; gin the maister wud lay on the tag twice as weel, it wud be fat he's sair needin',' said Robbie Mutch, somewhat savagely.

'Keep me, man!' exclaimed Mrs Mutch with a semi-hysterical accent and gesture, 'an' that's the wye that ye gae on! Weel, weel, aw mith speak to you aboot onything o' the kin'! Aw'm seer it's aneuch to fleg lessons oot o' a creatur's heid, to hear 's vera nain fader speakin' that gate.'

'They mith get lessons an' gae to the skweel tee than can mak' oot to herry craws' nests, an' traik aboot for oors i' the feedles deein' mischief,' said Robbie, in a milder key, as became the exigency that had emerged.

'Wasna ye never a laddie yersel', man, that ye wud hae the vera hert ca'd oot o' the littleane, tetherin' 'im till a bare dask the lee lang day, an' keepin' 'im as eident at a stent 's gin he war a man o' foorty?' asked Mrs Mutch, pathetically.

'Aw'm seer that loon hisna been three days rinnin' at the skweel sin' the gweed weather cam' in,' replied Robbie, parrying the personal appeal.

'An' foo cud ye expeck that creaturs wud like to be chaumer't up fae morn to even, gweed day an' ill, man, 's gin they war as mony bedalls nae able to leuk owre a door?'

It was impossible for the souter to make much of the argument, especially as his wife was again quite composed, and prepared to go on as long as he might find convenient and agreeable. But the souter had made up his mind that Sandy must be set to some useful work. And taking the youth by himself he submitted his proposal to him, which was that, summer being now at hand, Sandy should allow himself to be engaged as herd-boy to some of the neighbouring farmers. Now, although Sandy very heartily disliked the business of scholastic training, and had been tempted to desert the shrine of learning too frequently of late, on very doubtful pretences, in favour of employments that seemed more congenial to him, he was not a positively stubborn or disobedient youth; and as the proposed scheme of becoming a herd seemed to offer certain attractions, beyond that of freeing him of the growingly distasteful restraint of the school, he readily enough fell in with it. At an early opportunity thereafter he was engaged to herd the cattle of the farmer of Bowbutts accordingly.

The herd loon

The herd loon, sui generis, has become extinct; and improved farming is responsible for it. With high cultivation and the reclamation of waste lands, the practice of enclosing grew. The style of the cattle, too, was changed. They began to speak of the 'Teeswater' — which by-and-by they called the shorthorn — and other pure breeds; and these dainty animals were supposed to thrive better when kept in carefully fenced fields than roaming at large under charge of the herd loon, and restrained from straying into corn and turnip sections, and the like forbidden places, through dread of his club.

In my early time it was different. Fenced fields were the exception; and the mixed multitude of native bred cattle on each farm — at any rate, the cows and young cattle — were turned out day by day in a straggling troop to graze, now on the 'intoon rigs' during the early forenoon hours, and, later in the day, on the 'oot feedles',[3] where arable and waste land alternated in picturesque variety. The office of the herd, if duly performed, was by no means a sinecure. Over each separate animal, individually, great and small, the herd must exercise a certain moral discipline, alike for its sake and his own; for when it was otherwise, and they came to treat with utter disregard his loud calls to 'Keep back!' and to 'Come in owre!' and could be called to order only by a vigorous use of the club, propelled with all the force of the herd loon's right arm against their ribs; or, still worse, a fusillade of stones pitched at them, to the danger of their limb bones, the beasts got demoralised and learnt to 'range' as opportunity offered, in a fashion destructive both to the herd's comfort and their own well-doing as profitable stock for the herd's master.

The herd's club merits a passing word of notice. It was in the fashion of a policeman's baton, but bigger: a round stock roughly cut into shape, with a slight indication of a handle at one end. And to make the club serve its purpose completely there was cut out near the handle a mystic figure, sonething like an ill-fashioned monogram, known as a 'meltie bow', which, it was understood, saved the club from inflicting harm on the cattle if it chanced to strike them below the belt, as it were; also a rude figure of the herd himself, and in front of him certain symbols, thus: II I III V II II IV I I III X II II

The inscription on the club represented, 'Jockie an' 's owsen', and the full interpretation was this:

> Twa afore ane, an' three afore five;
> First twa, an' syne twa, an' four comes belyve;
> Noo ane, an' than ane, an' three at a cast;
> Double ane, an' twice twa, an' Jockie at the last.[4]

Such was the herd's emblem of office. By whom the symbols and legend which it bore were devised, is unknown to me. It must be owned that as a herd loon, Sandy Mutch turned out but poorly. True it was that the open air freedom of the herd's life, as compared with the close confinement of the schoolroom, had its own charm – if one could only have had combined with that perfect and entire freedom of action according to the dictates of one's own tastes and impulses. But even at herding that might not be. Nay, the very nature of herding implied the virtual surrender of the reasoning individual desire of the herd to the general instinctive preferences of the herded in all things right and lawful. An abnegation of one's self in their interest had to be made; and in honest performance of duty the virtues of unwearying patience, vigilant care, and a sympathetic apprehension of the bovine nature and needs had to be day by day exercised.

In the two first of these virtues, at any rate, Sandy Mutch was conspicuously deficient. For the quiet and sober continuousness of his new occupation, in truth, neither his training nor natural habits had well fitted him; and thus his herding was marked by 'fits and starts' of attention at one time, and of utter inattention and idleness at another, which accordingly put his master, the farmer of Bowbutts, in great wrath.

'Aw say, that loon wud provoke a vera saunt, a' 't a bodie can say till 'im. Fat does he mean girdin' the beasts into the barest neuk o' the faul'ies that wye!' and Bowbutts, putting his right hand up to his jaw, shouted a powerful shout to 'Wyn them doon the rigs, min, b' the side o' the corn!'

The herd and his cattle were half a mile off; but Bowbutt's lungs were of stentorian power, and it was evident the sound they had supplied his vocal organs with motive power to emit was distinctly heard, for the herd, who had been stretched at full length on the pasture, consulting his own ease and comfort, was seen at once to move in the direction of doing what he was bid. 'He's a weary ill herd that widdifu,' continued Bowbutts. 'Aw'm seer he mith 'a kent to lat them faur they wud get a gweed bite the day, to hae the creaturs weel fill't that I'm takin' to the market.'

''Deed, man,' said Bowbutts's wife – it was to her he addressed himself – 'Sawney's owre easy min'et to pit 'imsel' muckle about, oonless he be weel tell't aboot it. But he has gweed can amo' beasts fan he likes, f'r a' 'at'

'He's a sweir howffin; that's fat he is,' replied Bowbutts. 'Little to me wud pit 'im fae the toon.'

'An' fat better wud ye be o' that, man? Ye canna dee wantin' a herd,' said the goodwife.

'I've a gweed min' to sen' word till's fader, an' lat 'im ken fat aw think o' 'im; eeseless nickum!'

'Gae ye awa' an' rank yersel' than; ye'll get yer shavin' leems o' the skelfie ahin the saut backit, an' yer sark o' the heid o' the drawers; an' I'll get the beasts worn in aboot in a filie.'

Bowbutts did as he was bid; and the gudewife took the trouble to put herself in communication with the herd, to whom she forthwith imparted various judicious counsels in view of the duty before him that day; that, namely, of accompanying his master to market with certain cattle picked from the herd for sale, and which it behoved him accordingly to have well filled of food before commencing the journey.

In the prospect of getting off to the fair an hour or two thence, with Bowbutts riding on his pony, and himself driving four rough 'stirks' in front of him, which had just been pressed on his attention, Sandy Mutch felt a distinct elation of spirits; for he had much desired to vary his existence by some such experience. And when the other cattle had been housed, and they were fully started on their three-mile journey, he addressed himself to his task with a zealous earnestness that contrasted strongly with the inert and perfunctory style of his herding. The stirks, unaccustomed to be so driven, got wondrously excited. They scampered hither and thither, and leapt over the lower fences right and left, seeking the companionship of other cattle that they had sighted as they went along. But Sandy followed the chase with a will and to purpose, for while he ran vigorously, his tactical skill in out-manoeuvring the errant stirks when they once and again attempted to double and force their way homeward, astonished, and nearly excited the articulate admiration of even Bowbutts himself. And it was the same all through the hubbub of men and beasts during their stay in the fair. Sandy skilfully generalled his lot, kept them in the proper selling attitude, 'wi' their heids to the brae, laddie,' as Bowbutts had hinted to him, and even put in a fit word with would-be purchasers, when occasion demanded, during his master's temporary absence or engrossment in some incidental haggle. In short he gave unquestionable evidence of being in his element throughout; not excepting the interesting passage at the end, when Bowbutts having sold the last of the stirks, and got the lot clear off his hands, allowed Sandy to accompany him into the crowded canvas tent and partake slightly, while he discussed a final bottle of ale and a dram with a few of his cronies before setting out for home.

But as Bowbutts could not and did not go to the market every day, and as tending the cattle at home was not a duty to be well performed by merely intermittent effort, Sandy Mutch's character as herd, notwithstanding his undoubted success on the market day, was not in the least permanently bettered. Only this was noticeable, that Sandy had, with wondrous facility, taken a very broad and firm grip of what might be called the general principle of dealing in cattle. To his neighbour herd loons, with whom a good deal too much of his time was frequently spent, he expatiated at any length on the great sums of money that might be turned over in that way; and even uttered with confidence his opinion on the quality, weight, and other distinguishing particulars of given specimens of the bovine race that had come under his notice.

Meanwhile, Sandy Mutch, as has been said, was earning the title of a bad herd; and it was little comfort to the souter, as time went on, to find not only that Bowbutts declined a continuation of his services next season, but that the master to whom he had actually been engaged, before the summer was over mulcted him of good part of his fee in consideration of damage inflicted on a neighbour's corn crop through certain gross acts of carelessness on Sandy's part.

'That loon!' exclaimed the souter, 'he'll cairry a meal pyock yet, ere a' be deen, or ca' the kwintra sellin' besoms. He'll never mak's breid at nae honest han'iwark;' and it really seemed but too likely.

When Sandy Mutch had out-grown the herding stage, his promise of future usefulness did not seem greatly to improve. His father had long ago signified his belief that Sandy was dull in the head; and when his mother, whose belief in the lad was yet unshaken, suggested the expediency of his learning, if not the shoemaker trade, then some other skilled craft, the souter declared, wiih still stronger emphasis that before, that Sawney had 'nae han's', and it was no use people 'herryin' themsel's an' throwin' awa' gweed siller upon 'im'. The only path, therefore, that seemed open to Sandy, as the souter viewed it, was that of an 'orra man' about the farm: and in point of fact such was the capacity, varied by an occasional bout as an inferior and intermittently employed day labourer, in which he spent the next few years of his life.

The couper – preliminary essays

Inferior service rendered by Sandy Mutch, led naturally enough to inferior engagements obtained by him, and, of course, inferior wages resulting therefrom. He was not at all unfrequently out of employment, as has been already said, and being equally out of cash, he simply loafed about at home for the time being, duly attending country markets and all similar gatherings within reasonable distance, in search of interest and amusement. It frequently occurred to Sandy that trading in some shape in these markets would form a most congenial sphere of operations; but, then, he had no capital, and his credit among the whole range of his friends and acquaintances was not equal to a £5 note.

At last a crisis came that was destined to direct Sandy Mutch's whole future course in life. Sandy had engaged himself as servant to a man of no ascertainable character in respect of moral temperament and habits; and after he had for a few weeks endeavoured to fulfil his engagement, the man of no particular character, in a fit of unreasoning fury, saw good to curse and swear at him with a considerable amount of emphasis, because, as he averred, Sandy was not doing properly the piece of work on which he was engaged.

'Vera lickly,' replied Sandy, with much coolness, 'for it's the exact wye that ye bade me.'

'None o' yer impident chat here, sir, or I'll gar yer chafts cry knyp owre that ill-hung tongue o' yours,' said the master.

'Ye'll maybe better jist try't than,' was Sandy's answer, indicating, not altogether obscurely, that in him too the bellicose element existed in a latent state.

'Scoon'rel! D' ye think that ony maister 'll stan' that? Gae aboot yer bizness this moment, sir! Bonnie story that I sud nae only hae things connacht, but hae your ill win' to pit up wi' forbye.'

So Sandy's master had ordered him about his business, and Sandy went without further demur. But experience had made him wary in such matters. And thus feeling himself to be clearly in the right for once, he took the precaution of offering renewal of his services in presence of witnesses. This being bluntly refused, Sandy had recourse to his legal remedy.

'Ou jist lat ye 'im get a turn afore Shirra Watson again,' was the advice of an experienced acquaintance, whom Sandy saw fit to consult in the business. 'He's as weel kent there as he's respeckit to the ootwith; an' at ony rate the Shirra's aye a gweed freen to the servan'.[5] Ye sud get a haud o' yon muckle, lang-leggit chiel' 'at was awgent for me ance — fat d' ye ca' 'im? He was some dear to pay, but, man, he has an awfu' tongue; an' he did rive them up the richt gate. Gin ye dee that there's nae fear o' ye winnin' this time. No, no; I wud hae naething adee wi' that young chappies hardly oot o' the shall; they hae little rumgumption a hantle o' them, forbye't they're fear't to speak oot. An' fat's the eese o' a lawvyer gin he hinna a gweed moufu' o' ill jaw!'[6]

Accordingly Sandy Mutch, little to the comfort of the old souter, entered proceedings and summoned the man of no particular character into court; and with the best results. The excellent Sheriff took a favourable view of the case; and Sandy had the high satisfaction of being awarded his full wages and modified board wages, making together the sum of £12 sterling.

'Noo, loon,' said the souter, so soon as he had recovered from his astonishment at Sandy's unexpected good fortune, 'Noo, loon, ye'll gi'e yer mither a note, an' pit the lave o' that siller in'o the Savin' Bank, to be gyang water to ye at anither time.'

'Aw can dee better nor that wi't, ony wye,' replied Sandy, in a tone indicative of entire confidence in his own capacity as an economist.

'Better wi't!' echoed the souter, under some excitement: 'Aw wud like to ken fat wye ye can dee better wi't?'

'There wud be some eese o't lyin' i' the bank wi' nae owreturn, an' only a triffle onwal at the year's en'.'

The souter stared this time; and Sandy proceeded: 'Aw'm gyaun doon to the market the morn to see foo girsin' beasts 's sellin'; they'll be an upwith market shortly, or it chates me.'

The impulses of genius defy human forecast. Sandy Mutch's conduct had presented but a troublesome problem to his father hitherto; it had now attained the character of incomprehensibility. What could he think, or what could he say, about a son who was not merely impervious to his father's powers of reasoning, but had all at once spoken out with the air of a man entitled to talk down to the limited understanding of his benighted parent?

That evening, as the souter thought calmly over it, he could not avoid the reflection, that, provokingly stupid and disappointing as had been the conduct of his son previously, here, surely, was the climax of his self-willed folly in refusing to act on the barest rules of prudence even, in regard to the money so unexpectedly in his possession – rare commodity as it was in his experience. And his wife, who had been disappointed at not getting the 'note' spoken of by her husband, was not on this occasion inclined to dissent from his opinion. But Sandy was perfectly firm, and only became the more taciturn the more that fresh attempts were made to re-open the subject. In short he would have, and he took, his own way.

Sandy Mutch's first purchase, and with which he returned from the market of which he had spoken, was a biggish 'farrow' cow, speckled, with prominent haunch bones and rugged horns and not in 'high condition', as the dealers say. Sandy made the knowing people guess at the price; which they did, and hit above the mark considerably; and when Sandy told them that the actual price was 'a croon oot o' sax poun'', they agreed that the farrow cow was a great 'rug'; and as the purchase of the cow was directly followed by an equally judicious investment in a 'stirk', the public opinion regarding Sandy Mutch got perplexed. Then when Sandy at first opportunity sold the animals at several shillings of profit each, the public opinion got more perplexed still. And thus did matters go on week by week.

'Nyod that loon o' the souter's 'll bleck Willie Futtrit, the couper 'imsel', gin he haud on the gate that he's deein',' said an admiring acquaintance in view of certain of Sandy Mutch's business transactions. 'They tell me 't he turn't a stirkie 't he bocht a fyou ouks syne heels-o'er-heid i' the last market.'

But turning animals heels-o'er-head, technically, by doubling the purchase price, was not always easy, however sincere a man's intentions in that direction might be. And so it was that Sandy Mutch's transactions at times threatened to go somewhat stiffly in the opposite direction. He had gone to An'ersmas Fair,[7] and in his eagerness to do business walked out the Glentons Road to meet sellers bringing their cattle to the fair. They were a primitive set the dwellers in the Glentons; far off any public highway, little disturbed by communication with the outer world; and thus left to grow up as 'great nature,' in the shape of rugged hills and brattling burns, fashioned them. Sandy Mutch had not walked far when he met a Glentons crofter, with his broad blue bonnet, his coat of hodden grey, furnished with metal buttons the size of a George III penny piece, and his knee breeches, and ribbed stockings.[8] The crofter led a little half Highland-looking cow, in a hair-plaited halter; and his unsophisticated white-haired boy, who had never hitherto witnessed such a stirring scene as that presented by An'ersmas Fair, went behind, carrying his father's hazel stick, to drive. The crofter asked £4 for his cow; and Sandy Mutch offered £3. The crofter declined, and they moved on toward the fair. A quarter of a mile had pretty well exhausted Sandy's vocabulary of depreciatory adjectives as applicable to the cow, and it had also advanced his offer by five shillings. The crofter wavered, but slightly. He still stuck to his price, and merely spoke of 'a gweed luckpenny'[9] as the only deduction he would make. They had got to the place where the market 'customer' stood collecting the twopences exigible for every cow, quey or steer that passed; and they stopped till the coppers should be paid, and a red keil mark put on the cow's hind quarters, in token thereof. A rapid summary of the cow's deficiencies, uttered with some vehemence, followed by a final offer of 'three-pun-ten', ultimately overcame the Glentons man, and a bargain was struck in the very 'mou' o' the market'. Sandy Mutch's object was, as indeed his ardent and confident hope had been, to re-sell the Glentons man's cow forthwith, and realise at least ten shillings off the transaction. But, to his intense disappointment, no one seemed disposed to look at the cow with the purpose of buying her. The day was wearing on, and so far from this hope being realised, he had not yet been offered his own price. The farmers did not wish to have a Highland cow, and the coupers who passed sneered at it as a 'nochty beastie'.

'Nyod, Sawney, ye're brunt for ance wi' that carlie, ony wye: the beastie's nae richt, min,' said Willie Futtrit, handling the cow, and making the Glentons man's boy, who was now in sole charge during his father's temporary absence, lead it out a short space.

'He upheeld it, at ony rate,' answered Sandy.

'Uphaud, or no uphaud, she's as hide-bun 's an aul' wecht, min. Fat time did she graw better o' the stiffness laddie?' asked Mr Futtrit, addressing the boy.

'She wasna never onweel,' was the boy's perplexed reply.

'Dinna ye tell me, noo. Ye've leern't yer lesson brawly, aw daursay; but ye'll better jist tell the trowth aboot 'er.'

The boy persisted in an indignant denial of the old couper's suggestion; but Sandy Mutch felt himself touched on the point of honour. Here was an animal dexterously bought from one of the most unsophisticated-looking of men, and which yet in open market, would not fetch its own price. Sandy was stung by the remarks of the senior coupers, and he determined to get out of his false position.

If he had known the business a little better, he would have taken care to swallow his chagrin, and simply knock the best luckpenny he could out of the seller. He did not do that, but returning to the Glentons man, he roundly and hotly accused him of selling him, as a sound cow, an animal which was a confirmed 'piner', and all but worthless. The Glentons man stoutly denied the accusation, which was loudly re-asserted amid a thickening group of sympathetic onlookers.

'The beast's as soun' 's ever a beast was; and there's nae a handier creatur i' the market – I'll tak' my aith upon 't,' said the owner of the cow.

'Macksna,' retorted Sandy Mutch. 'ye'll keep 'er for me. I'll hae naething adee wi' 'er;' and he made to move off, as he spoke.

'Get the joodge o' the market – get the joodge o' the market,' cried the onlookers, who by this time had got keenly interested in the squabble. 'He canna be alloo't to brak' the man's market that gate.'

One or two of the crowd bustled off to fetch the judge of the market, who was soon found in the person of Tammas Rorison, the banker and 'baillie' of the burgh, who happened also to be agent for the owner of the market stance, and custodian of the 'market customs' at An'ermas Fair.[10] The banker was a man of middle height, but greatly more than medium rotundity, whose strongly marked face was encumbered with little in the way of beard, beyond a pair of strictly defined whiskers in the middle of his cheeks, although his head was crowned by a dense crop of stiffish hair, inclined to red in colour, but now sprinkled with grey. A stout tuft of this hair was always brushed up right in front, and when the banker stood erect, put his legs together, and hooked his thumbs into the arm-holes of his waistcoat, which was his favourite attitude, he bore a curious resemblance to an enormously overgrown seal set upon its tail.

'Fat's adoo – fat's adoo?' asked the banker; 'ony chiel' fechtin', or fou?'

It was explained that a trading dispute only had occurred.

'Ou ay, some coupin' transaction. Fesh them this gate, oot o' the thrang a wee bit, an' we'll seen sattle that.'

Tammas Rorison, the judge of An'ermas Fair, was a man whose power in his own domain was as potently exercised as that of many rulers; and on being summonded before him, Sandy Mutch not only felt impelled to obey without demur, but also that his capability of defence was at the same time sensibly diminished. The judge straightened himself up in his usual attitude, and heard the story of the seller of the cow. He then called for Sandy Mutch's statement.

'Weel,' said the judge, 'I wudna won'er nor ye've promis't something owre an' abeen fat the beastie's worth; but that's nae rizzon for brakin' yer bargain, man. Fat? – a fau'ty beast is 't? We canna tak' your word for that, ye ken. The beast's there as ye see 't. Fat proof hae ye o' 't bein' a piner? Willie Futtrit! Weel, peer man, I daursay Willie's word wud be jist as gweed's his aith aboot buyin' or sellin' a coo; an' like aneuch he wud swear black an' blue till obleege a neebour, though he never saw the coo in 's life afore. But I think we'll aiven be deein' wantin' 'im this turn. Come ye awa' an' pay the man for's beastie; an' see an' mak' yer best o' 't. Fowk's nane the waur o' some bocht wit files.'

There was no appeal from the judge of the market; and the Glentons man got his money accordingly; the only bit of threatened revenge, when the man asked at what time he would take possession of his purchase, being the declaration from Sandy Mutch that he 'wud gar 'im stan' there wi' 't till sin-doon', as 'a' law' allowed him to do; a threat which he did not fully carry out, for the simple reason that it would have been inflicting punishment on himself equally with his opponent.

The couper full fledged

The transactions recorded, though all very well for a beginning, and giving good promise of greater things to come, could not long satisfy the ambition of a man who had the true cattle-couping spirit within him.

Besides certain annual fairs, there were within a radius of eight or nine miles several markets that occurred at much shorter intervals. At each and all of these Sandy Mutch was a regular attendant. Occasionally he bought an animal or two, and sold them again before he left the market; occasionally, too, he made a plunge and bought several. In this latter case he at once threw himself abroad for buyers in a seemingly cursory, yet not unknowing, way.

'Weel, I mith brak' the lottie to obleege an acquaintance, though I canna sell the lave sae weel – will ye gi'e 's a bode?'

If the man gave a 'bode' for one or two 'stirks', Sandy would loudly declare that he had offered less for what formed really 'the pick' of the lot than the average 'owreheid' price to himself. How far the statement might square with the facts, he would know best himself, but in any case when he got in tow with a buyer, or buyers, he knew that he was in a fair way to sell out again, or bring his stock to such reduced dimensions by the end of the market as would enable him to clear scores by receiving cash with one hand, and paying it over with the other. Occasionally, too, it happened that he neither bought nor sold. His object was profit, and unless he encountered a man with whom he imagined he could drive a bargain somewhat under the market price, that object could not be served. He was not always successful, even to the extent of holding his own, for it would happen now and again that another couper, or other tricky person, would contrive to land a faulty beast upon him, of which he could get quit only by making a loss; and at times the balance of wits was so even between buyer and seller that he found himself in the position of being obliged to re-sell even a 'fau't-free' beast at exactly the same price as he had paid for it, and that perhaps after undergoing the trouble of taking it home from one market and out to another, not to speak of its board meanwhile. But in any case it was business, bargain-making, and among the set to whom Sandy was now getting fully assimilated there was a strong belief in the simple 'owre-turn o' siller' as a commercially wholesome proceeding apart from questions of productiveness or profit.

They were not a particularly reputable set, those coo-coupers. Mostly bleared, dilapidated-looking elderly characters; generally, not invariably, of the male sex; fond of tobacco and snuff, and fonder of whisky. Their wits were sharp enough, and their language was not choice, though it was a general belief that amongst them downright 'leein'' and systematic deception were not practised on such an elaborate and complicated scale quite as among their contemporaries who dealt in old and half-worn horses.

In the earlier part of his career, both rapid manipulation and an occasional 'hitch' from a brother couper were needed to enable Sandy Mutch to meet his engagements in making payments. But a strong report once and again sent abroad of large profits secured by certain transactions by and bye gave distinct form and body to the impression that Sandy was a prosperous trader; and his credit rose in a wonderful way. Nobody now doubted his verbal promise to pay, hardly even the bank as represented by its local agent, Mr Tammas Rorison. He had now begun to purchase larger cattle from the farmers, and happy indeed was the seller who could secure his best 'bode' when he was really of a mind to buy; for it was known that Sandy Mutch would not 'haggle' over a few shillings, inasmuch as if he bought at a full price he would sell to equally good purpose, and despatch of business was of consequence to a man like him. In summer he rented a field or two of pasture grass; in winter he purchased a number of acres of turnips for the sustenance of stock. And as locomotion a-foot did not adequately serve the exigencies of his increasing business, he got a horse and gig for personal use. His 'machine', as Sandy termed the gig, became familiarly known, not only at the markets, but at many a substantial farm-stead, where Sandy Mutch was an occasional caller in quest of stock to buy, and where he was ever a welcome guest, received on a footing, if not of perfect equality, certainly of entire familiarity, and his judgement deferred to in matters of bovine economy.

That this rapid and steady rise in his fortunes should beget a little envy in the minds of some of the less generous of Sandy Mutch's contemporaries, and the less successful amongst his rivals, was, of course, natural. There were those who even asserted that certain of his transactions were no cleaner than they ought to be; that in addition to over-reaching simple people without remorse when he got the opportunity, he had not scrupled to resort systematically to any of the underhand devices known to the lowest of his class that would serve his end for the time. These people also spoke of Sandy as 'a peer ignorant slype', who 'mith ken aboot a nowte beast weel aneouch b' guess o' ee; but for ony kin' o' beuk lear cudna tell ye a B fae a bull's fit,' and as being at best but the daily companion of a set of very questionable characters.

Like many of the candid things that our friends say about us, if the spirit of these utterances was somewhat harsh, their substance was not perhaps far from the truth. But then what need for 'book lear', if a man felt no sense of loss, and suffered nothing in pocket or general credit by its absence? And it was just this special power of measuring and estimating cattle by 'guess o' ee', that constituted Sandy Mutch's distinguishing faculty in a business point of view, and enabled him to get on. It would have puzzled him hopelessly to be asked to calculate the value of a carcase of beef — the number of pounds weight and the price per pound being given as the two factors; yet with the live animal before him, Sandy would, by a sort of intuitive mental process, fix its 'dead weight', as it stood, with surprising exactitude, and attach the value accordingly as regulated by 'ripeness' of flesh, current price, and so on. It was by the assiduous exercise of this inborn faculty that he had made his rising reputation.

Sandy Mutch's mother was amply satisfied with her son. Sandy was to her now simply a man of large business and ample means, through whose relationship to her she was entitled to a sort of reflected glory. And, to do him justice, Sandy had of late shown a certain readiness to recompense maternal attention to his needs, by now and again handing over to his mother a proportion of the loose silver and copper coinage that occasionally accumulated in his trouser pockets. His home was still chiefly under the paternal roof, though in marketing and otherwise he was much absent; and if this made his domestic habits less regular than might have been desirable, there was a great deal to be allowed for in the case of a person of such importance in the community. To the old souter, the matter wore a less gratifying aspect. His desire would still have been to see his son addict himself to some form of honest industry whatever it might be, and he was far from certain that 'couping' cattle was to be strictly so defined.

'He'll coup till he coup ower the tail i' the gutter some day; an' that'll be seen yet,' said the souter.

'Man, wud naething satisfee ye,' said the souter's wife, in reply. 'Aw'm seer he's a muckle ta'en oot man by'se fat he wud 'a ever been sittin' wi' the lapstane on 's knee. Fat has a' your nain hard wark, an' a' yer heid o' lear deen for 's? Little mair nor get the bare bit an' the dud, an' keep a sober aneuch reef abeen oor heids. Fat for wudna the laddie try something that fowk can mak' a livin' at?'

The souter was, as usual, talked down but not convinced, and he merely added, 'Be the mailin gryte or sma' fowk sud win their livin' b' the honest eese o' their han's, fan they hinna ta'en patience to be qualifeet for deein' 't wi' their harns. It'll come to nae gweed wi' 'im ere a' be deen.'

It might be; only the potential facts were against the souter, meanwhile at least; for was it not the case that by common consent Sandy was doing a thriving business, and bidding more than fairly to be one of the prosperous men of the place: that he had already virtually risen out of the rank of the mere coo-couper, and gained a sort of indirect recognition even from men of the status of Patrick Ellison Scurr, Esq, the great grazier and dealer,[11] who had oftener than once effected a purchase of 'stores' through the medium of Sandy as a sort of agent.

The couper down

[Willie Futtrit accuses Sandy Mutch of sharp practice at a cattle market. The two fight, and the police are called. Sandy finds himself before the Sheriff Court on a charge of assault. Defended by a cunning lawyer, he escapes with a light fine.]

There was only one circumstance connected with the court case over which Sandy Mutch grieved. 'Time's money wi' me, ye see,' was an observation which Sandy, in common with other men whose thoughts are toward a great future, had, about this period of his life, got into the habit of making; and surely it could not have happened more awkwardly, even had the public prosecutor and the Sheriff been filled with malevolence against him than that the court should have been fixed for a 'St Saar's day'.[12] But so it had been; and Sandy Mutch had been broken of one of the great days of the season, in a trading point of view; for St Sair's came but once a year, and he had trusted to doing a large stroke of business on that day. Sandy complained of his disappointment much and loudly at the time, and for a long while after; for the dried-up state of the pastures, and the critical position of the turnip crop, had brought about a juncture of affairs by which feeble men were paralysed, and only the bold and perspicacious found themselves in their element. Two days later, and a copious rain had changed the conditions, and made buying or selling an easy matter for any man with a single pennyweight of brains in his skull. Of course, fortune was still before him for the winning, and Sandy Mutch was not the man, by any means, to give in the chase faintly; but lost ground at times is hard to regain. So argued the couper.

And surely it were more than the conditions of this mortal life permit that even the most brilliant career should not at one point or another suffer temporary eclipse. It is, in the very nature of things, a phase of the inevitable; which, however, like the passing cloud on the sun's disc, serves only to make more magnificent the undimmed power of the luminary, when it has emerged from the momentary shade. It was hardly to be anticipated that Sandy Mutch would be for ever exempt from the adverse contingencies of a trader's life accruing in one way or another. Neither was he; for by and by rumours got abroad that Sandy, as a business man, had on a sudden found himself in deep water.

'Ye dinna mean to say 't the couper's fail't?'

'Ay, man, the couper's broken.'

'Keep's an' guide's, fa wud 'a thocht o' Sawney Mutch sittin' doon noo!'

'Weel, min, he was gyaun a gryte len'th for a chiel' that begood wi' an aul' coo or twa less nor half-a-dizzen o' year syne; as you an' me tee min' weel.'

'Ay, but loshtie, man, Sawney was thocht as gweed 's the bank ony day wi' the fairmers. There's fyou wud bleck 'im amo' nowte beasts, buyin' or sellin', lat aleen a fair swap; an' he's hed a gryte owreturn o' siller.'

'Owre muckle, aw doot. He had been sen'in them to Lunnon b' the dizzen ilka ither ouk, hale-wheel, this file, lippenin' to the tae lift to relieve the tither; an' syne wi' the fu' han' in a backgaen market, Sawney begood to fin' oot that he had wun to the en' o' 's tether.'

'Man, it'll mak' an' unco reerie i' the kwintra side. Fat'll they dee wi' 'im? Will they jile 'im?'

'Hoot-toot — jile 'im! Nae fears o' that. They war tellin' me that it wud be sowder't up, mair nor lickly. Man, they canna weel affoord to lat 'im gae to the gowff. Mony a gweed raik o' siller has he paid for beasts; an' ov coorse severals o' them wud lickly be cautioners, or hae len'it sooms till 'im.'

'The bank keeps the like o' 'im up af'en.'

'Ou ay; an' the bank'll ken fat for, come o' ither fowk't like.'

'Weel, I'm taul', at ony rate, that there 'll be fat they ca' a 'composition' — payin' them sae muckle i' the poun' aff o' han' like.'

'To lat Sawney win to the road again, in coorse?'

'N — weel, aw cudna say aboot that; aw'm some dootfu', min. It's nae sae easy gettin' yersel' gaither't fan ance ye're flung o' your braid back.'

'There was a heap o' them liket to deal wi' 'im, though, raither nor the regular butchers, an' that – men't they hed transackit wi' never so lang, an' 't hed aye the siller ready i' their han'. Ye see they aye thocht Sawney wud rin raither abeen the market price afore he wud wunt a lottie o' beasts.'

'Jist like the fairmers; they dinna ken fan they get the vailue o' fat they're sellin'; an' 'll rin their risk o' dealin' wi' ony weirdless loup-the-cat for the sake o' a skinnin' mair nor fat a thing's really worth.'

'Ay, man, they ken richt foo to grip at a' that they can get, though it sud be never so oonrizzonable or wheety like; an' neist time they'll jist gae as far the tither gate drammin' thegither, haudin the gill stoup upo' a'body that comes within cry, an' near han' strivin' aboot fa'll be latt'n' pay maist o' the drink.'

These sentiments, uttered by a couple of interested contemporaries, indicate not inaccurately the position of affairs, and the tone of public feeling in relation to Sandy Mutch's pecuniary difficulties. In his time of growing prosperity Sandy had found no difficulty in obtaining liberal 'accommodation' from Tammas Rorison the banker. While paper of his to a certain amount was kept floating by the use of sundry names of farmers amongst whom he transacted business, the banker could not in the case of such a valuable and desirable customer – who, if mismanaged or disobliged, might have got into the hands of the rival banker – hesitate to grant, at his own risk, an occasional overdraft not covered by any outside security. And now that Sandy had suffered what he termed a 'back-jar', he was just a little confused as to the amount of either his liabilities or assets, book-keeping and accounting, in even their simplest forms, being arts to him utterly unknown. Naturally enough the banker, who had had opportunity of knowing his man sufficiently well on more sides of him than one, knew also much better than any one else how the liabilities stood, and by taking Sandy in hand personally, as a sort of an informal trustee, he next got at the assets with sufficient accuracy to enable him to declare, as he did without any long delay, that the composition must be six and eight pence in the pound. The creditors were asked to approve of this, and they approved in a general way accordingly. It was understood that the paper drawn in Sandy's favour would all be made good at the bank, or several other failures must occur. An undesirable event this latter, and not an inevitable one if things were judiciously gone about. So the banker hinted, and the banker knew and could handle the material he had to deal with as well as any man. Some of the 'accommodations' were just a little inconvenient of adjustment. There was Burnside, for example, who had given Sandy accommodation for £25, being the season's rent of a grass field; and Sandy had obliged Burnie in a similar way with £28 to clear his twelve months-old manure account. Deprived of Sandy's name on both bills, Burnie felt he should be in rather a tight place with his Martinmas rent to meet, and a hard 'scrape' to get that up; but then, by Sandy's failure, the smaller bill, as the banker pointed out, could happily be reduced to £17 in place of £25, and by a

determined push among men circumstanced like himself, Burnie, for corresponding favours granted by him to them, got those obliging neighbours to
take up a side of the two bills, and, like himself, hope on. True, the trifle of
discount went against him; but otherwise Burnie did not feel himself worse
than before. He was still a solvent man, he understood, and he pitied Mutch,
'peer stock', who had 'fa'in' i' the rive' so undeservedly.

Some folks there were, who, when matters were arranged, said the banker,
though he had not sought to 'rank' in the list of Sandy Mutch's creditors, had
contrived to keep himself and the institution he represented pretty well
scatheless; but in conceding fresh 'accommodations', as he had done in
certain cases, it was held undeniable that the banker had acted a very friendly
part to those agriculturists who were involved in the couper's failure. No
doubt there were grumblers among the outside creditors. Two or three
persons who had sold cattle to Sandy a week or two before he was known to
be bankrupt, threatened to be unpleasant. They had got no payment
previous to the stoppage, and now they had to accept six and eightpence per
pound over the bank counter, in place of the full 'notes', bating a 'luckpenny'
and the usual allowance of 'bargain ale'. These grumbled loudly, and seemed
determined to cherish a feeling of ill-usage in the matter, despite the banker's
sharp rebuke of their unreasonableness; yet was it felt by the general public
that Sandy Mutch's 'sittin' doon' had been attended with less disastrous
effects than could have been anticipated, considering the extent and
unexpectedness of the collapse; and that these good results were largely due
to the banker's skill there was no room to doubt.

Up again

To Sandy Mutch, personally, the event of his failure brought a certain
measure of discouragement. Deprived of his gig, which he had honourably
given up, with the animal that drew it, for behoof of his creditors, he was
again reduced to mere pedestrian activity. Of course, he was quite destitute
of cash; and Tammas Rorison, the banker, who was for the time being very
shy on that topic, when his client endeavoured to approach it, simply urged,
'Hae patience, Sandy, man; an' keep yer een aboot ye. It wudna leuk sair to
be gyaun aboot wi' a fu' pouch eenoo.'

In the circumstances, Sandy Mutch found it beyond his compass just yet
to do even a limited business in swine dealing, which had presented itself to
his mind as a hopeful and more easily attainable field than that of trading in
larger cattle. And so, for a time, he again loafed about his native hamlet,
finding shelter under the paternal roof and awakening wrathful, but as
hitherto ineffectual criticisms of his habits by his father the souter.

But Sandy must have in his hand somehow; and thus, in course of a few months, he was again to be seen bustling about in the cattle markets. The scope of his operations was different, but trafficking in cattle was still his care: and at the close of the market, he was ordinarily to be seen collecting and taking the charge of 'droving' to the 'Toon',[13] or elsewhere, the lot purchased by one of the men who did a considerable business as a butcher and grazier. And not exclusively as a common drover, paid at the rate of half a crown a day and his drink, when employed. By common consent, Sandy had a large measure of skill as a buyer of stock; and it was not in reason that this his talent should be allowed to rust utterly. Sandy had been once and again trusted to do a stroke in buying in his master's behalf, when his master, for reasons sufficient to himself, wished to keep in the background, and not reveal his identity to the seller.

There was another line, too, open to the man of no capital and an equal amount of principle; only it must be prosecuted as a conjunct business; and in this wise: two of the fraternity, or better still, three, met at the opening of the fair, and, by common understanding, promptly fixed on a likely lot of grazing beasts in the hands of some small farmer – if a verdant person, so much the better. Couper number one first 'priced', and offered for the lot in a matter of course way. He would keep the 'exposer' in hand up to his station in the market, and then subject the beasts to a fresh handling, thumping them about freely with his stick, and candidly expatiating on their weak points, but winding up with, 'Still an' on, aw'll stan' to my bode – the aiven notes an' a gweed luckpenny back – but ye'll need to mak' up yer min' aboot it. Nae man 'll mak' 's siller oot o' them; only aw'm jist needin' something o' the kin' mysel' the day.'

He has offered, say, £20, and the price asked for the stirks is £25. The exposer is half indignant and wholly disappointed at the couper's appreciation of his stirks; but the couper does not put himself about for that; and after badgering the man for half an hour or so he sums up: 'Weel, here's my han' (he extends the palm accordingly), 'a twenty-pun note, an' I'll lea'e the luckpenny to yoursel'. It's mair nor the creaturs 's worth to ony ane; mere hunger't atomies, an' a backgaen market tee.'

'I'll raither tak' them hame again,' exclaims the irritated owner of the stirks.

'An' ye'll get it adee, man, an' tak' less siller neist time – but please yersel',' retorts couper number one, who now retreats, giving 'the wink' to couper number two; and couper number two has hold of the man accordingly before any other buyer can put in a word. Couper number two bids him ask £20 and he'll maybe make an offer. – 'Ye seerly dinna ken fat wye the market's gyaun min. Offer't twenty poun' already! Nae fear o' ye.'

'The man's nae oot o' cry yet that offer't it,' exclaims the seller.

'Weel, man, there wus twa feels; and the ane that refees't the siller was the biggest feel o' the twa,' is the reply of couper number two, 'The man's kent that ye wusna wantin' to sell.'

'He kent brawly't aw wud sell, gin I gat vailue far my beasts.'

'Ye dinna ken fat yer speakin' aboot, min; lat's hear a price't fowk can bid ye something, an' nae waste my time an' lose yer market baith.' Couper number two is less reputable-looking and more scurrilous of speech than couper number one even; and he keeps an uncommonly sharp look-out lest any bona fide dealer who would really buy the stirks at their full market value should indicate a disposition to hang on, waiting his chance. The least appearance of anything of the sort he violently resents as a dishonourable attempt to break his marketing. In due course couper number two, who has persecuted the owner of the stirks for three-quarters of an hour, gives place to another of the same 'kidney'. It may be number three, or quite as likely number one returned again, the essential point being to keep outsiders off until the owner of the stirks either capitulates or is seen to be hopelessly obstinate.

'Weel, laird, are ye gyaun to tak' siller yet?' asks couper number one; and he adds an emphatic declaration anent his own good-natured softness in ever again 'lattin his een see' the laird after the treatment he had previously given him.

'Nae the siller that ye offer't ony wye,' replies the owner of the stirks, in an apparently decided tone.

But the couper knows what all this is worth, and what may be the result of a renewed assault, and he continues his attack. If the man is in circumstances that compel him to sell, he like enough begins by and by to waver in his resolution, which the couper quickly perceives, and loses no time in trying to drive home his bargain by generously offering to 'refar it to ony man that kens the vailue o' beasts i' the market, this minit.' Only a prompt conclusion either way is, he hints, imperative.

The root principle of this mode of trading, of course, is simply to step dexterously in between the legitimate buyer and the seller; keep the latter closely in hand under a series of assaults, till, through dint of sheer chicanery, a bargain has been concluded, and then fall back on the regular trader, or other bona fide buyer, to re-purchase at market price, and by so doing put the first buyers, who, to a certainty, have not as many shillings in pocket as they have promised to pay in pounds, in funds to 'clear their feet', and allow them to profit in proportion as they have been successful in getting their purchases at under value. Sandy Mutch at an earlier stage of his career had on his own account attempted a little of what might be termed sharp dealing. And he now participated in a few partnership transactions of the kind just described; but, to do him justice, he did not go heartily into the line. The amount of 'plunder' was not always enough to be satisfactory; occasionally its division could not be effected with perfect pleasantness, when the drink had been allowed for; and, besides, it tended on the whole to obscure his credit among his friends rather than otherwise, inasmuch as Sandy was never able to point to an individual achievement of a satisfactory sort that he could really say was his own; while his purse remained about as lank as before, and he made no real headway in business. But where there is a sufficiently pronounced will, a distinct way is sure to show itself in due course. And thus it came about that an opportunity for independent trading turned up by and by.

That fell disease, pleuro-pneumonia, visited the region and committed serious ravages among neat stock, to the terror of the farmers and graziers, who had not then the benefit of paternal legislation in the shape of regulations concerning contagious disease amongst animals. In the circumstances a panic ensued.[14] When the disease attacked their stocks they knew that probably three-fourths of them would die if prompt measures were not taken; and naturally the ordinary run of dealers and butchers fought shy of purchasing diseased beasts, or those that presumably had been in dangerous proximity to them. It was here that Sandy Mutch's talent and spirit of enterprise availed him. He now went boldly into certain speculative cattle transactions, the exact nature and conditions of which he did not openly proclaim; only he was understood to have embarked somewhat largely in the killing and dead meat business. He certainly forwarded quantities of dead meat to the market, and when his 'returns' had come to hand, he paid those from whom he had bought at rates fixed by himself, and which they were bound thankfully to accept.

In course of time cattle disease had disappeared from the locality, but not so Sandy Mutch's resuscitated business. He was again as well in heart as ever, and his familiar form seldom absent from any of the district markets as they occurred. He now bought steadily and in increasing values, often at the close of a market paying down in ready cash to the amount of several hundred pounds.

'He's an exterordinar chiel', Sandy Mutch; foo he has wun to the road again! They tell me he's better upon't nor ever,' said Bowbutts, who rather loved to gossip a little about his old herd at a time, viewing him as one of the remarkable men of the place.

'An' weel fell's 'im,' replied his neighbour Gowanwall. 'It was jist menseless the siller't he made aff o' diseas't nowte, aw b'lieve.'

'Is't possible, man? Weel, fa wud 'a thocht that fan he was herdin' my beasts, noo?'

'Weel, I'm nae biddin' ye believe me; but there's aye some water faur the stirkie droons, ye ken; an' there wus severals that I ken that he ca'd owre beasts till, an' flay't them an' tyeuk them awa' to the toon i' the seelence o' the nicht in a cairt; an' that didna leuk owre weel.'

'An' wud the carkidges raelly been ta'en to the market, no?'

'Weel, I'm jist tellin' ye fat aw'm tellin' ye — I wudna wunt to jeedge nae man.'

'At ony rate, he's winnin' in amon' a lot o' the muckle fairmers again.'

'Ou ay; fan a chiel' has the siller in's pouch he'll hae little diffeekwalty o' gettin' a hearin' an' be thocht a hantle o'. It's nae lang sin' some o' 's aul' cronies wud 'a hed muckle adee to ken 'im, an' he hedna been pointet oot to them.'

'That's jist the wye o' the wardle, man; but Sawney winna brak's nicht's rest aboot that, gin the bools be rowin' richt wi' 'im amo' the nowte.'

'But fat d' ye think, man? – they tell me that he's gyaun to tak' a fairm 'imsel', gin he hinna deen't else.'

'Gyaun to tak' a fairm! Ye're seerly jokin' noo, Gowanies.'

'Jokin' or no jokin', his bode was neist to the heichest for Mull o' Meadapple the tither day.'

'Ex-ter-ordinar!'

'Ay; an' it chates me gin he binna gettin' 't tee.'

'Weel, that does cowe the gowan fairly! Sawney Mutch takin' ane o' the best pairts i' the kwintra-side. Man, there's nae a place like it far girsin' beasts roon an' roon; lat aleen corn an' the green crap.'

'An' Sawney didna need 's mither to tell 'im that.'

'An' he's raelly ta'en the Mull o' Meadapple. Na, that will be news to oor gudewife; she hed aye a kin' o' notion o' the loon, for as droll a breet's he was.'

'Ye see fat it is to hae a freen' i' the court, man. There was a perfeck merdle o' them aifter 't; but Sawney hed gotten the banker to pit in a word for 'im wi' the new factor bodie – he's ane o' that Aberdeen lawvyers, ye ken, an' jist kens as muckle about grun' 's my pipe stapple there.'

'Ov coorse; but he'll ken the richt side o' a shilling brawly, and fat wye to screw't oot o' fowk, rizzon or neen. There's fyou o' them fa's back at that.'

'Aw b'lieve ye're aboot richt there, Bowies. "Well," says the factor, "but Maister Mutch is not the highest." Ov coorse, they hed it advertees't "the highest offer may not be accepit." "I un'erstan'," says the banker, "but gif it's nae passin' a tenpun note, Maister Mutch wud lea'e 'imsel' in your han'." I got this, ye ken, fae them 't hed it fae some o' themsel's. So it's nae ca'd aboot clype.'

'Lat ye the banker aleen. He kens as weel aboot takin' grun' as ony o' them. He's factor't a hantle 'imsel' in's time, as weel 's a' ither thing.'

'Ou ay; he's nae a blate ane, Tammas, we a' ken that.'

'So Sawney's gettin' the Mull toon!'

'Weel, I'm taul' it's as gweed's sattl't. Ov coorse it was thocht that the factor mith 'a try't gin the tither man wud draw up a bit aifter 'im; but he hed behav't vera honourable to Sandy, it wud appear.'

'Vera honourable, as ye say,' observed Bowbutts, somewhat equivocally.

'Nyod, man, it's mervellous fat enfluence 'll dee, espeeshally i' the takin' o' grun',' added Gowanwall.

'In fack, there's nae gettin' o' a pairt warth hae'in hardly wuntin' 't, there's sae mony seekin' them, an sae mony quirks o' ae kin' or anither afore ye can be seer. Hooever, the couper 'll be fairly at the gate wi' the best o' them fan he's in'o Mull o' Meadapple.'

NOTES

1. Excerpted from W Alexander, *Life Among My Ain Folk* (Edinburgh, Douglas, 2nd edn, 1882), pp 85-109, 120-32.

2. This brief description of elementary education in an early nineteenth-century Aberdeenshire country school, with its concern for reading, writing, 'coontin'' and the shorter catechism, is a version of an account first published in one of Alexander's 'Sketches of Rural Life in Aberdeenshire' (*North of Scotland Gazette*, 25 March 1853). It is expanded in several chapters of *Johnny Gibb of Gushetneuk*. See also I J Simpson, *Education in Aberdeenshire Before 1872* (London, Athlone Press, 1947).

3. Before arable land was consolidated in enclosed fields it was divided in two qualities. Infield ('the intoon rigs') was heavily manured and bore grain crops every year. Outfield ('oot feedles') saw little manure apart from the dung of wandering cattle in the winter, and relied on long periods of fallowing to maintain whatever fertility it enjoyed. See W Alexander, *Northern Rural Life* (Finzean, Robin Callender, new edn, 1979), pp 29–32, and I Whyte, *Agriculture and Society in Seventeenth-Century Scotland* (Edinburgh, John Donald, 1979), passim.

4. I know no other description of the Aberdeenshire herd's club, with its mystic and inscrutable inscription. No doubt we are indebted to Alexander's youthful years on the farm for this intriguing account.

5. William Watson, Sheriff-Substitute of Aberdeenshire, did indeed take a keenly sympathetic – if rather paternalistic to modern eyes – interest in the problems of farm servants and similar groups. His major achievement was to found industrial feeding schools for Aberdeen street urchins.

6. Alexander rarely pays any lawyer a compliment: lawyer and factor were too closely linked for his taste.

7. Andermas Fair was held at Rayne on the fourth Tuesday in each November. See G.S. Keith, *A General View of the Agriculture of Aberdeenshire* (Aberdeen, Brown, 1811), p 550. Rayne lies close to Alexander's youthful stamping-ground in Chapel of Garioch, and this long anecdote reeks of personal experience or oral transmission.

8. Alexander may appear to be ridiculing the Glentons crofter through his out-dated clothes. Not so. We soon learn that the crofter is a more admirable character than Sandy Mutch – not that that is any great achievement – and his clothes strongly recall Johnny Gibb's habitual garb. Since Johnny is the measure of moral excellence in rural Aberdeenshire, we are not to despise this crofter. Alexander is up to his usual tricks: pervasive irony, and making one book talk to another.

9. A nominal sum of money returned, for luck, by the seller to the purchaser.

10. The judge of the market had powers to arbitrate on disagreements. His decision was supported by the might of a couple of attendants with rusty halberds. Note Alexander's sly comment on Rorison's monopoly of influential local offices.

11. This gentleman appears more prominently in another story in *Life Among My Ain Folk*, pp 1–83. The criticism of Scurr in that story showed considerable bravery on Alexander's part, for his career recalls that of 'the grazier king', William McCombie,

Tillyfour; the cousin of Alexander's old patron, the first Scottish tenant farmer to sit in parliament, and a power in local Liberal circles.

12. St Sair's Fair, held in the last week of June, was among the largest annual fairs in the Garioch.

13. Aberdeen.

14. The biggest panic came in 1865, when rinderpest rather than pleuro-pneumonia ravaged Aberdeenshire herds. Rents for large farms, principally devoted to cattle feeding, dropped like a stone. This outbreak was controlled by a novel and rigorous slaughter policy, underpinned by adequate compensation: the model for modern disease control methods. This was the brainwave of William McCombie, Tillyfour. See W Alexander, *The Rinderpest in Aberdeenshire: the Outbreak of 1865, and how it was Stamped Out* (Aberdeen, Free Press, 1882).

Glossary

Abeen	above
antrin	occasional
ation	stock; kindred
aught	eight
ava	at all
audiscence	*a hearing*
back	to address a letter
backgaen	falling
back-jar	a setback
bail(l)ie	magistrate; cattleman
bairn	a child
bake-board	a kneading board
bann	to curse; to swear
baul	bold
bedall	a bedridden person
begood	began
bide	to stay
big	to build
blaewort	a bluebell
blate	sheepish, bashful
bleck	to puzzle, to surpass
bode	to bid; a bid
boll	a measure of volume
booet	a lantern
bools	marbles
bothy	that part of a farm steaing in which *bothied* male farm servants both slept and cooked their own food
bounds	patience
bow	a bool (a measure of volume)
bowstring	a form of snare
brae	a hill, a slope
braw	good; strong' brave
breeder	a brother
breeks	trousers
breid	bread (usually this means oatcakes)
brose	a staple food, gruel based on oatmeal

buirdly	burly
but and ben	the characteristic two-roomed rural Aberdeenshire cottage; the *but* is the kitchen, the *ben* a parlour or best room
but-bed	a bed in the kitchen
ca'	to drive; to work
can	sense
cannasbreid	a small space (literally, the breadth of a canvas)
carkidge	a carcase
carl	a man
caup	a turned wooden bowl
cautioner	a backer
chafts	chops; jaws
chaumer	a room; farm servants' sleeping apartment
chiel	a man; a fellow
clype	gossip
confeerin'	suitable; corresponding
connach	to spoil; to destroy
coom	sloping
coup	to trade; to deal
cowe the gowan	to overcome and humble
crack	a talk; a chat; to talk
creel	a basket
cryl knyp	to go smack
dargin'	day labouring
dautie	a pet
deece	a kitchen settle
deval	to cease; cessation
divot	a flat piece of turf
dog-dirder	whipper-in; kennel attendant
doon-sittin'	establishment; bankruptcy
dottl't	senile
dram	a drink
draught	a load
dubs	mud; filth
dud	a cloth
dyker	a wall-builder (usually a day labourer)
eenoo	even now; just now
eident	industrious; diligent
fa	who
fae	from
fan	when
fat	what
fauchin'	ploughing
faul'is	folds formed by dividing unenclosed land with hurdles

faur	where
feal	turf; peat
fecht	to fight; a fight
feck	most; the majority
fesh	to fetch
feu	a perpetual lease at a fixed rent; to give or take such a lease
file	while; an occasion
fire house	a house with a fire in it, thus an inhabited house
flay	to skin
fleg	to beat
flit	to leave
fog	to make a profit
foo	how
foreman	the most senior horseman: on smaller farms he would take on the *grieve's* (qv) role
forenicht	the evening
fou	drunk
frem't	strangers; people not of one's kin
gar	to force; to oblige
gardies	the hands or arms
gast	a fright; a shock
gatefarrin	presentable
gey	considerable
geyan	rather
gill stoup	a large communal drinking vessel
giv	if
gird	to drive
girdle	iron griddle
girse	grass
gloaming	twilight
goodman	a farmer (usually holding more land than a crofter)
goodwife	a farmer's wife
gowff	ruin; destruction
graith	harness
green craps	root crops (usually turnips)
greet	to cry; to weep
grieve	the managing servant on a large farm
grip	greed
grun'	ground; land
gudge	a stout, thick-set fellow
gudewife	see *goodwife*
gullie	a (large) knife
gweed	good
gweeshtens	an exclamation of surprise

gyaun	going
gyte	mad; demented
haill	whole
haiver	to talk foolishly or incoherently
halflin	a lad
hantle	a considerable quantity or number
harns	brains
haumer	to walk clumsily
herry	to harry; to seek and destroy
hin(d)most	last
hingin' lum	a wooden chimney projecting from the wall
hir't	seasoned; made palatable
hizzie	a hussy
holipie	humpy; mis-shapen
hoot	an interjection of surprise
howfflin	a clumsy senseless lad
ilka	each; every
inhaudin	one who declines to leave
jaud	a jade
ken	knowledge; to know
kist	a chest containing clothes and other personal possessions
kitchie	a kitchen
korter	a quarter (of an oatcake, for instance)
kwintra	country
kwite	a coat
kyaak	a cake
kye	cattle
laird	a landlord
lave	the rest; the remainder
lear	learning
leems	things; implements
lick	to beat; to chastise
lippen	to trust
loon	a lad; a boy
loshtie	an interjection of surprise
loup the cat	an itinerant man (originally a travelling tailor)
lug	an ear
macksna	it makes no difference to me
maet	food
meal	oatmeal
mearie	a mare
menseless	unbelievable
merdle	a crowd
minnons	minnows

muckle	big; large; much
nae	not
near b'gyaun	mean; niggardly
neep	a turnip
neuk	a corner
nickum	a mischievous boy; a wastrel
niz	a nose
nochty	inconsiderable; worthless
nowt(e)	cattle
ongrutt'n	choked back tears
onwal	interest on a loan
oot-wark	field labour
orpiet	peevish; querulous
orra	odd
orra beast	an odd horse (not one of a pair, that is)
ouk	a week
owre	over; excessively
pawky	sly; cunning
peeak	to cry peevishly
peer	poor
pickle	little
pilget	a struggle
pirl	to move gently
police	a pot holder
pottage	porridge
pyock	a sack
quean	a girl; a maiden
raik	to care; a considerable amount
raith	a term; a quarter of a year
ram	a heavy stick, usually gnarled and knotty
ramsh	hasty; rash
rank	to prepare; to dress
reerie	an uproar; a clamour
rig	a strip of arable land
rive	to dig; to rouse; a ditch
roch	rough, coarse
roup	an auction
row	to roll
rowd	round
rowle	to rule; a rule
rug	to pull; a bargain
rumgumption	common sense
sair	sore; painful; oppressive
sark	a shirt

aut backit	a salt box
cault	scolded
clate	a slate
harries	contentions; quarrels
hell't	dug; thrown
heetin'	shooting
hortsome	lively; entertaining
c	such
ller	silver; money
pper	a supper; to give supper to
kailie	a slate pencil
kirpit	splashed
ype	a contemptible man
matchet	a small and insignificant person
nifter	a sniff; to sniff
ober	plain; plainly
ocht	sought; ordered (drink)
oo	sow
orra	sorrow
outar	shoemaker
owder	to solder; to patch
owens	a staple food made from oat husks
peer, speir	to ask; to question
preein'	spruce; neat; smart
amackie	a little stomach
apple	a stem
av't aff	procrastinated
ech	to cram
eer	a stir
ent	a task
ilt	a handle
irk	a bullock
ob-thackit	straw-thatched (a *stob* is a Y-shaped piece of wood used to hold the straw in place)
oot	stout; healthy
reen	yesterday evening
rippet	striped
veir	lazy; insolent
ving	a rotating iron bucket, allowing a pot to be hung from a hook before moving the pot over the fire
ne	then
ck	a lease
'en-aboot	cultivated
g	a strap

taties	potatoes
tchil	a child
teen	a child
thackit	thatched
thole	to suffer; to endure
threep	to insist
threave	a measure of cut grain, on or off the straw
toon	a town; a farm steading
traik	to trek
truein'	playing truant from
truncher	a trencher; a large plate
up throu	upland district
upwith	rising
wardle	a world
wark steer	a plough ox or cow
waur	worse
wecht	a weight
weel-faur't	well-favoured; handsome
weirdless	worthless
wile, wyle	to select
widdifu	a scoundrel (literally, one fit to be hanged)
worn	brought
wrocht	worked
wyn	to bring; to send
yoking	a period during which plough animals were harnessed for work